ELIE WIESEL

ELIE WIESEL
Between Memory and Hope

Edited by
Carol Rittner, R.S.M.

NEW YORK UNIVERSITY PRESS
New York and London

Library of Congress Cataloging-in-Publication Data
Elie Wiesel : between memory and hope / edited by Carol Rittner.
    p.   cm.
  Includes bibliographical references.
  ISBN 0-8147-7410-5 (alk. paper)
    1. Wiesel, Elie, 1928–   —Criticism and interpretation.
I. Rittner, Carol Ann, 1943–
PQ2683.I32Z66   1990
813'.54—dc20   89-13180
                                                        CIP

New York University Press books are printed on acid-free paper,
and their binding materials are chosen for strength and durability.

c 10 9 8 7 6 5 4 3 2

Book design by Ken Venezio

For my Mother and Father who gave me life,

For the Sisters of Mercy who give me life, and

*For Concilia Moran, R.S.M., and Sondra Myers
who have enriched my life.*

In gratitude.

Contents

How does a Jew in the concentration camp of Nazi Germany read Psalms 22 and 23?

Foreword

Carol Rittner

"Tell me what you are doing," the Rabbi said in a soft voice. I told him I was writing. "Is that all?" he asked in disbelief. I said, yes, that's all. His expression was so reproachful that I had to elaborate and explain that some writings could sometimes, in moments of grace, attain the quality of deeds.

— ELIE WIESEL, *Legends of Our Time*

For more than thirty years, Elie Wiesel has wrestled with his haunting memories of the Holocaust: "How can we speak of it? How can we not speak of it?"[1] Prodded by his conscience to tell the story, Wiesel, the survivor-witness, struggles with Wiesel, the writer-witness, to reveal the enormity of the nightmare—without betraying the dead. Beginning with his autobiographical memoir, *Night*, each of his books reflects the battle between silence and revelation that animates his work.

Like the hero in his novel, *A Beggar in Jerusalem*, Elie Wiesel has become a necessary connection between past and future. Somehow he has found a way to sustain a "spirit of resistance" that is able to stay loyal to the suffering that gave it birth. As Terrence Des Pres wrote in *The Survivor*, "The conflict between silence and the scream, so prominent in Wiesel's novels, is in fact a battle between death and life, between allegiance to the dead and care for the living."[2]

The essays in this book affirm Elie Wiesel's "care for the living." He writes stories, but not just any kind of stories. Wiesel's stories "are conceived somewhere between the facts of destruction and a

ix

faith in creation. Somewhere between hell and heaven, his stories begin and end and begin again."[3]

Wiesel's goal is always the same: to invoke memory as a shield for the future, to create a more humane and moral world where people are not victims and children no longer starve or have to run in fear. As Egil Aarvik, chairman of the Norweigan Nobel Committee, said in 1986, when Wiesel received the Nobel Peace Prize,

From the abyss of the death camps he has come as a messenger to mankind —not with a message of hate and revenge but with one of brotherhood and atonement. Elie Wiesel is not only the man who survived, he is also the spirit which has triumphed. In him we see a man who has gone from utter humiliation to become one of our most important spiritual leaders and guides. . . . It is vital that we have such guides in an age when terror, repression and racial discrimination still exist in the world.[4]

Somewhere between memory and despair Elie Wiesel offers a word of hope to a world short on hope. And, moment by graced moment, he helps to create a world in which peace is possible.

Although it is true that one cannot separate Elie Wiesel, the survivor-witness from Elie Wiesel, the writer-witness, the essays in this volume are intended to focus on his work, and on the literary, theological, and philosophical issues that emerge from it, rather than on him. The essays in *Elie Wiesel: Between Memory and Hope* were written by Jewish and Christian scholars from a variety of disciplines and perspectives and were prepared specifically for this project. These essays affirm Elie Wiesel's stature as an artist and his care as a person for other human beings.

Like all projects, the preparation of this book was a collaborative effort. All of the contributors generously responded to my invitation to prepare an essay for the book. I would like to express my gratitude to each one.

I especially would like to thank Elie Wiesel for his contribution. For more than thirty years, he has struggled to give voice to silence. I am awed by the results.

I would like to thank Random House, Inc., for granting us permission to quote from Elie Wiesel, *A Jew Today*, Copyright © 1978 by Elirion Associates, Inc.; Irving Abrahamson for permission to quote from Irving Abrahamson, ed., *Against Silence: The Voice and Vision of Elie Wiesel*, Copyright © 1985 by Irving Abrahamson; and Hill and Wang for permission to quote from Elie Wiesel, *Night*, Copyright © 1960 by MacGibbon and Kee.

Thanks also to Kitty Moore, senior editor at New York University Press, who is the essence of graciousness and professionalism. I also want to thank Professors Leo Goldberger and George Schwab, respected scholars and friends, for their guidance, and Dr. Jean Duchesne (Paris), Dr. Rosette Lamont (New York), and Lydia Davis (New York) for their assistance with the translations from French. Finally, I would like to thank Leslie Wu, a lovely and generous young woman, who carefully prepared the manuscript.

Notes

1. Elie Wiesel in conversation with Carol Rittner, August 1988.
2. Terrence Des Pres, *The Survivor* (New York: Oxford University Press, 1976), 36.
3. Mary Jo Leddy, see chap. 5 of this book.
4. Egil Aarvik, "The Nobel Presentation Speech," in *Elie Wiesel: The Nobel Peace Prize* (New York: Summit Books and Boston University, 1986), 4–5.

ELIE WIESEL

1

The Solitude of God

Elie Wiesel

Solitude. Does there exist a more anguishing problem for human beings, for the Creator, for the Jew? At once necessary and crushing, solitude both affirms me and rejects me: what would I be without it, what would become of me if it were my only prospect? Created in the image of God, human beings are, like God, alone. And yet human beings can hope, they must hope. Human beings can rise, they must rise, go beyond themselves to merge with or recover themselves in God. God alone, in fact, is condemned to eternal solitude. Only God is truly, irreducibly alone.

This is a subject of passionate interest to the Hasidic and mystical Masters. For them, God is often to be pitied. Yes, God inspires not only love and piety, justice and respect, but also compassion and pity. More precisely, human beings, in opening their hearts and souls to the disquieting and exalting mysteries of creation, cannot help feeling pity, in the purest sense of the term, for the Creator: pity for the Father who suffers with His suffering children and sometimes makes them suffer; pity for the weary Judge, transcended by His own severity: pity for the King whose crown is so often dragged through the dust, whose word is ill heard, misunderstood, misinterpreted; pity for the Lord who is everywhere, always, in every thought, in every thing, in every action, even in pain, even in evil, even in want, even in the absence that agonizes human beings, prisoners of one another and all of them prisoners of their own solitude.

For what would a human being be if he were not, in his heart of hearts, a living appeal sent out toward another to break through his own solitude? If he succeeds completely, he will be diminished by it:

1

he will live in duration and not in time. But what is more, can he undertake such an action if he knows beforehand that it will not succeed, or, worse, that it must not succeed?

Adam, solitary, had no problem: that was his problem. "It is not good for man to live alone," God decreed. So then Adam discovered his companion Eve by his side. Was she his problem? No, he himself was the problem, he himself confronting Eve: before, his solitude had weighed on him; now, he missed it. Before, he did not know he was alone; now he had learned about it. Henceforth, he would live in this vicious circle: the less alone he was, because someone lived with him, the more aware he was of his solitude. The solution? There is none, there cannot be one. This is why solitude is the basis of so many philosophical enquiries and so many religious movements. I say "I" without knowing to what, or rather to whom, I am referring. Who am I? The one speaking or the one listening? The two forms of myself, the two selves, are separated by a wall that only an absolute and immortal consciousness would be capable of scaling, perhaps of dominating. On both sides, the self lives alone. And yet . . . each is rooted in the solitude of the other! This is why a certain Jewish tradition forbids the use of the singular "I": only God can say "I." God alone defines Himself in relation to that "I." Only God has no need of emerging from Himself to be Himself.

But I am interrupting this meditation. Whatever happens, it brings us back to ourselves.

As a child, in my little Jewish town buried in the Carpathians, I was afraid of solitude; for me, it meant abandonment. At the end of the day I would wait for my parents to come home, just as I had waited for my teachers and schoolmates to appear in the morning. And what if something had happened to them? Above all I did not want to find myself alone, cut off, excluded from their experiences, even if they were unhappy ones. Vaguely I knew that my one chance of survival was to belong to my family, my community: to live or survive outside seemed inconceivable to me. To put it another way: I accepted collective solitude but not individual solitude.

Collective solitude did not frighten me; I was used to it. Hadn't it existed ever since Egypt, since Sinai? Wasn't it inherent in our very condition? For a long time, weren't we the only ones in a pagan and idolatrous society to believe in a single God, to receive His laws, to remain faithful to Him? Weren't we the only ones in a violent world to oppose murder, falsehood, covetousness, slavery, and, above all, humiliation, the worst form of slavery?

But within this order, isolation of self did not mean exclusion of the other, and certainly not denial of the other. In conformity with the Jewish tradition, we believed that the Torah, the essence of Judaism, was, naturally, good for the Jews, that it helped to keep their particularity alive, fruitful. In other words we believed that because of their chosen path, their identification with the Torah, Jews had the power to fulfill themselves under the sign of the truth. But at the same time, non-Jews could, by following their own chosen path, attain the same degree of truth. They could, starting from their singularity, accede to universality. So that to be Jewish meant: to be and to live, not in opposition to others, but by their side. The pagan prophet Bileam meant to curse us by consigning us to isolation; in fact, his malediction turned into a blessing.

Then, in time, it turned back into a malediction. The term *levadad yishkon* came to mean, no longer isolation, but exclusion. And at every level: exclusion from society, from history, and, lastly, from humanity. Is there any need to repeat the frightful litany? The ghettos, the privations, the pogroms, the absurd, hateful accusations, the racial and religious persecutions through centuries of Christianity, throughout Christian lands, the Nazi altars known as Auschwitz and Treblinka . . . What did my ancestors and their descendants die of, if not the fact than humanity had decided to exclude them, the better to trample them underfoot, deform and annihilate them?

The process was simple and terribly effective! Our virtues were identified and misrepresented to the point of caricature. Then we were blamed for our caricatured manners, modes of belief, and ways of living. Our fidelity was transformed into servitude, our faith into despair, our desire for difference into a desire for exclusion—in short, our solitude into isolation. Sometimes I no longer know which should surprise us more: the solitude imposed on us from outside or the stubbornness with which we have tried to break through it.

Our methods of resistance were many and various: we devoted ourselves to study not only to acquire an ancient knowledge, but also to meet our precursors there; because of them, we felt less alone. And this is the secret and the power of the Talmud: its characters are alive, present. They speak to us as though they were our contemporaries, as though our problems concerned them and theirs us. I follow Rabbi Shimon bar Yohai into his cave and he is less alone, and I too; I listen to Rabbi Akiba and his voice touches me, as the voice of Rabbi Zeira stuns me. Their present is not my past, but my present.

If the Hasidic movement won such rapid victories, if, in the eighteenth century, it succeeded in implanting itself within so few years in so many scattered Jewish communities from the Dnieper to the Carpathians, it is because it was a response to, and perhaps even a cure for, solitude. A Hasid is never alone; even when he is alone, he has his Rabbi, his Master, with him, in him; he has only to recall his Rabbi's Sabbath face to dissipate his solitude. If life weighs on him too heavily, if he feels discouraged, depressed, he has only to tear himself away from the daily life of the remote villages and go to the Rabbi's court. There, he will find himself back among friends, companions rich and less rich, erudite and less erudite: together they will sing, together they will dance, together they will celebrate Jewish solidarity, faithfulness to God and His creatures, together they will affirm their conviction that, for better or for worse, human beings have received from heaven the dubious gift of suffering the most implacable of solitudes and having the means to surmount it, transform it into hope. The joy, the happiness I felt, as a child and an adolescent, among the Hasidim, with our Master, on the evening of a simple Sabbath or on the occasion of a special festival, has never been equaled since. And if, even now, I often feel overcome with longing, it is a longing for those gatherings, that joy, that fullness: no solitude, no suffering could resist it.

I remember, yes, I remember certain Hasidim back there in the kingdom of night. There, we experienced the ultimate end of all experiences. There we crossed the limit of anguish, and solitude, and the struggle against them. An anguish beyond anguish . . . A solitude within solitude . . . Naked despair . . . Sadness stripped of all embellishment, all language, all outward appearance: that was what composed our world. If you only knew how many, and of what quality, nearly slipped and fell. . . . Reduced to the state of victims, fathers and sons turned on each other suddenly, enemies, because of a crust of bread. Friends and brothers tore each other apart for a spoonful of soup, an instant's respite, a thicker jacket. If you only knew how many of the kapos were liberal intellectuals, how many of the intellectuals were sadists! Yes, that was the way it was: many made the wrong choice. Forgetting all the principles of their educations, they were put to the test and failed. But the men and women with religious convictions, the resistance priests, were able to stand fast: none of them agreed to collaborate in order to save their skin. And that was equally true, even more true, of the rabbis: none of them—I repeat: *none of them*—consented to take the little power offered him to live—or live better, and longer—at the expense of his companions, his brothers and sisters in adversity. On the contrary, they displayed an abnegation that left the killers perplexed and, in a sense, stupefied. As for the Hasidim, they raised themselves higher than the heavens by their spirit of faith and solidarity: their common prayers on New Year's Day, their decision to celebrate with joy—yes, you read it correctly: with joy—the festival of the Law. And all this occurred in places where, by trying to dehumanize their victims, the killers ended by dehumanizing themselves. . . . Even today, my reason totters: it cannot grasp the hidden meaning, the brutal truth of what I saw—on one side, a humanity so pure, on the other, a humanity so low. How was it possible? How was it plausible to pray to God at Birkenau, in the shadow of the chimneys? How could we invoke God on the ruins of His creation?

I deal with these subjects in my stories. In other words: they obsess me even in my writing. As a storyteller, I turn solitude into an act against solitude.

What is writing? I appropriate words that belong to everyone. At that moment, I have made them mine; they bear my sign and my seal. Each of them reflects me, either condemns me or remains faithful to me. The bond between me and the words I use becomes charged with being: I am alone with them, but I would be more so without them.

Sooner or later, they become my reason for living and working. Whence their ambivalence: when they sing, I rise to the heavens; when they are gray and humdrum, I am lifeless.

Every creator experiences the same feelings of extreme ambition and depression. Samuel Beckett writes "as a last resort." Rabbi Nahman told stories in order to turn them into prayers.

If a different "I" could write my stories, I wouldn't have written them. I wrote them in order to give evidence. My role is that of a witness. Hence the solitude that weighs on each of my sentences, and on each of my silences. Every book is at once my first and my last book. And every story tells about the life and the struggle of the first and the last Jew, who have in common their solitude. Not to tell stories, or to tell something else, would be to betray them, abandon them, and worse: bear false witness. Whether I write of Moses or Jeremiah, Abraham or the Baal Shem Tov, it is my contemporary who signals to me and to whom I signal: they come to our rescue.

Did they also come to our rescue in the time of darkness? Our solitude in those years was unprecedented. Abandoned by human beings, forgotten by God, the Jewish man and woman felt driven out of Creation. Then, during a time as empty and gaping as the maw of a beast, Jews were forced to ask themselves the question: Is this the end? In one sense, we could answer Yes. It was the end of an era, the end of an illusion. Perhaps it was even the end of the world— except that it takes time to understand these things.

Orwell was not just a writer, he was also, in his own way, a prophet: was it by chance that he chose the year 1984 as a turning point? I don't think so. One has only to lapse into complacency, and to yield to forgetfulness, for the fallout of Auschwitz to cause tomorrow's Hiroshima.

But you will ask me: what about the Messiah in all this? Well, I still believe in him. I believe in the Messiah with all my heart, even more than before. But his coming depends on us. As the texts of the Kabbalah say: it is human beings and not the Lord who will determine the hour when the redeemer will come and the way in which he will come.

Which brings me back to my opening proposition, where I spoke of pity toward God.

Naturally, like everyone else, I have known what it is to be angry and I have raised my voice in protest. I don't regret it. But with the passing of the years, I have come to understand the twofold questioning that modern man has to undergo: just as I have the right to ask the Judge of all men and women, "Why did you allow Auschwitz to happen?" He also has the right to ask us, "Why did you spoil my creation? What right had you to cut the trees of life to make of them an altar to the glory of death?"

Suddenly you think of God in His luminous, heavenly solitude, and you begin to cry. You cry for Him and over Him. You cry so much that He too, according to Talmudic tradition, begins to cry, so that your tears and His meet and join together as only two melancholy solitudes, thirsting for presence, may join together.

—Translated by Lydia Davis

2

Elie Wiesel: A Thirty-Year Dialogue Between Hope and Despair

Daniel Stern

I am tempted to begin with the ending of *Night*, the most eloquent statement of despair in Holocaust literature—and one of the most eloquent in world literature. *Night*,[1] as every schoolchild now knows, was Elie Wiesel's first book: a memoir of which it has been said, one reads it once with awe and twice at one's peril.

Why such an extreme statement? Is it because *Night* evokes the life of "the kingdom of night" of the concentration camps so vividly, so painfully? The answer is more psychological than literary. I believe the secret of that book's astonishing power to move us consists of two riddles wrapped around each other.

First, *Night* forces the reader to experience the horrifying daily life of Auschwitz through the eyes of a child—though the tale is written by a grown man. And, second, it mysteriously expresses the despair of the child and the man, years later, writing about the child, at one and the same time. From the incident in which a young boy is left to slowly strangle to death before the assembled prisoners, to the beating to death of the child's father in the bunk below—during which the boy remains silent—we witness events so extreme that we accept the extreme central scenario of the book: that a pious Jewish boy enters Auschwitz and leaves so totally bereft of hope that implicitly God and Man are permanently indicted. I would have to turn to Ivan Karamazov's theological and metaphysical despair to find a match in modern literature. (Ivan uses as an example the torments and tears of a child locked up in a closet by a cruel parent. Such an injustice tempts him to "return his ticket to God." Though suffering is always suffering, and that of a child perhaps the most poignant, it is clear how far we have come from the world of Dostoevsky: from closets to gas chambers.)

The thirty years between the publication of *Night* and the year in which I write these words have seen both the Holocaust itself and the young protagonist of *Night* travel extraordinary journeys. The Holocaust has become in the minds of some a kingdom to be divided up by scholars who claim it, by scoffers who deny its historical reality, and by a new generation, which includes the first generation of the children of survivors, a generation who may soon have *their own* children.

The boy, Wiesel, has traveled a journey from Auschwitz to Stockholm, from the degradation of the Holocaust to one of the grandest successes: the Nobel Peace Prize. Yet his vision of the human condition—and the Jewish condition which he views as inextricably linked to it—is far more complex than is suggested by many of the scholars and critics who comment on his work. The path I would like to trace in this essay is the jagged one that Elie Wiesel has followed, oscillating between hope and despair, in a number of his books, in a cantata with the deeply paradoxical title of *Ani Maamin*[2]—*I Believe* —and in his personal speaking path around the world. This last plays a special role in Wiesel's mission, since, wittingly or unwittingly, he has inspired hundreds of thousands of people to a renewed sense of hope and belief. Many of these people have been shocked and moved to pity and despair by reading his work, yet have been moved beyond hopelessness after a direct encounter with the author, when he speaks to them in public, after having spoken to them in the privacy of his books.

Conventional wisdom has it that Wiesel has triumphantly returned from the "dead," that is, from despair to hope. If this is true, just what *is* the nature of its truth? How gradual was the return to hope? How deep is it? Is it confined to humankind? Is it confined to God? Is it a compromise; is it an illusion? And, most importantly, is there a moment, a year, an incident, anything that can pinpoint this change, this development?

A generation after the Holocaust, I suggest that if this commitment to hope was going to happen, it was far from a fait accompli. The telling of the story had finally begun—but its effects on both the world at large and on the survivors themselves were still very much in doubt. That is why I shall choose as a first illustrative quotation something far less "grand" than *Night*. Instead, let me invoke a small story about the telling of a tale (and the selling of a tale) and what it means to the listeners as well as to the teller.

It is taken from the book titled, appropriately, *One Generation After*. The story is called "First Royalties"[3] and is divided into two parts that complement each other perfectly. In a concentration camp a boy so young he is "barely out of Yeshiva" encounters an older man who advises him to "protect his soul." If he does this, the body's safety will somehow follow. How do you achieve this? By study, of course. Study what? The Talmud, of course. But how—no books, no tractates to examine? Simple, the older man says—by using memory. The older man knows the tractates by heart. They study together, learn, and survive together until one day the older man is removed from the work detail. The boy never sees him again.

The second part of the story is an incident in which a tough Block Leader—a Czech Jew with a sense of irony—sets up a literary contest. He offers a prize of two bowls of soup to the prisoner who tells the best story. When his turn comes, the boy refuses. The Block Leader is incredulous. No wish to invent a story so as to get enough to eat so that he might survive. The boy says, no thank you, sir; not only have I no story I wish to tell, but I have just eaten. This, the Block Leader, says, is truly mad. Eaten? Here? Today? And at this point the unnamed boy begins to describe the meal he has just attended in his imagination. "The dishes, the wines, the fruits, the desserts. By inviting him to the feast I reminded him that it was Friday night. The Shabbat meal. White tablecloth, silver candlesticks. The serenity, the joy."[4]

And the boy sings a moving prose poem of a Shabbat dinner that enchants the small circle of listeners—Block Leader and prisoners alike. It is a great success and he is nominated the winner by acclaim. He takes the two bowls of soup—the first royalties of the future writer—to his bunk. "And the nausea welled up inside me, uncontrollable, overwhelming. I had the oppressive feeling that it was my story itself I was swallowing—a story impoverished and diminished for having been told; its source a memory grown dim and less and less my own."[5]

I invoke this despair at the telling of the tale, even though it is not yet the telling of the great tale of the destruction of an entire people, but merely the sharing of a private memory, as the sounding of the theme. For thirty years that boy will, in various guises, tell stories and in various literary, theological, and metaphysical ways react with a kind of powerful anxiety. As if the unthinkableness of the event had made it untellable and unsharable, as well. Yet it must be told and shared. Perhaps the price was the existential nausea that, paradoxically, has never left the subtext of each telling.

Bear in mind that the audience, over the years, is a changing one, including the early, uninterested public, the other survivors, and even the people who wish to be sympathetic but cannot, or do not wish, to comprehend the enormity of such suffering. Among these listeners we must also include, naturally, God, Himself, a God who appears, at times to be utterly indifferent, and at other times to engage in a bitter ironic dialogue with various characters who speak for Wiesel. Though the most interesting audiences are the all-too-human ones such as Pedro, a kind of attractive nihilist who challenges every possible belief, in *The Town Beyond the Wall*,[6] and the Rabbi at the end of *The Gates of the Forest*[7] who urges joy on the despairing young survivor who is far from ready to tell his tale or to accept either joy or belief.

Thus, there is a continuing tension between the tale of total terror that demands to be told, but that is corrupted and diluted by the very act of telling, and by the hopelessness of being understood in a way that does not diminish the experience being related. This tension lasts for years and runs through many of Wiesel's early books.

It is only when we read two books, quite well along in Wiesel's canon, that we begin to approach some kind of resolution of this tension. *The Testament*,[8] published in 1981, and *The Fifth Son*,[9] published in 1985. Wiesel's output is too prodigious for generalizations. However, it seems to me that not until the novels of the eighties are there families taking center stage in his fictional universe. This is not a small issue, not a mere technical novelistic matter. It has a central relevance. Until now we have Wiesel's typical protagonist, alone, except for fleeting emotional and sexual experiences, wifeless and childless, a rootless, wandering survivor engaged in a quest without boundaries and without hope. It is essentially a quest for an answer. Why? How could this happen? And it is without hope, since to find an answer that would satisfy this survivor, either history would have to turn backward and the Holocaust be canceled, or a human being—or God—would have to answer the two impossible questions: How? Why?

The encounters of the prototypical hero are brief, temporary, and impermanent. Protagonists, such as Michael in *The Town Beyond the Wall* and Gregor in *The Gates of the Forest*, wander and question, shell-shocked survivors asking directions in a world suddenly bereft of signposts. It is hard to tell which would be the greater obscenity: the permanent absence of a definitive answer, or anything that might pass for an explanation of the astonishing cruelties let loose upon millions of innocents.

Hence, the preoccupation in all of these novels with asking questions and telling stories, and with a proliferation of events involving temporary mutes. Other writers, for example, Samuel Beckett and Harold Pinter, have emphasized silence—its temptations, its attractions, its final impossibility. But alone among contemporary authors, Wiesel uses silence as a continuing metaphor. And the theme of voluntary and involuntary muteness is one of his favorite ways of expressing the paradox of the purity of silence and the eternally compromised need for speech—another expression for telling the tale. The eternal oscillation between speech and silence becomes a kind of metaphor for the oscillation between hope and despair. Michael is tortured but remains silent. Gregor plays a mute who terrifies the audience of a Christian passion play when he suddenly speaks. And, we may recall that after the young boy in "First Royalties" tells his story, he feels it has been diminished—become less his own—because it has been told.

It is as if all speech, all answers and the telling of all tales have become fatally compromised. Why?

Much has been written by others, survivors and historians, about this question. Paul Celan, for example, calls into question the validity of language itself, once human speech has been used to plan and implement a "Final Solution." Others have questioned the nature of the telling of tales as a road to understanding, once the Author of the story of the Universe itself has been challenged, subverted, and questioned, where does that leave all the lesser stories of our daily existence?

In Wiesel's work, there is often the question, To whom shall I tell the story? "I alone have escaped to tell you" is the subtext. In *Night*, his earliest work, there already appears a certain Moshe, the Madman who returns to Sighet to tell of the disaster that is befalling the Jews of Europe, but he is not believed. He is the first of many witnesses who have a tale of awe to tell, a tale no one wishes to hear. In the parallel historical realm, it is now a commonplace to recognize that indifference to the Holocaust and its survivors was the rule rather than the exception, one of the reasons it took years for the survivors to break their silence. But even then it was to a world that could not *or did not wish to* comprehend the full magnitude of what had happened that the story was told.

Those who experienced the Holocaust had no need to tell the tale to each other; indeed, it remained for years their dark secret. Those who stood by while it took place had no wish to hear of it; and those who did want to know, to learn were so stunned by the magnitude of the suffering that they were compelled to turn away, almost against their will. And those who had participated, or who had sympathy for the persecutors rather than for the victims, became the ultimate unwilling audience. That is, they denied that the tale was true, adding a kind of demonic blasphemy to the fate of the reluctant witnesses. As for God, who was present, or absent, throughout the event, did He require reminding?

The two books, *The Testament* and *The Fifth Son*, are watersheds marking a unique historical moment. The moment I refer to is the birth and growth of the second generation of survivors. It is difficult to pinpoint the beginning of this generation, either as a historical reality or as a voice, a group demanding to be reckoned with, but perhaps the mid-seventies will do as well as any other. And it is part of my thesis that their appearance as a reality, as a force, has a bearing on the artistic and spiritual development of Elie Wiesel's

work from then on and is a key element in what can be described
as his movement from despair toward hope, from rebellion toward
reconciliation.

Another element influencing Wiesel's work is the return of the
Russian Jews to the stage of history, an event that has resulted in a
wave of hard-won immigration of Soviet Jews to Israel and to the
United States, an event prefigured and in part set in motion by
Wiesel's book *The Jews of Silence*.[10] It is possible to see two historical
events converging to push a despairing witness, in thrall to silence,
into fresh speech and fresh action. Here was a new story to tell—a
story still happening, whose outcome might still be influenced for the
good, if the tale were told and if the world listened. In this respect,
both issues are related: The slaughtered millions of the Holocaust
had endured their fates and were gone, but the fate of the Jews of the
Soviet Union and the children of the survivors were both still in
question.

The first of the two novels, *The Testament*, takes place, for the
most part, in Russia, but also in the Berlin of the 1920s, Paris of the
1930s, Spain during the Civil War, and finally, in Russia of World
War II and after. The second novel, *The Fifth Son*, takes place in
Brooklyn and Germany. What links them?

The Testament is told by a father to a son. *The Fifth Son* is told by
a son about a father. In the first book, a son turns mute; in the second
book, it is the father's silence that is in question. Their differences
are as interesting as their similarities. *The Testament* is a historical
novel, a long narrative with many characters and a *mise en scene* that
is no less ambitious than the entire political landscape of the twentieth century.

It is ostensibly the story of Paltiel Kossover, a Russian poet who,
in his spiritual and political Odyssey embodies the twentieth-century
adventures, and it contains the fullest treatment in Wiesel's work—
and one of the fullest anywhere—of the Jewish messianic commitment to the world revolution of communism and its tragic outcome. It
also touches on Zionism, the Spanish Civil War, the Holocaust, and
the Soviet oppression of the Jews. In scope, it is one of the most
ambitious of Wiesel's novels. Yet the underlying themes remain the
same as in the briefer, more existential novels. Kossover's poems are

unpublished (silence). There is the watchman, Zupanev, who tells Kossover's son, Grisha, of the "secret testimony" of Paltiel Kossover's trial as a Zionist spy by the Soviets, after he naively returns to Russia (another form of silence), as well as Kossover's secret testament to his son. And in one of the most overt ironic situations, Kossover's son, Grisha, has taken a vow of silence as a kind of protest over the mysterious confusions of his father's life.

In a way, it is as if Wiesel had gone back into the deep recesses of modern history in order to paint in the missing background of the current situation of the Soviet "Jews of Silence." It is unique in the Wiesel fictional canon for the fullness of its brilliantly rendered historical background and its rich play of political ideas. And it being Wiesel, there is always the edge of the theological and spiritual dimension present or impending. But it stands as an important movement in his career as a novelist, weaving as it does the earlier themes of the hopelessly compromised telling of the tale into the broad sweep of the tale of history itself.

The next novel, *The Fifth Son*, bears the dedication: *For Elisha and all the other children of survivors*. I mention this because it bears, somehow, on the particular melody I am trying to isolate from the large symphonic texture of Wiesel's fiction. From the first page it is clear that we are seeing dramatized in a novel, perhaps for the first time, what had, in recent years, become a much-talked-about and written-about phenomenon: the bitter refusal of many survivors to tell the tale of their suffering to their children, and the bitter, anguished response on the part of this first generation, in the face of this silence.

By the time *The Fifth Son* was published, numerous articles had been written on the subject—psychiatric papers, scholarly books, even psychiatric conferences had been convened to examine this syndrome. At about the same time as the book was published, an international organization of Children of Survivors was formed. As far as I know, *The Fifth Son* is the first work of fiction to dramatize what, apparently, is a widespread conflict between the survivors and their children.

The texture of *The Fifth Son* is as taut and spare as *The Testament* is broad and encompassing. Reuven Tamiroff, a modest, unassuming

Jewish refugee who earns his living as a librarian, lives in Brooklyn
with his son. He is silent on everything the world considers important: matters of fact. What happened to the Jews of the ghetto
Dawarowsk? Why is Tamiroff's wife, Rachel, in a hospital, probably
an asylum, dying of grief? Is it related to the fact that her oldest son,
Ariel, had been murdered years before by an SS officer? (It is one of
the tales that Reuven Tamiroff refuses to tell his surviving son.)

That son gains the glimpses he does of these matters, mainly
through two friends of his father's: both inspired inventions. Simha-
the-dark, and Bontchek; two of the ironic commentators who pepper
Wiesel's fictions like bitter, laughing prophets. The game of silent
survivor and searching, desperate child that has by now been so well
documented in life, is played out painfully by Reuven and his son.
The son's obsession grows until he learns of his father's encounter
with an SS Officer, Richard Lander, nicknamed "The Angel," as in
"Angel of Death." Indeed, Lander caused countless deaths, including that of the older Tamiroff child, Ariel. Ariel, too, becomes one of
the son's obsessions, the child who died instead of him. Of particular
interest is the fact that, in the haunting denouement in which the son
searches out Lander to finally commit the act of vengeance his father
had failed to commit years before, it is the survivor's child, the
second generation, who bears the burden of the tale.

To return again to the post-Nobel Wiesel the world knows: the
paradigm of Yeats's poem "Among School Children" in which the
poet speaks of himself as a "smiling sixty-year-old public man." For
like Yeats, Wiesel is a great poet of sorrow who has challenged God
and man on behalf of the humiliated of the world. And his smile at
an ironic moment during one of his lectures has become as precious
to his audiences of today, as was his revelation of an irreconcilable
despair to readers of a generation ago. Just as he has disseminated a
terrible knowledge too awful to be comprehended, so too has he now
disseminated a kind of hope—mostly, perhaps, by example. By a
persistent honesty in the face of cruel man and silent God, an honesty
so profound that he has not given an inch in his battle against those
who wish to vulgarize suffering, let alone those who wish a too-easy
accommodation with a universe ruled by such suffering. This is a
man whose voice seems to have spoken for so many nonsurvivors, as

well as, for example, those people of good will who did not wish to
see an American president honor the SS along with their victims at
the Bitburg Cemetery. The man whose insistence on hope for the
hopeless of today (not of the past) shares equal emotional and spiritual space with his sense of timeless tragedy.

And yet, whence the source of this developing home in *him?*

The answer I am proposing is, perhaps, finally rather simple. I
believe that the birth of a child to a survivor, of a generation of
children of survivors, brought about a leap of faith—as paradoxical
a leap as is suggested by the Kirkegaardian imagery the term evokes.
Once the solitary wanderers, with smoke and ashes in their hair and
eyes, were no longer alone in the chain of human creation, perhaps
everything changed. The cries of babies that grow into the tormented
questions of adolescents, why should they not change the rules of the
game between man and God, at least for this one generation that has
been tried as perhaps no other generation in history?

To remind any reader of Wiesel about how deep his hopelessness
was, how profound the quarrel with God and His universe, one has
only to turn to those most moving pages in *The Gates of the Forest*, to
the scene at the end in which Gregor, lost in his darkened universe,
confronts the Hasidic Rebbe of Brooklyn during Simchat Torah.
In this encounter the author has his character recount, to my knowledge for the first time, the now famous story of the *D'in Torah* at
Auschwitz, a trial in which a Rabbi called three of his colleagues
together and indicted God for the crime of murder. The unanimous
verdict: guilty.

Gregor is remorseless in telling the story to the Rabbi: "After all,
He had the last word. On the day after the trial, He turned the
sentence against his judges and accusers. They, too, were taken off
to the slaughter. And I tell you this: if their death has no meaning, then it's an insult, and if it does have a meaning, it's even
more so."[11]

Gregor drives and drives the Rebbe until he responds: "So be it!"
he shouted. "He's guilty; do you think I don't know it? That I have
no eyes to see, no ears to hear? That my heart doesn't revolt? That I
have no desire to beat my head against the wall and shout like a
madman, to give rein to my sorrow and disappointment? Yes, he is

guilty. He has become the ally of evil, of death, of murder, but the problem is still not solved. I ask you a question and dare you answer: 'What is there left for us to do?' "[12]

Gregor did not, and could not, answer the Rebbe. Elie Wiesel, in the intervening years, has answered, not with rhetoric but with art and action. The telling of the tale that once filled his young protagonist with nausea now is told and retold by a new generation of survivors' children. And, in Stockholm, on 11 December 1986, he delivered the Nobel Lecture: "Hope, Despair, and Memory." He begins with the traditional prayer *Ani maamin:* "*Ani maamin,* I believe . . . I believe in the coming of the Messiah . . . I believe in the hope for a future, just as I believe in the irresistible power of memory."[13] And he concludes with words that I would like to believe validate the thesis presented here, a thesis that tries to document through the fictional art of this Master, the journey from the abyss of despair to the tentative new ground of hope:

The only lesson that I have learned from my experiences is twofold: first, that there are no plausible answers to what we have endured. There are no theological answers, there are no psychological answers, there are no literary answers, there are no philosophical answers, there are no religious answers. The only conceivable answer is a *moral* answer. This means there must be a moral element in whatever we do. Second, that just as despair can be given to me only by another human being, hope too can be given to me only by another human being. [Hu]mankind must remember also, and above all, that like hope and whatever hope signifies, peace is not God's gift to his creatures. Peace is a very special gift—it is our gift to each other. And so *Ani maamin*—I believe—that we must have hope for one another also because of one another. And *Ani maamin*—I believe—that because of our children and theirs we should be worthy of that hope, of that redemption, and of some measure of peace.[14]

This movement from despair with humankind and God toward hope for humankind is, although not a simple movement, unmistakable. In adapting the classic *Ani maamin* to embody belief in and for other humans and the ensuing line about being worthy of that hope because of our children—these are Wiesel's significant additions to the ancient prayer of belief.

Freud tells us that actions quiet anxiety and that even unbelieving political masses tend to believe that their children embody their immortality. Wiesel's life and career describe an evolution from solitary witness to spiritual leader, from solitary wanderer to rooted father: an extraordinary thirty-year journey from despair toward hope.

It is in the bearing witness, in the telling of the untellable tale, that Wiesel's voice has brought light where once there was unrelieved night. But all these arguments adduced above are only partial explanations.

The rest is the mystery of art.

Notes

1. Elie Wiesel, *Night*, trans. Stella Rodway (New York: Avon Books, 1960).
2. Elie Wiesel, *Ani Maamin: A Song Lost and Found Again*, trans. Marion Wiesel (New York: Random House, 1973).
3. Elie Wiesel, "First Royalties," in *One Generation After* (New York: Pocket Books, 1978), 105–14.
4. Wiesel, "First Royalties," 112.
5. Ibid., 114.
6. Elie Wiesel, *The Town Beyond the Wall*, trans. Stephen Becker (New York: Avon Books, 1964).
7. Elie Wiesel, *The Gates of the Forest*, trans. Frances Frenaye (New York: Avon Books, 1967).
8. Elie Wiesel, *The Testament*, trans. Marion Wiesel (New York: Summit Books, 1981).
9. Elie Wiesel, *The Fifth Son*, trans. Marion Wiesel (New York: Summit Books, 1985).
10. Elie Wiesel, *The Jews of Silence*, trans. Neal Kozodoy (New York: New American Library, 1967).
11. Wiesel, *Gates of the Forest*, 195.
12. Ibid., 196–97.
13. Elie Wiesel, "The Nobel Lecture: Hope, Despair, and Memory," in *The Nobel Peace Prize 1986* (New York: Summit Books and Boston University, 1986), 21.
14. Ibid., 31.

3

Elie Wiesel:
Between Jerusalem and New York

George Schwab

For some strange reason, I chose the Diaspora.
                              —ELIE WIESEL

Asked where he felt most at home, Elie Wiesel replied, "In Jerusalem, when I am not in Jerusalem."[1] Because there are no obstacles to his settling there, the question that comes to mind is, How can Elie Wiesel, an observant Jew, a concentration camp survivor, a devout supporter of Israel, and one of the most eloquent spokesmen that Jewry has ever produced, reside in New York and not in Jerusalem? When I asked myself whether it is possible to attribute his decision to choose the Diaspora[2] to the age-old ambivalence that Jews have displayed toward living in Israel in fear, perhaps, that congregating in one place will serve as a prelude to national persecution leading to group extinction, I turned to his writings for evidence as to his thinking. Never having read him in depth before, I even labored under the erroneous impression that the traumatic concentration camp experiences of this man of frail appearance precluded him from facing additional ordeals, especially those associated with a severely embattled Israel. On the other hand, I concluded, a partial and perhaps even a satisfactory answer might be obtained by looking at his oeuvre from the perspective of the Holocaust survivor turned committed writer and activist.

Born in 1928 in the small town of Sighet in Transylvania, Elie Wiesel's childhood was shaped by his Jewish home as a member of a devout Jewish family. According to Elie Wiesel, the world that was transmitted to him and that he willingly and lovingly embraced centered on the warmth of his home, on the Hebrew Bible, Hasidism, the Talmud, and other commentaries. Had it not been for the Second World War, it is doubtful that he would have stepped out of this context, except for one thing. Displaying strong artistic inclinations as a child, he knew that he "was going to write even before the war" but was not certain what he was going to write about. In all likelihood, he added, it would have been a "commentary on the Bible or on the Talmud."[3]

While there is a continuity, one with its own complexities, between the prewar and the postwar Elie Wiesel, as far as his commitment to Judaism is concerned, his traumatic experiences at Auschwitz and Buchenwald, the butchery of part of his family, and the slaughter of Jews, experiences so overwhelming that words can neither capture nor convey the horror, engendered in him a change in direction that was not merely accentual. The trauma that the critical interruption of his normal life brought about led him to question God. Though never going as far as Nietzsche in declaring that God was dead, he nevertheless concluded that God's failure to intercede in the tragedy of His people is tantamount to His having abandoned them.[4] Unable to rely on Him, Elie Wiesel concluded that He was a "God in whom I no longer believed."[5] With his belief in God shattered, his family gone, and his life and dreams turned to dust, his very being became dominated by war and slaughter. Said he: "My universe is the universe of the survivor."[6]

Maintaining other aspects of the Jewish context, Elie Wiesel was brought to France from Germany soon after the war. Though dreary postwar Paris was no hospitable place to one whose companion had been Auschwitz, in Paris and at the Sorbonne, his intellectual horizons broadened decisively.[7] Just as one can argue that Elie Wiesel's career as a novelist was sealed in Paris where he discovered, read, and was inspired by literary giants such as Kafka, Dostoevsky,

Camus, and Sartre, it can also be shown that existentialist components contributed to his opting for the Diaspora. It was congenial to
him because it dovetailed with his Hasidic heritage with its emphasis
on fellowship and hope "to hopeless Jews."[8]

The metaphysical consciousness that gripped the imagination of
gloomy postwar France was certainly existentialist, which was, above
all, a set of beliefs agreeable to any intellectual in search of the
meaning and purpose of life. Although Elie Wiesel did not share the
existentialist assumption about the nonexistence of God, his conclusion regarding God, which he reached in Auschwitz because of
Auschwitz, did converge, at least initially, with the existentialist
belief in the purposelessness of the universe. Rather than the creation of an irreparable void, within the context of a nonexistent God,
[Sartre insisted that *precisely* because there is no God, everything on
earth becomes possible.] According to him, this "is the very starting
point of existentialism."[9] What follows in the Sartrean configuration
is that human beings are forced to define themselves, to make themselves. In the words of Sartre,

When we say that man chooses his own self, we mean that everyone of us
does likewise; but we also mean by that that in making this choice he also
chooses all men. In fact, in creating the man that we want to be, there is
not a single one of our acts which does not at the same time create an image
of man as we think he ought to be. To choose to be this or that is to affirm
at the same time the value of what we choose, because we can never choose
evil. We always choose the good, and nothing can be good for us without
being good for all.[10]

In accord with Elie Wiesel's Hasidic provenience and the existentialist focus on and commitment to man, on man actively and positively defining and determining himself, and thereby his fellow men,
he has noted that having survived the Holocaust by chance, he felt
compelled or "duty-bound to give meaning to [his] survival, to justify
each moment of [his] life."[11] This means the necessity of always
transmitting to others what had transpired. Not to do so, "not to
transmit [the] experience [of the Holocaust]," said Elie Wiesel, "is to
betray the experience."[12] It will be shown, however, that this is only
one level in his multitiered thrust, the prerequisite to attaining his
overarching goal.

Having formulated his purpose of committing to paper the magnitude of the calamity for the annals of Jewish history,[13] a further goal, if not his final one, that can be extrapolated from his writings is his commitment to sensitize the world to the severity of the crimes committed against the Jewish people and make the horrors stick, so to speak. I have deduced this resolve from his writings, from his depiction of slices of the Holocaust, and from his reminding the world that although "not all victims were Jewish . . . all Jews were victims."[14] The scope of the crimes, the inadequacy of language to capture events of the Holocaust (not to speak of the impossibility of storifying the Holocaust in its entirety), combined with the incapacity of the human imagination to grasp and to comprehend the little that language can convey, led Elie Wiesel to characterize the Holocaust as the central "event of this century and perhaps of all the centuries."[15] The uniqueness of the Holocaust, which resides in its universality, that is, the condemnation of Jews to death everywhere, thrusts the Holocaust to the forefront of history and reaffirms the historicity of the Jewish people, which Elie Wiesel reinforces by turning to biblical times. What emerges is a conception of history that is neither linear nor cyclical. He oscillates between two poles, between two singular events: Sinai and the Holocaust. According to him, "Auschwitz was a unique phenomenon, a unique event, like the revelation at Sinai."[16] Thus just as the Covenant between God and the new nation established a pact between the Deity and His people that had implications that far transcended the new nation that was born in consequence of the Exodus and the Wandering, the Holocaust, "the dark face of Sinai," as Elie Wiesel calls it,[17] transcends the tragedy of Jewry.

The historicity of the Jewish people imposes duties on Jews and non-Jews alike, according to Elie Wiesel. As far as Jews are concerned, everyone is "responsible for the past and the future of [his people] because [every Jew] carries within himself the vision of Sinai and the flames of the *Khourban* [the Destruction]."[18] Going beyond the Jewish context, he reminds the world that in order to begin to fathom the dehumanized dimension that the war assumed, the severity of the crimes committed against Jews, Auschwitz must always be remembered and used as a frame of reference. And here Elie Wiesel issued a warning that, I believe, revealed his overarching goal. Said he: "The only way for the world to save itself is by remembering what it has done to my people and, beyond it, to other people. . . . There could have been no Hiroshima, symbolically, without Auschwitz."[19] "To forget Auschwitz is to justify Hiroshima—the next Hiroshima. It is a paradox: Only Auschwitz can save the planet from a new Hiroshima. . . . We recall ultimate violence in order to prevent its recurrence. Ours then is a twofold commitment: to life and truth"[20] —an affirmation that accords with the imperatives of the Covenant, with the stress on fellowship in Hasidism, and with the philosophical components of existentialism. To use Robert McAfee Brown's telling formulation, the aforementioned succinctly encapsulates Elie Wiesel's move "from Jewish particularity to human universality" without, of course, ever compromising on the former.[21]

That we might thus fail to remember the past and the danger that this would spell for the future have led Elie Wiesel, an unshakable believer in the power of the written word, to recast the purpose of literature and the task of writers. He has argued that whereas before the Holocaust writing for art's sake, for the sake of beauty, might have made sense, Auschwitz has made the world aware that it no longer does because "beauty without an ethical dimension cannot exist." The world, he said, has witnessed what culture without an ethical content did to Germany during the war. What the Nazis called culture lacked "any ethical purpose or motivation. I believe in, the ethical thrust, in the ethical function, in the human adventure in science or in culture or in writing."[22] Based on the implications of the Holocaust, writers, Elie Wiesel insists, "must write with that as background, as criteri[on]. Once he takes this as a background, as a yardstick, he will be careful in writing. He will not prostitute his words; his responsibilities are such that they are paralyzing."[23]

In summary, unable to turn the clock back to the world that existed before the destruction and convinced that the world is racing toward another destruction, he has set himself the task of doing everything possible to help avert ruin. Said he: "I continue to write [teach, speak, and demonstrate] because I am trying to prevent the catastrophe."[24] But in contrast to Nietzsche, who believed in repudiating the past as a thing "so threatening that it has to be forgotten," Elie Wiesel affirms it. Without memory, he believes, people would operate in a void and their endeavors would be meaningless. [25] In the words of George Santayana: "Those who cannot remember the past are condemned to repeat it."

Although the discussion does not directly illuminate the answer to the question why New York and not Jerusalem, it will contribute to an understanding about why Elie Wiesel made his choice to live in the Diaspora. He himself is vague on the why. The clues he provides are scanty. He speaks of wanting to go to Palestine after his liberation from Buchenwald but of being prevented from doing so because of the British policy that severely restricted Jewish immigration. "From that point on," he said, he was "ready to go anywhere"[26] and ended up in France. When the state of Israel was created in 1948, a "messianic event with which [he] wanted to be associated,"[27] he volunteered to fight for the beleaguered state but was rejected for medical reasons. Undeterred, he went to Israel as a journalist, staying a couple of weeks. He returned to Paris and resumed his studies, continuing to work as a journalist for an Israeli newspaper in order to support himself. [28]

As a journalist he traveled widely, and while working in New York in the mid-1950s, he was hit by a taxi and, in his words, "was given up."[29] The accident, which led to his becoming an invalid for almost a year, brought him into conflict with the French bureaucracy, which insisted that he return to France to have his visa extended, notwithstanding his confinement to a wheelchair. Despondent, Wiesel reacted favorably to a suggestion made by a sympathetic American immigration officer who proposed that he become an American citizen as a way of solving the visa problem. [30] He stayed and eventually became a citizen. "Since then," said Elie Wiesel, "I'm grateful to America. Even when I oppose some of the Administration's policies I do it out of a sense of gratitude toward this country. Nowhere else —with the exception of Israel, of course—did I encounter such a human attitude."[31] In reply to Harry James Cargas's question: "But why New York?" Elie Wiesel said:

In the beginning I had to stay in New York. I was a journalist accredited to the U.N. My paper paid for my being in New York. That lasted, until, I think, 1966 or so. When I gave up journalism, I had to choose some other means. For very practical reasons I chose New York . . . [because he accepted a distinguished professorship at the] City College which rearranged and changed everything. [32]

That these practical explanations cannot constitute a satisfactory answer to the question is obvious. A more plausible key is provided by Elie Wiesel's admission that his "true self [does not] belong . . . to France . . . to America, [or] to any other place,"[33] a trait characteristic of Diaspora Jews. Denied for centuries the right to plant genuine roots in the Diaspora, Jews have never fully felt at home anywhere. Until recently their precarious situation was not even translated into defining political power and authority in territorial terms. The core of Jewish identity was religion and, in more general terms, Jewishness. Because the creation of the state of Israel in 1948 did not lead to the mass exodus of Jews from the Diaspora to the Holy Land, the mind-set of Diaspora Jews did not change appreciably. True, construed as a safety valve, a haven to which to run in case of danger, Israel has to some extent drained the angst of Diaspora Jews in open-society countries. The new element to enter the discussion in consequence of the creation of Israel centered on the relationship between the Jews of Israel and those of the Diaspora. Stung perhaps by the collective denigration of Diaspora Jews by the Jews of Israel for not ascending to the Holy Land, Elie Wiesel took an unequivocal stand. Said he: It is his "absolute conviction that the oneness of [the Jewish people] is of an ontological nature. Whoever chooses one against the other cannot be defined as truly Jewish. Whoever attempts to oppose Israel to the Diaspora, or vice versa, will inevitably betray both."[34]

However significant this statement may be in absolving conscious and subconscious guilt feelings on the part of Diaspora Jews, and thereby rationalizing their choice to remain, and however important the statement may be in revealing his own decision, the case of Elie Wiesel is more complicated. Underlying this justification is his commitment to live a dedicated life, one inspired and nourished by the Hasidic commitment to the "ideals of humanity [and] to the ideals of brotherhood,"[35] which he has garbed in existentialist imperatives. Thus, in contrast to the Hasid of Pshiskhe, who, unknown to himself, according to Elie Wiesel, lived a "philosophical event, or engaged in a philosophical debate,"[36] Elie Wiesel consciously lives both. Obsessed to apprehend a world that is better than the world that was and so recognized by the Nobel Committee that awarded him the Nobel Peace Prize in 1986, he tirelessly continues to write, teach, speak, and demonstrate. Aware that he may not be reaching "large sections of the public"[37] but obstinately determined to do so, he used all of his Nobel prize funds to establish in New York a vehicle "to promote the cause of human rights and peace throughout the world," The Elie Wiesel Foundation for Humanity. As one who has mustered and channeled emotional, intellectual, and financial resources to attain the ultimate objective of a humane and peaceful world, he has left himself no choice other than to continue on the path that he has followed since the 1950s. In short, a self-imposed agenda like that of Elie Wiesel's precludes him from working anywhere but a world metropolis.

New York, a hospitable open city rich in ethnic life, a center of Hasidism and a model for Jerusalem and the Middle East insofar as the three Abrahamic religions live in peace, an international cultural and intellectual hub, the headquarters of the United Nations and the communications capital of the world, is a cosmopolis in the news everywhere, is sui generis as far as the furthering of Elie Wiesel's vitally necessary commitment is concerned. It dovetails with his overlapping thrust: transmitting what transpired, sensitizing the consciousness of the world to the crimes of Auschwitz, and appealing to world public opinion on the necessity of recalling consummate violence in order to prevent catastrophe. Even if the first can be adequately attained from Jerusalem, the second and the third cannot, I believe. The committed writer and activist that Elie Wiesel is, coupled with his unalterable determination to advance, amplify, and beam his highly charged cause around the world, can best be fulfilled in New York — a city that has no peers.

Notes

1. Elie Wiesel, "The Itinerary of Elie Wiesel: From Sighet to Jerusalem" (1972), television script published in *Against Silence: The Voice and Vision of Elie Wiesel,* ed. Irving Abrahamson, vol. 3, p. 8 (New York: Holocaust Library, 1985).
2. Ibid., 6.
3. Harry James Cargas, *In Conversation with Elie Wiesel* (New York: Paulist Press, 1976), 87.
4. Elie Wiesel, *Night,* trans. Stella Rodway. (Toronto: Bantam, 1986), 31, 32, 42, 62, 64, 65, 66.
5. Ibid., 87. For an answer to Carol Rittner's question of the apparent paradox of his rejection and affirmation of God, Elie Wiesel recently put it as follows: "It is . . . true that I said my God was 'murdered.' I can say that it was true for that moment [in *Night*], that it may be true for certain moments, but it is no longer true for my entire life. We have to believe in the Deity, that God is alive because we are alive and our lives are intertwined." "An Interview with Elie Wiesel," *America* 159, no. 15 (19 November 1988): 398.
6. Elie Wiesel, "How and Why I Write" (1980), in *Against Silence,* ed. Abrahamson, 2: 117.
7. Cargas, *In Conversation,* 79.
8. John S. Friedman, "An Interview with Elie Wiesel on 'The Art of Fiction,' " *Paris Review* 79, no. 91 (Spring 1984): 138, 162.
9. Jean-Paul Sartre, *Existentialism,* trans. Bernard Frechtman (New York: Philosophical Library, 1947), 27.
10. Ibid., 20.
11. Quoted by Abrahamson in *Against Silence,* 1: 15.
12. Wiesel, "How and Why I Write."
13. Abrahamson, *Against Silence* 1: 10–13.
14. Elie Wiesel, "Does the Holocaust Lie Beyond the Reach of Art?" (1983), in ibid. 2: 125.
15. Elie Wiesel, "The Holocaust and the Anguish of the Writer" (1973), in ibid., 66.
16. Cargas, *In Conversation,* 8.
17. Elie Wiesel, "From Holocaust to Rebirth" (1970), in *Against Silence,* ed. Abrahamson 1: 240.
18. Elie Wiesel, "On Being a Jew" (1967), in ibid., 246.

19. Elie Wiesel, "On Silence, Words, and Salvation" (1980), in ibid. 2: 122.
20. Wiesel, "Does the Holocaust Lie Beyond the Reach of Art?" 126.
21. Robert McAfee Brown, *Elie Wiesel: Messenger to All Humanity* (Notre Dame: University of Notre Dame Press, 1983), 193.
22. Cargas, *In Conversation*, 86–87.
23. Ibid., 87.
24. Wiesel, "On Silence, Words, and Salvation."
25. Ibid.; Elie Wiesel, "To Deepen Memory," in ibid. 3: 157; Elie Wiesel, "The Focus Is Memory" (1979), in ibid., 161–64.
26. Cargas, *In Conversation*, 76.
27. Ibid., 89
28. Ibid.
29. Ibid., 63.
30. Ibid., 64.
31. Ibid.
32. Ibid.
33. Elie Wiesel, "The Use of Words and the Weight of Silence" (1973), in *Against Silence*, ed. Abrahamson 2: 77. In a recent dialogue with Philip de Saint-Cheron, Elie Wiesel put it as follows:

> Personally, I consider myself a Jew and an American simultaneously, and still, I love Israel with all my heart; and still, I write in French. I am close to all these countries. It is the Jew in me who is American, it is the Jew in me who loves France, and the Jew in me who wholeheartedly and from the depth of his soul loves Israel. Perhaps there was a time when we had to make these geographic choices. Today, geography has become irrelevant. *Le mal et l'exil: Recontre avec Élie Wiesel* (Paris: Nouvelle cité, 1988), 215.

34. Elie Wiesel, "Two Images, One Destiny" (1974), in *Against Silence*, ed. Abrahamson 1: 297.
35. Elie Wiesel, "The Baal Shem Tov" (1972), in *Against Silence*, ed. Abrahamson 3: 81.
36. Friedman, "Interview with Elie Wiesel," 138, 139.
37. Abrahamson, *Against Silence*, 1: 17.

4

An Interview with Elie Wiesel

Carol Rittner

Born on 30 September 1928 in Sighet, Romania, Elie Wiesel is no ordinary writer. A survivor of the Holocaust, he stands in the place of his experience, yet never seems to lose faith in God, in decency, or in the human effort to build a more humane world for all people.

His hard-won faith, fashioned out of his experience of the Holocaust, is one of this century's great acts of faith. While Wiesel rejects the very notion of "God is dead," he challenges Jews and non-Jews alike to confront the real difficulty, which he maintains is not to live in a world without God, but to choose to live in a world with God, even while facing the evil, suffering, and mystery of the Holocaust.

When he was given the 1986 Nobel Peace Prize, Egil Aarvik, chairman of the Norwegian Nobel Committee, called Wiesel "a witness for truth and justice" who has come from the abyss of the death camps "as a messenger to mankind—not with a message of hate and revenge but with one of brotherhood and atonement. . . . In him we see a man who has gone from utter humiliation to become one of our most important spiritual leaders and guides."[1]

In a time when spiritual authority is often ineffective or called into question, Elie Wiesel's reconstructed belief in God, humanity, and the future—in spite of the past—is a source of inspiration to Jews and Christians all over the world. Convinced that "humanity's fate is not sealed; that everything is still possible," he is equally convinced that "it is up to human beings to build on the ruins, with the ruins, a

30

hearth, a shelter, a dwelling in which life will be celebrated and not profaned, in which the future will not be accompanied by anguish."[2] It is a compelling conviction challenging him—and us—to take human history seriously.

Rittner: What does it mean to be a Jew today?

Wiesel: To be a Jew today is like being a Jew three thousand years ago, except that conditions have changed. Deep down, I should basically feel exactly what a Jew in the time of King David felt, meaning, the Jewish people have received the Law, which doesn't make us superior to any people nor inferior to any people, but we have received the Law and the Law must be shared with other people. We must not force it on others, but we should offer it to them.

To be a Jew is to remember. In the time of David, I would have said, "I remember Joshua, I remember Moses, I remember Abraham." And today, I say, "I remember David. I remember Solomon." To be a Jew is to remember as far back as possible, but that also goes for anyone who is not Jewish. Everyone has a memory that began before his or her own.

To be a Jew is to be a human being. If there is one word I would like to imprint on everything I do, it is the word, "humanize." A teacher should "humanize" his or her students, a book should "humanize" its readers, and so forth. Questions, too, must "humanize," not "dehumanize."

In *Messengers of God* [New York: Random House, 1976], I said that the mission of the Jew was not to make the whole world Jewish but to humanize it, to make it a warmer, more hospitable, more human, more welcoming world. That is true for every individual Jew as well as for all the Jewish people, but again, I would say that this also must be true for others in their own way. My mission and your mission are the same: to humanize the world.

R: One of the most searing and devastating passages I have ever read is in your memoir, *Night,* published in 1958: "Never shall I forget that night, the first night in camp, which turned my life into one long night . . . Never shall I forget those moments which murdered my God and my soul and turned my dreams to dust." On the one hand, you say your faith was "consumed," yet, on the other, not only in *Night* but in so many other things you have written, you also seem to affirm God. How do you explain such an apparent paradox? Have you ever regretted writing *Night*?

W: Oh no. I think *Night* is probably my statement which will survive the many things I have written during the past thirty years. It's true that it is a paradox, but I have made it so intentionally. On the one hand, I do say that "night" remains with me; on the other hand, I didn't remain with that "night."

It is also true that I said my God was murdered. I can say that it was true for that moment, that it may be true for certain moments, but it is no longer true for my entire life. We have to believe in the Deity, that God is alive because we are alive and our lives are intertwined. It is true that I said that my life was reduced to dust. It was true then, it may even be true for some moments now, but it cannot be true forever.

If I had written nothing else, I think *Night* would have been a statement of total despair, but I kept on writing in order to show that while I stand by every word, every comma, every silence in that book, one must continue. Having said that, what now? We must do something with life, with people, with spiritual ambitions.

R: What do you mean by "spiritual ambitions"?

W: To a religious person, to me, since I come from that background, everything must be translated in spiritual terms, which means into a quest for truth. We are here to search for truth about God, about human beings, about life. And that truth should neither hurt nor diminish anyone; quite the opposite; it should elevate everyone; it should bring people together, not separate them. There is a point where peace and justice are synonymous, where all the lofty ideals and ideas converge. To reach that point is a spiritual ambition.

R: Have you changed in the three decades since writing *Night*? Perhaps I should really ask, have you changed over the years since being liberated from Buchenwald in 1945?

W: Deep down I haven't. Deep down I remain the same person I was. Older, of course, but still the same person, asking questions, waiting for answers, searching for the child I used to be. On a superficial level, I am less intimidated than before, but I am still as timid, as bashful, as shy as before. Of course, I have acquired more words. I've told more stories, which means that I also have read more stories, but I belong to a strange generation. When I came out of Buchenwald in 1945, I was sixteen, but I was already old. Those of us who died there more than once understood what our death could do to people who witnessed it. What else could I learn that I had not already learned?

R: It is true, of course, that the death camps of the Third Reich no longer exist, but concentration camps continue to exist in various parts of the world. I wonder if we have learned anything since 1945?

W: Ours is the most cursed and blessed century in history. It's the most cursed because of what it has endured. Blessed, too, because strangely enough, if it learns from the event, from the Holocaust, it may use its experience to save the future.

The message is: Learn from experience. Everything should be related to the event, but nothing should be compared to it. It must maintain its uniqueness, otherwise, who knows what will happen? The danger is always cheap comparisons, easy analogies. Those who didn't experience it will never know what it meant to experience it. For them, it is easy to reduce it to a normative notion, to say, "It's like . . ." something or other.

I don't wish to be in a position in which it seems that I am begrudging another's suffering. On the contrary. I respect another person's suffering more when I respect the individuality, the genuineness of his or her suffering. I think every group and every person has the right to be remembered, but why play with comparisons and analogies, why mix sufferings together?

When Christians began talking about the Holocaust, remembering the victims, it was the Jews they remembered. Why? Because of the enormity of what happened to the Jewish people. They felt there was something theological, something ontological about the Jewish tragedy. Later on, because they remembered so well the Jewish tragedy, they began also to remember the other victims—the Gypsies, communists, homosexuals, and so on.

Go back and read the writings. Forty years ago nobody even remembered the other victims. Yet, there were resistance fighters, many Polish and Ukrainian inmates, even German resistance members who suffered at the hands of the Nazis and their collaborators. No one mentioned the others, no one spoke about them, but because the Jewish tragedy during the Holocaust had such an impact, it somehow broadened its own base so that non-Jewish victims of the Nazis began to be remembered, which is natural, which is important, which is good—provided there is no confusion. Confusion works against memory.

R: You have been writing and teaching for many years. Are the roles intertwined for you?

W: Not only do I think that the roles of writer and teacher are intertwined, but for me it is the same role. The teacher in me is a writer and the writer in me is a teacher.

R: Do you find young people as receptive to what you have to say today in 1988 as they were when *Night* was published in 1958? What values would you like to pass on to your students?

W: My first goal is to inspire students to respect one another, which means they should be there to help each other, not to judge one another. Never, in my presence, has a student been humiliated. If it happens that a student makes a fool of himself or herself, instead of laughing, the other students rush to their defense. This is the first and most important value I want to pass on to my students: respect, that students would respect every fellow student and every fellow human being. How can I ask them to respect the dead if I don't ask them to respect the living? And the other way around.

I began writing and publishing in 1958, then I began teaching. I really don't see a difference. Most of my readers are young, just as all of my students are young. This is the most rewarding part in my life. Most of the letters I receive from around the world, 80 to 90 percent are from young people— teenagers, collective letters from classes, and so on. Somehow,

I feel I can speak to them, and they are ready to receive what I have to offer.

R: For whom do you write?

W: This is a question every writer must ask himself or herself. First of all, I write for those who are not here. I said it thirty years ago, and I say it again: those whose presence I feel behind my back and who look over my shoulder are severe judges. Under their gaze, I must tell the truth. On a different level, I write for young people. My main concern is for young people to whom I have to transmit and unto whom I have to entrust things they cannot physically bear carrying. Perhaps another way of saying it is that I really write for a combination of those who are not born yet and those who are no longer alive.

R: You once said, "Whatever I have learned in my life is questions, and whatever I have tried to share with friends is questions." In your view, what are some of the key questions of our time?

W: First, and perhaps most important of all, the question of survival: How can we use the knowledge and the experience and the memory of the past to insure the survival of this planet? Unless we do something with those memories I think we will be crushed by them.

Sartre used to say that human beings are condemned to be free. I would paraphrase that and say, we are condemned to save the world with our memories. The question is: How? In other words, how do we manage to humanize destiny?

R: Do you find any sources of hope in the world today?

W: It's a paradox. I find enough sources of despair by opening the newspapers every day, or listening to the news. Yet, at the same time, every day I find new sources for hope. Each time a person surprises me by remaining human, by offering a gift, being generous, resisting evil, and surely by fighting evil, I am grateful to God, grateful that I am the contemporary of that person. This is truly a reason for hope.

The same reason that drives me to despair drives me to hope. When I think of what we have forgotten: so many people have been forgotten, so many events have been neglected and buried.

And yet, at the same time, the obsession with memory has never been greater than now.

Never before, I think, have so many students been so aware of so many injustices in the world, and many are willing to do something about them. Of course there are "ivory tower students," but there are also students ready to be influenced, ready to be inspired. They are looking for people to admire, for books to inspire and challenge them. That is surely a source of hope today.

R: In your view, is evil a noun or a verb?

W: It's both. It's everything. I think evil has many faces, but I would say that all of these faces have masks, and beneath the mask there is indifference. That is what all the faces of evil have in common: indifference. And the moment you start tearing off the mask, good has a chance because you are already fighting. It's easy to fight evil. It's enough not to be indifferent.

Every individual actually can fight evil, and even at times vanquish evil. We saw this practically during World War II and the Holocaust when some Christians and other non-Jews tried to help Jews. Here are a few people who made a difference. They had no armies, they had no power, they had no protection. They were all alone, and yet they defeated evil by fighting indifference.

R: There are Jews and Christians who have criticized you because in their opinion you have not spoken out strongly enough against the abuses suffered by Palestinians in the Israeli-occupied West Bank. Why is it so difficult for you to speak critically about these matters?

W: First of all, as you know better than anyone, because you have read them, I have written and spoken out about these abuses. When I heard about the incident in which four Arabs were buried up to their necks, when I heard about Israeli soldiers being told to break the bones of Arab protesters, I spoke up with pain and anger. I voiced my protests in newspapers and on television; I spoke publicly to Jewish groups all over the country.

Last May I went to Israel to meet with various people, includ-

ing political leaders and military officers about these matters. I
asked many questions: How long can this situation go on? What
do these moral principles mean that we speak about so often?
What will the future bring to Israel?

I went to Gaza where I met with a well-known Palestinian
lawyer, Fayez Abu Rahme, the uncle of the assassinated Abu
Jihad, who before his death was one of Arafat's chief aides.
When I returned to New York, I immediately wrote an article
which was published on the Op-Ed page of the *New York Times*
["A Mideast Peace—Is It Possible?" 23 June 1988]. In every
article I have written about Israel and the Middle East, I have
spoken against such abuses. The fact of the matter, however, is
that some people want me to do more, and they want me to do it
their way. I have gotten many letters saying that I should be the
spokesman for the Palestinians, but that cannot be: I'm much
too Jewish. I am too linked to everything that is Jewish—to
Jewish destiny, Jewish life, Jewish survival—I cannot disasso-
ciate myself from the Jewish people, the Jewish community. I
have always said it is through my Jewishness, through my link
to the Jewish people that I am associated with humanity. Without it, I would have no base in my own life, in my own consciousness.

R: But isn't it true that your criticism of Israel tends to be a little
reserved?

W: It's true that I am reserved in my judgment when I speak about
Israel, but let us wait a little. After all, the Jewish people is
3,500 years old; the Jewish state is only 40 years old. Forty
years in the life of a people 3,500 years old is not very long.
Remember, for 2,000 years we were in exile. We never had
power, we never abused other people's rights. Now we have
power, and it is not so easy. When injustices occur, the Israelis
don't like it. They are against it. That is true of almost everyone
except for a few extremists, fanatics whose names—even men-
tioning them would be a disservice to the Jewish people—are
an embarrassment to the Jewish people. But I am convinced that
with the passing of a few days or a few months, Israel itself will
find ways of correcting this situation. We should have faith in

the Jewish people. We will work it out. We cannot do it in one day. Show me a place in the world — even one — where solutions are found in one day.

It took eight or ten years to find a cease-fire between Iraq and Iran. A million people were killed there. More than a million. When Hussein fought the PLO in Black September, some say 15,000 people were killed in one day. That does not mean that I justify the actions that occasionally occur in Israel. Not at all. I simply say, Look, I believe in the Jewish people. Humanity and morality for us are important. Even if for political reasons certain things are happening which I don't like, which I cannot bear, I still have faith in the Jewish people.

R: A few days after your Op-Ed essay was published in the *New York Times*, you published another, entitled, "Pope John Paul II and His Jewish Problem," in the *New York Post* [28 June 1988, 27]. Some Catholics, including the editors of *America*, took exception to your criticism of the Pope — not the criticism of his failure to mention the Jewish victims when he visited Mauthausen, which was an astonishing omission — but your statement that the Pope "never mentioned the Jewish victims during his first Auschwitz visit nine years ago." Could you explain your comment and criticism?

W: The Pope has made many statements and has given many homilies, but I as a Jew must respond as a Jew should respond to his first visit to Auschwitz. Perhaps our expectations were too high, perhaps it was too much to hope that this man who lived in Poland, who had seen so much suffering, who had seen so much, would be more open, more moderate, more compassionate?

It hurts me to say this, but really, at Auschwitz, a place where nearly four million people were killed, most of them pious Jews, the word "Jew" does not appear in his homily. Why didn't he say "Jew"? The "children of Abraham" were taken there? Jews were taken there. The "children of Abraham" were gassed there? Jews were gassed there. The "children of Abraham" lost their children there? Jewish children died there.

And what about my other criticism? Why didn't the *America* editorial mention about the so-called gift?

R: You mean Pope John Paul II's comment about Jewish and Christian suffering in places like Mauthausen being a "gift to the world"?

W: Yes. Look, I do not want to engage in polemics. I wish I did not have to write the piece that was published in the *New York Post*. I wish that a Christian had written it. I'd rather build bridges than show what separates Jews from Christians, as I am convinced, deep down in my heart, that the Pope, too, is interested in opening doors, in building bridges, but I must be honest. I hope that when I speak, I speak with respect about him and about all who believe in Christianity, but I think this respect should be shared, should be mutual.

Why did I find his comments about suffering in places like Mauthausen so offensive? Because it is a tragedy of such magnitude, one which we haven't even explored yet, we haven't even felt yet — it will take generations to realize what happened — and simply to say it was a "gift" to humanity diminishes the weight of the tragedy. Again, I respond as a Jew. I understand: as a Catholic, his feelings are different. After all, Jesus died and from the Pope's viewpoint, his death was a gift to humanity. But when the Pope spoke about Jews — and also about Christians — he evoked them together. How can I, as a Jew, accept what he, as the leader of Catholics, said about Jews?

In the Jewish tradition, every death is always a blemish on creation, a catastrophe. Occasionally in Talmudic literature we find the Tzaddick, the "just man" whose death expiates the sins of that generation, so to speak, but that is a rare occurrence. Usually we say that when a Tzaddik dies, it is a sign that he will bring misfortune on the world. The death of every person, especially of many people, is a misfortune, not a "gift." Therefore, I must voice my dissent about the word "gift." It is not the proper word in this context.

I remember a year earlier Cardinal O'Connor, who is a close friend of mine, used the same expression, after visiting Yad

Vashem in Jerusalem. I spoke to the Cardinal, and I asked him: Why did you say that? Why didn't you use the word "lesson" instead of "gift," then there would be no problem. If you had said that the sufferings must teach us something, that this tragedy is a "lesson," I could accept it. But to use the word "gift," it means that the guilty are not guilty. They should be rewarded. Those who killed the Jews should be rewarded for offering such a gift to humankind. Of course I understand that it was meant as a positive remark, but you must understand how it sounds to me, as a Jew.

Maybe the official and profound theological attitude of the Vatican is to see the Jewish tragedy as a "gift" in the sense of a unification with the Christ who died. Well, I must tell you that many Jews would also find this objectionable. To say of these Jews, many of whom were pious, religious Jews, who would have given of their lives in order not to convert to Christianity, to say that their suffering was united with Jesus Christ, surely you must see how offensive such a statement is. It is as though all of a sudden posthumously they had been converted to Christianity.

R: What hurts you and what gives you hope in the dialogue between Christians and Jews?

W: What hurts me is the misunderstanding that results when Christians and Jews try to find a rapprochement for the wrong reasons. It hurts because it's condescending, and we must do away with condescension. Respect, mutual respect, should be the name of our link. When I experience it, it gives me hope, because then I do not have to play games. I don't have to put on masks. I can be the person I am, with my foibles, my virtues, with my memories, my fears. There are memories that weigh on both of us, and yet, I can say, Look, we are equals. When I meet the same attitude toward me from Christians, it gives me hope.

R: How would you like to be remembered?

W: As a Jew, naturally. As a witness. As a good father.

New York   9 August 1988

Notes

1. Egil Aarvik, "The Nobel Presentation Speech," in *Elie Wiesel: The Nobel Peace Prize* (New York: Summit Books and Boston University, 1986), 4–5.
2. Elie Wiesel, "Opening Remarks" at the Conference of Nobel Laureates, "Facing the Twenty-first Century: Threats and Promises," Paris, 18–21 January 1988. Unpublished.

5

Between Destruction and Creation

Mary Jo Leddy

Elie Wiesel's stories are conceived somewhere between the facts of destruction and a faith in creation. Somewhere between hell and heaven, his stories begin and end and begin again.

This somewhere "in between" resembles neither the middle ground inhabited by the morally neutral nor the imaginary realm constructed by other writers. To locate Wiesel's stories is to discover a dislocating dilemma that shapes all of his writings. It is a profoundly religious and moral dilemma.

The extremes of this unresolved dilemma are indicated in the very structure of his book, *The Six Days of Destruction: Meditations Towards Hope*. [1] As coauthor (with Albert Friedlander), Wiesel's contribution to this book is a series of six short stories about the destruction that was the Holocaust *(Shoah)*. These stories are meant to complement the lighting of the six candles during the Yom Hashoah service in memory of the six million Jews who were murdered during the Nazi era. Each of these stories is preceeded by a quotation from the book of Genesis that recounts one of the six days of creation, and by a prayer composed by Albert Friedlander. Unfortunately, the moving prayers articulated by Friedlander, seem disconnected, not only in style but also in substance, from the stories written by Wiesel. The prayers to the God of creation seem to emerge significantly unscathed from the fires of destruction in Auschwitz.

Nevertheless, the structure of this book, the interspersing of the six days of destruction with the six days of creation, does indicate the existential relationship, between these two realities, which exists throughout Wiesel's writings. Although Wiesel explores this relationship in various ways at various times, it remains an unresolved relationship. Wiesel seems to resist imposing any easy resolution of the problematic relationship between a belief in creation and the burden of the experience of destruction in the twentieth century. He also seems to resist the temptation to deny the connection between creation and destruction, a connection as mysterious in its origins as it is real in its consequences.

The Six Days of Destruction provides a point of departure for reflecting further about the significant religious and moral dilemma that underlies Elie Wiesel's writings.

The opening words of Wiesel's first story of destruction sound uncomfortably familiar. He removes any protective distinctions between the tales of destruction and creation with what can only be called a religious resolve. These two types of stories punctuate each other. The two stories are, in the end as in the beginning, one story. The story of the destruction that was the Holocaust is the inversion, the perversion, of the story of creation:

And it came to pass in those days that terror denied all languages and frontiers. It became a universe of its own. In those days, it imprisoned and mutilated its victims and their dreams, and then reduced them to ashes. It deprived human beings of the sun, the heart of happiness, and the soul of salvation. In those days, it ruled in the high and the low places. Its reign seemed eternal. (17)

This inversion of the familiar story of creation seems to suggest that Wiesel's experience of destruction in Auschwitz plunges him into a dark night—a night that happened not only in the twentieth century but also, somehow, at the beginning of the world. The seeds of destruction were planted in the garden of Eden. At the dawn of creation, there was the possibility of moral darkness. "For God, for reasons his people do not understand, had finished his work too soon, before depriving Evil of its power" (63).

Creation and destruction. Few would dare to tell the story of such promise and such peril—the story of goodness forever in peril and of evil forever compromised by its reliance on creation for its very existence.

Wiesel dares to tell such a story—not because he can but because he must. His writings contain many reflections on the dilemmas of bearing witness to the horrible reality of the Holocaust. He struggles with the inadequacies of words, with the ambiguities of silence, with the impossibility and yet the necessity of communicating the reality of evil. His choice to write was at once a religious and moral and political choice. To have remained silent would have granted dignity to the innocent dead while denying the possibility of dedication on the part of the living. To have remained silent would have robbed evil of its investment in normalizing discourse but at the expense of discounting the resilient voice of the good.

Few of us have had to face the depth of the moral dilemma of having to choose between speaking or remaining silent. Few of us are so sensitive to the sacredness of the Word, of words and their creative power. Few of us are so aware of the web of deceit and denial that can be woven by words and of their destructive power. Not many feel the acute difference involved in choosing between respecting the sacredness of silence or resisting the complicity of silence. Wiesel has chosen to write and his life gives weight to his words.

Although the visit with the French novelist François Mauriac seems to have been influential in Wiesel's decision to break his vow of silence about the Holocaust, one does not know exactly the day or the hour when he made such a choice. Perhaps Wiesel himself does not know exactly when, or how, or even why. Yet, a choice was faced somehow, somewhere, as surely as Adam and Eve shouldered the burden of choice once they shared in the knowledge of the difference between good and evil.

Wiesel has shared in the terrible knowledge of evil. His first book *Night*, the book in which he breaks his vow of silence, has challenged countless readers to share in the shattering knowledge of evil as it became known in the heart and soul of a young child. To see Auschwitz through the eyes of a child is to see the reality of evil revealed from its most telling perspective.

Never shall I forget that night, the first night in camp, which has turned my life into one long night, seven times cursed and seven times sealed. Never shall I forget that smoke, Never shall I forget the little faces of the children whose bodies I saw turned into wreathes of smoke beneath a silent blue sky.

Never shall I forget those flames which consumed my faith forever.[2]

Wiesel's latest book, *The Six Days of Destruction* is another description of evil through the eyes of the victims. They are people with names and faces . . . Hava and Baruch and Leah and Sheindl and Rose. Unlike some philosophers and theologians, Wiesel does not define evil. He does not debate "the problem of evil." Rather, he describes evil in its shapes and faces, in its sounds and smells. It is an incomplete description—one that would take six million stories of destruction to tell . . . and more. Yet, this is the beginning of the knowledge of evil. After reading Wiesel's descriptions of evil, one can no longer remain innocent or ignorant of evil except by choice. Wiesel's description of the destructive fires of Auschwitz forever challenges Augustine's notion that evil "is the absence of good." Evil was present and real at Auschwitz because of the enforced absence of Jews from this world.

Wiesel knows how the innocent and the good were rendered powerless by the crushing reality of evil. Knowledge such as his threatens to overwhelm faith. The only prayer Wiesel can offer at the beginning of the Sabbath must include the full realization of the six days of destruction. "Thou, O Lord, who has conferred on us the faith in the week which has passed and in the one to come, why has Thou allowed the killer to come between us and Thee?" (63).

In this prayer, Wiesel gives voice to the deepest doubt that arises for the religious person (whether Jew or Christian) once they have shared in some knowledge of the evil of the Holocaust. This anguish is unrelieved by the fact that, while there were religious (Christian) roots of such destruction, it flourished in the postreligious modern world. For a religious person, the shattering of faith in humanity coincides with a shattering of faith in God—who made men and women in the image and likeness of Divinity.

Yet, Wiesel's writings are also marked by a profound sense of the difference between good and evil. The knowledge of this difference seems, paradoxically, born of faith. His words, as his faith, first took shape within the world of eastern European Jewry—a world that breathed with a sense of blessing. Wiesel's descriptions of the small town of Sighet, in which he grew up, convey the memory of a world that sang and studied, danced, and divined out of gratitude for the gift of life and creation:

I shall never forget Shabbat in my town. When I shall have forgotten
everything else, my memory will still retain the atmosphere of holiday, of
serenity pervading even the poorest houses: the white table cloth, the
candles, the meticulously combed little girls, the men on their way to
synagogue . . . As it enveloped the universe, the Shabbat conferred on it a
dimension of peace, an aura of love.[3]

At that time, in that universe, everything seemed simple . . . I knew
where I was, I knew why I existed. I existed to glorify God and to sanctify
his Word. I existed to link my destiny to that of my people, and the destiny
of my people to that of humanity. I existed to do good and to combat evil.[4]

This was the world of Sighet. Wiesel remembers that world and
seems to look on it and say, "It was very good." If, in his first book,
he writes, "Never shall I forget that night," by 1978 he writes, "I
shall never forget Shabbat in my town." The memory of goodness and
grace does not diminish the reality of night but rather deepens it.
Only one who grew up with God in such a world would mourn its
destruction forever.

In his insightful exploration of Wiesel's writings, Robert McAfee
Brown detects a significant shift in emphasis in Wiesel's 1962 book,
The Town Beyond the Wall.[5] After this book, Wiesel begins to
write not only about the world in which he was almost destroyed
(Auschwitz) but also about the world in which he had his beginnings
(Sighet). "I am seeking my childhood. I will always be seeking it. I
need it. It is necessary to me as a point of reference, as a refuge."[6]
The one world does not cancel out the other. "Of course the mystery
of good is no less disturbing than the mystery of evil. Man alone is
capable of uniting them by remembering."[7] One of Wiesel's most
moving prayers is that which binds him back to the God of his
beginnings: "I no longer ask You for either rest or wisdom. I only ask
you not to close me to gratitude, be it of the most trivial kind, or to
surprise and friendship."[8]

The beginnings of Wiesel's life took place in a world mediated by
meaning. That world of meaning has been destroyed. Yet, Wiesel's
deep sense of the difference between meaning and meaninglessness
has remained. In this determination of that difference lies his contribution to the human community. In refusing to give meaning to the
destruction of the Holocaust, he has helped to restore some sense of

what is meaningful in this world. In marking out the limits of meaning, he has set a certain boundary on meaninglessness.

Joblike, he has lamented before God the meaninglessness of the Holocaust:

> There were many periods in our past when we had every right in the world to turn to God and say, "Enough. Since you seem to approve of all these persecutions, all these outrages, have it your way: let your world go on without Jews. Either You are our partner in history, or You are not. If you are, do Your share; if You are not, we consider ourselves free of past commitments. Since You choose to break the Covenant, so be it."
>
> Yet, And yet, and yet . . . We went on believing, hoping, invoking His name . . . We did not give up on Him.[9]

And yet, and yet . . . In sharing his despair of God with God he has, in spite of himself, in spite of God, reaffirmed the real locus of the struggle for meaning. He has done this in an age when faith in God grows as dim as the knowledge of the difference between good and evil.

Wiesel's stories describing the destruction of the Holocaust are never destructive in themselves. One searches in vain for any sign of cynicism about God or human beings. There is disappointment, despair, and anger—but never cynicism. Wiesel has chosen to write, I suspect, not only out of fidelity to the victims but also out of small but real faith in those of us who are his readers. Perhaps he believes that the best in us will bear with the worst in us. Perhaps he believes that we may yet determine the difference between good and evil with our lives.

Many have commented on Wiesel's books as examples of the paradox of literary creation—of something written out of nothingness. Yet, the analogy between aesthetic creation and the divine activity described in the biblical story of creation seems to obscure the quality of the relationship between destruction and creation in Wiesel's writings—it is a moral rather than a literary relationship. His books are not novels but rather the testimonies of a witness who seeks to rescue through memory those who would otherwise remain consigned to holes of oblivion. He writes so that we will never forget the victims of the Holocaust—neither the miracle of their creation nor the fact of their destruction. "If the role of the writer may once have been to entertain, that of the witness is to disturb, alert, to waken, to warn against indifference to injustice."[10]

Wiesel's stories, which remain within the realm of the unresolved relationship between creation and destruction, nevertheless invite us to a moral resolve. They create within us the possibility of knowing the difference between good and evil and of acting on that difference. This is why it was most appropriate that he received the Nobel Prize for Peace rather than the Nobel Prize for Literature. His words and his witness invite moral creativity. What kind of moral creativity? He refers several times to Albert Camus's exhortation, "One must create happiness to protest against a universe of unhappiness."[11]

For Wiesel, there is a fragile but real possibility that the world could be animated by creation rather than devoured by destruction. "We only have the question. But it is we who must turn it into a prayer. A call to combat evil. A warning against indifference. A song which, in spite of everything, will try to justify the first gleam of a hope which is yet to be born."[12]

Wiesel's stories leave us, in the end as in the beginning, with the freedom to choose between creating or destroying. For us as for him, that choice makes a difference in this world.

Notes

1. Elie Wiesel and Albert H. Friedlander, *The Six Days of Destruction: Meditations Towards Hope* (Mahwah, N.J.: Paulist Press, 1988).
2. Elie Wiesel, *Night* (New York: Avon Books, 1969), 44.
3. Elie Wiesel, *A Jew Today* (New York: Random House, 1978), 8.
4. Elie Wiesel, "Recalling Swallowed-up Worlds," *Christian Century* 98 (27 May 1981): 609.
5. Robert McAfee Brown, *Elie Wiesel: Messenger to All Humanity* (Notre Dame: University of Notre Dame Press, 1983), chap. 3.
6. Wiesel, "Recalling Swallowed-up Worlds," 609.
7. Elie Wiesel, *The Gates of the Forest* (New York: Avon Books, 1973), 254.
8. Elie Wiesel, *One Generation After* (New York: Random House, 1970), 189.

9. Wiesel, *A Jew Today*, 164.

10. Elie Wiesel, "A Personal Response," *Face to Face: An Interreligious Bulletin* 6 (1979): 36.

11. Quoted in Elie Wiesel, *The Town Beyond the Wall* (New York: Avon Books, 1969), 127.

12. Ibid., 61.

6

Silence—Survival—Solidarity:
Reflections on Reading Elie Wiesel

Dow Marmur

I became aware of the Holocaust when I was eight or nine years old and would listen to the news coming through the only radio in the *kolchoz* in Uzbekistan where my parents and I spent most of the war years. As the Red Army spokesman reported on the extermination camps and the millions of dead, the adults around me almost invariably concluded that it could not possibly be like that; it must be Soviet propaganda to fuel hatred against the German enemy. Even if, in the course of the year between the end of the war and our return to our native Poland, we had not heard from any of our relatives, my parents, like many others who were with us, still believed that the family, if not intact then at least still numerous, would be waiting for us when we returned. When the truth finally dawned on them, they were silent. It was an awesome silence.

I think of it whenever I recall Aaron's silence (Lev. 10:3) upon hearing that two of his sons had been devoured by the "strange fire" they offered up in the sanctuary. But in the biblical tale, at least, Aaron's silence is explained. We knew of no reason for what we found; our silence was not the result of self-control, but came out of an inability to utter words when confronted with the truth of the fires of the crematoria.

Those who themselves survived the camps were also unable to speak. When, a couple of years after our return to Poland, we emigrated to Sweden and lived with many of those who had been rescued by the Swedish Red Cross in the final days of the war, I was

50

once again struck by the silence. The survivors spoke among themselves, but not to outsiders, because "they" would not understand.
When people would hear of the horrors of the camps, some Swedes,
including Jews, would say to survivors that things hadn't been that
easy in Sweden either. After all, shoes had been rationed during the
war. One former camp inmate was actually asked by a fellow Jew
who had been spared the ordeal whether it was *very* difficult to obtain
kosher food. In the face of such questions and such reactions, what
else could there be but silence?

Jan Karski, courier between the Polish underground and the Allies, attempted to alert the Free World to the plight of the Jews by
giving an eye-witness account of what was happening in the Warsaw
ghetto. Prominent American leaders declared that they found it impossible to believe him. If they found it impossible, what could one
reasonably expect from ordinary folk, including ordinary Germans?
In the 1960s a German pastor, Dieter Schoeneich, and I had initiated
a reconciliation program between Protestant youths in Germany, all
born after 1945, and Jews in Britain, where I was working at the
time. There were not enough Jews in Germany for that kind of
program. One of the recurring questions Jewish hosts asked their
German visitors was, "What did your parents know?" Perhaps they
knew much but would not admit it because of the amnesia that comes
from guilt. But perhaps they did not know in the way others did not
know, and in the way those Jews listening to the radio in a remote
Uzbek *kolchoz* did not know. In the face of such "ignorance," silence
seemed inescapable. Every attempt at use of language failed because
it sought to express the unthinkable.

Language also failed because, ultimately, language itself had been
debased. That is a central theme in the writings of George Steiner.
He explains this attack on the German language by declaring, "I
believe that the matter of the relations between language and political
inhumanity is a crucial one; and . . . I believe that it can be seen
with specific tragic urgency in respect of the uses of German in the
Nazi period and in the acrobatics of oblivion which followed on the
fall of Nazism."[1]

Disbelief did not only come to those who mourned the victims, or
to those who descended from the perpetrators; sometimes it affected

the victims themselves. In an exchange between Emil Fackenheim, the theologian of the Holocaust par excellence, and Elie Wiesel, its best-known witness, at a symposium on Jewish values in the post-Holocaust future, the latter recalled a question he was asked, whether he really believed what had happened to him. Wiesel: "Well, Emil, I do not believe it. The event seems unreal, as if it occurred on a different planet."[2] That is, incidentally, one reason why "revisionism," invariably vicious and malicious, is so painful to the survivors. It abuses their silence.

Yet, in the face of such "disbelief," silence remains the only humanly possible response. Wiesel's concluding words in his opening statement at the same symposium—"That is the problem, that is my fear: perhaps whatever we try to write and say about Jewish values and Jewish experience has no relationship to either."[3]— prompted the chairman of the event to summarize the contribution of the other participants—besides Wiesel and Fackenheim, George Steiner and Richard H. Popkin—that "we pretty much agree that the ultimate reaction is silence."[4]

Silence may have been inevitable, but it was also unbearable. That is why, paradoxically, survivors had to speak and—those who had the gift—to write, if for nobody else than for themselves: to make themselves believe the truth. Even if they could not speak to outsiders, perhaps they could speak to each other. And they did. I spent my adolescent years in the company of camp survivors. I do not remember them talking of much else; they told of their experiences again and again; it was necessary for their existence, their survival. They recalled death and suffering in order to be able to live.

The late Dr. Shammai Davidson's research on the so-called survivor syndrome is significant. Comparing groups of survivors in Israel and in California, he found that, although the latter were much more affluent and successful, the former seemed happier. He concluded that this was because survivors living in California found it difficult to speak of what had happened to them in the camps, because the cultural milieu was not conducive to such testimony. On the other hand, it was proper and easy to speak in Israel, because the culture encouraged the talking and the sharing. Silence may have been expedient in one's business dealings in the New World, but, apparently, dangerous for one's mental well-being. Similarly, parents who set out to spare their children, born after the war, their gruesome experiences caused them more anguish than those who shared with the young the truth, and thus could go on together like Abraham and Isaac on their way down from Moriah.

Hence the centrality of Yad Vashem and all the other monuments in Israeli public life. They are national shrines designed to honor the memory of the martyrs and to provide survivors with opportunities to grieve together. They also make it possible to break the silence and thus survive. Although many of those who have spoken and written, not least Elie Wiesel himself, insist that they recognize in their speaking the purpose of why they survived, it may be legitimate to put it differently: not that they survived in order to speak, but *they speak in order to survive.* Even if nobody "out there" wants to listen, survivors have to speak in order to live. Thus the paradox of speaking and writing about silence: uttering words to demonstrate that nothing can be said.

When speaking and writing is no longer possible, there seems little point in going on. Is that why Paul Celan, Piotr Rawicz, Primo Levi, and many others took their own lives? Is that why a painter and Holocaust survivor I got to know refused medical treatment and died prematurely? Perhaps it was because he had given his testimony, said everything there was to be said; perhaps it was because he could not give his testimony and, therefore, could not live any longer.

The difference between living in order to tell the tale and telling the tale in order to live is significant. The latter suggests that survival is the primary aim of us all, particularly of those who were spared the gas chambers. Fackenheim's famous formulation, his 614th commandment, which originated at the symposium referred to above, speaks for it: "The authentic Jew of today is forbidden to hand Hitler yet another, posthumous victory."[5] He must survive as a Jew. The survivors who testified to their ordeal made it possible for themselves to stay alive. We who were not there are duty-bound to encourage them to tell and tell again in order to spare them from annihilation and save ourselves from dangerous ignorance.

Elie Wiesel may have described the reason for his own writing as a way of justifying his survival, rather than a means of survival, but his actions point in a different direction. The title of his book about the Jews in Soviet Russia may be *The Jews of Silence*, but the content is about the Jews as survivors. What he had to tell about them, in fact contributed to their survival. Silence may be inevitable at times, but survival is the purpose always.

The transformation of silence into the struggle for survival is a long process. In its final stages it reflects what Robert Jay Lifton has described as "the survivor's *struggle for meaning*, for a sense of inner form."[6] But survival constitutes also a break with silence, a transformation into a new paradigm. In the same way as the silence of Aaron was soon to be followed by his assertiveness (Lev. 10:16–20), so was the silence of individual survivors transformed into the collective assertiveness of the Jewish people. It became, in Lifton's language, "the survivor mission."[7] Whereas individuals could either keep silent and give Hitler posthumous victories, or speak and live, the Jewish people had to *act* in order to survive: hence Israel. But such action also came to challenge the events that led to the silence in an effort to make sure that the tragedy would not happen again. The State of Israel is not a consolation but a transformation. The Holocaust was the final and most cruel manifestation of a Jewish world ruled by anti-Semitism; silence was the natural response to that. Israel is the beginning of a new era, characterized by the rebirth of Jewish assertiveness in which survival is the primary aim; the response now is determined action. That is why the existence of Israel is so central to "Holocaust theologians" as diverse in their interpretations as Eliezer Berkovits, Emil Fackenheim, and Richard Rubenstein.

Assertive action can easily deteriorate into triumphalism and fanaticism. When that happens, the Holocaust becomes an emotive tool in the rhetoric. The silence of the victims and the survivors is being debased by the deafening noise of propagandists and demagogues. That is why we have to ask the obvious question: Survival—for what? The first, and perhaps second, generation after the *Shoah* will be satisfied with Fackenheim's rationale: not to give Hitler a posthumous victory. But what about future generations? Will this negative answer be sufficient, or will they seek positive reasons for Jewish survival? When—not *if*, but *when*—they do, we must tell them what all the generations of Jews that came before them were told: Care for the stranger, for you were strangers in the land of Egypt. Survival, even in suffering, leads to solidarity with all who suffer in order to alleviate the pain and thus help to "mend the world" so that suffering will be no more.

It is not a coincidence that the man who formulated the 614th commandment is now also a resident of Israel and the author of a seminal book called *To Mend the World*. Already in the 1967 symposium, Fackenheim insisted not only that "we are, first, commanded to survive as Jews, lest the Jewish people perish," but also that "we are forbidden, finally, to despair of the world as the place which is to become the kingdom of God, lest we help make it a meaningless place in which God is dead or irrelevant and everything is permitted."[8] And Elie Wiesel, having testified to the need for silence and the imperative of survival, turned in solidarity to the oppressed of other nations. As a survivor he not only had a duty, but also a right to speak and to act to prevent a universal holocaust as well as to alleviate personal suffering anywhere in the world.

Reflecting on this discussion of Wiesel's work, and paraphrasing his message, Robert McAfee Brown writes:

The particularity of Jewish suffering can never be remembered only as an end in itself; it is a foretaste of what can happen to any person, any people. If Jews can be burned, so can others. To start with a concern for his own people—as Wiesel always does—is never to end there; it becomes, in turn, a starting place for concern for all peoples. The most Jewish of writers becomes the most universal among them.[9]

In this Wiesel reverses the logic of prophecy. Whereas the prophets address Israel out of the actions of the nations, "the most Jewish of writers" of our time speaks to the nations out of the experience of Israel. He had broken his silence not only to survive by honoring the dead, but also to prevent the death of others.

In a thoughtful paper, Fred L. Downing points to a development in the writings of Wiesel.[10] Recalling his early years in Sighet,

Wiesel writes as the *homo religiosus*. In his effort to find meaning in survival, he becomes a *homo poeta*, "man, the meaning maker," in which he reveals "a heroic effort to deny death ultimate victory" and pointing to "a courageous and prolific human project to reconstruct and restructure meaning on the ruins of a former life-world." This, finally, manifests itself in Elie Wiesel, the *homo publicus* when this "private and sensitive man is driven into the realm of public advocacy for the purpose of the public enactment of a vision and the building of a more just and humane society." Although Downing does not put it this way, it may be legitimate to identify the *homo religiosus* as the Jew of silence in the face of God's unfathomable will, an Aaron-like figure; the *homo poeta* as the writer-survivor in search of meaning; and the *homo publicus* as the eminent Jew of our time who expresses the solidarity of his people with all who suffer out of his own and his people's indescribable pain.

The final chapter of Marc Ellis's book *Toward a Jewish Theology of Liberation* is called "From Holocaust to Solidarity." Recognizing the shift from silence to survival in Jewish life, Ellis speaks of "the need for empowerment as a religious response to destruction."[11] He believes that Jewish thought today must not center around anti-Semitism because "the slogan 'Never Again' too often becomes the rationale for refusing to trust and to risk,"[12] whereas solidarity demands precisely such trust and such risk. We must tell the tale not only to honor our martyrs of the past but also to prevent martyrdom, in the present and in the future: "The new urgency, represented by the 'burning children' of all peoples, calls us to this rediscovery with a bewildering urgency: As much as any time in history, the world needs this witness, and at the crossroads of our own history, so do we."[13]

Robert McAfee Brown speaks the same language when he compares Wiesel's *The Town Beyond the Wall* to a short story by Camus in which "the conclusion leaves unresolved whether a word written in tiny letters on the center of an artist's canvas should be read as *solitary* or *solidary*." Brown adds: "The shape of one letter was the infinite distance between isolation and community, between darkness and light."[14] The shift from solitary silence via survival in search of meaning toward participatory solidarity is indicative of a conclusion that makes living possible for the survivor, even after he has told his tale. And it makes living possible for all of us because the one who has been through hell has addressed us. Those who have followed Wiesel's example have made the same journey from darkness to light. Paradoxically, by becoming conscious of the prospect of a global holocaust, life has gained more depth—despite the awareness of the danger, or perhaps because of it.

Robert McAfee Brown sees in this transformation of silence to solidarity a truly religious pilgrimage: "We have seen that the cumulative journey of the first five books [by Wiesel] was from solitude to solidarity, from looking into the visible face of death to looking into the invisible face of God."[15] God alone has the truly universal perspective; human beings can only speak out of their own narrow world and limited experience. But by seeking to reach out to the world at large through our particularity, we begin to perceive "the invisible face of God." Showing solidarity thus becomes the stuff out of which the theology of liberation is made—not only the liberation of others but also the liberation of self. It is in this universalist dimension that the survivor finds purpose, meaning, and challenge. The survivor now knows the answer to the question, Survival—for what? and can teach us its significance.

The silence of Aaron in the face of tragedy was soon transformed to assertiveness; he had to speak in order to survive. In time he became the role model for all: "Be of the disciples of Aaron, one that loves peace, that loves mankind and brings them to Torah." (Avot 1:12) The formulation is deliberately universalist. The man who has suffered and survived is able to care for humanity. We are urged to follow in his footsteps.

Does it matter? Can the powerless speak? Can survivors be heard or are they invariably ignored? Why speak at all? Indeed, why survive? Answer: In order to testify; in Walter Brueggemann's terminology, to make history. For Brueggemann, the Bible is not about *recording* history but about *making* history, because "the history-making process in ancient Israel is done through *the voice of marginality* which is carried by prophetic figures and those with whom they make common cause."[16] The most prominent among them is Jeremiah. "My thesis, thus, is," writes Brueggemann, "that *Jeremiah as a voice of marginality is a history-maker in the sense that the kings could not be,* though he stands outside the time-line and outside every head-line."[17]

Elie Wiesel, the survivor, identifies with Jeremiah. At the end of his portrait of the prophet, he tells of how Jeremiah defied the king. Then he adds, "And what are we doing, we writers, we witnesses, we Jews? For over three thousand years we have been repeating the same story—the story of a solitary prophet who would have given anything, including his life, to be able to tell another kind of tale, one filled with joy and fervor rather than sorrow and anguish."[18] But he could not because he was called to higher things. "The history makers," writes Brueggemann, "are those who have the capacity and courage to *disclose* the human process. The dominant voices, however, are those which want to *close* the human process in the interest of order and the protection of a monopoly which always needs to be guarded." He adds, "Where history making ends, society is at the edge of losing its humaneness."[19]

Wiesel broke his silence in order to survive, but—by his own admission—he writes and speaks in order to testify. Much of that testimony, together with the testimonies of other survivors, has made history precisely because it stood up to "the dominant voices" that clamor for the status quo, for the atrocities, to continue—against Jews and non-Jews alike. The call to solidarity overpowers them, however; the voice of God is the voice of liberation, and Wiesel is one of its carriers. His message, articulating the message of the Jewish people, which includes suffering but transcends it, contains the voice of God, that in its ostensible marginality makes history.

The attempt to make solidarity, not survival, the ultimate reason for breaking the silence in the face of the Holocaust is also a deliberate effort to counteract those political forces that, within Jewry, see the *Shoah* as the moral validator of actions calculated to separate Jew from Gentile, as well as those manifestations of power that, outside the Jewish community, view the Holocaust as the barrier between Jew and non-Jew. The Jews who insist that the Holocaust be invoked to validate everything we do, right or wrong, and the non-

Jews—Christians, Muslims, and secularists—who insist that we have to cease to speak of the Holocaust to gain recognition are Holocaust abusers: the former by separating solidarity from survival, the latter by separating survival from solidarity. Both nationalist extremists, with their slogan Never Again! and international "revisionists," who insist that it never happened, abuse the Holocaust.

Each time we refer to the quest for survival in relation to the existence of Israel, we are in danger of linking the two in a logical sequence in which the Holocaust justifies Israel. This is, of course, historically untrue, though it may be at times politically expedient. Wiesel makes the point repeatedly: the Holocaust is not a reason for Israel; Israel is at best a consolation for the Holocaust and an opportunity to care for the world precisely because Jews can call a fragment of that world their own.

Similarly, it may be less than prudent to quote Elie Wiesel's statement that even survivors themselves did not always believe what had happened to them. For it can be taken in "evidence" by the Holocaust deniers. Yet I included the reference as an illustration of the magnitude of the experience—not as an indication that the events never happened—and also for another reason: to remind ourselves that disbelief and denial come easily to us in the face of suffering and danger. Both lead to silence. Therefore, we have to help each other to be on the alert in our common endeavors to prevent a future global holocaust. We have to speak to live and to let live. Survival leads to solidarity, and solidarity leads to survival. Silence has to be overcome, despite the pain of speaking. Elie Wiesel has shown us how to do it.

Notes

1. George Steiner, note on republishing "The Hollow Miracle" in his *Language and Silence* (Harmondsworth: Penguin, 1969), 136.
2. "Jewish Values in the Post-Holocaust Future," *Judaism* 16, 3 (Summer 1967): 285.
3. Ibid., 284.
4. Ibid.

5. Ibid., 272.
6. Robert Jay Lifton, "The Concept of the Survivor," in *The Future of Immortality* (New York: Basic Books, 1987), 241.
7. Ibid.
8. Fackenheim, in "Jewish Values," 273.
9. Robert McAfee Brown, *Elie Wiesel—Messenger to all Humanity* (Notre Dame: University of Notre Dame Press, 1983), 16.
10. Fred L. Downing, "Autobiography, Fiction, and Faith: Reflections on the Literary Religious Pilgrimage of Elie Wiesel" (Paper presented at "Remembering for the Future," the International Scholars' Conference, Oxford, July 1988), 1441–1455.
11. Marc H. Ellis, *Toward a Jewish Theology of Liberation* (Maryknoll, N.Y.: Orbis Books, 1987), 111.
12. Ibid., 114.
13. Ibid., 122.
14. Brown, *Elie Wiesel*, 80.
15. Ibid., 99.
16. Walter Brueggemann, *Hope Within History* (Atlanta: John Knox Press, 1987), 55.
17. Ibid., 56.
18. Elie Wiesel, *Five Biblical Portraits* (Notre Dame: University of Notre Dame Press, 1981), 126–27.
19. Brueggemann, *Hope*, 57.

7

The Memory of Self and the Memory of God in Elie Wiesel's Jewish Consciousness

Marcel Dubois

Meminisse sui, meminisse Dei
— SAINT AUGUSTINE

"To remember oneself is to remember God."[1] This sentence expresses, in a radically new fashion, as far as Plato was concerned, St. Augustine's own experience of Platonic recollection. Augustine, no doubt, would have been very surprised if someone had told him that the origin of Plato's insight was Jewish.

It is clear, however, that here the Christian Doctor correctly expressed the nature of the Jewish experience of memory. The historical reference to the past—a past lived out in the sight of God—was the means of rejoining God's presence through an act of theological memory inspired by faith.

If this formula of Augustine's sums up the spiritual experience of Judaism, it also provides a key for the understanding of the religious intuition that underlies the entire work of Elie Wiesel.

It has been said that Elie Wiesel is the "standard-bearer" of the Jewish memory of the *Shoah*. The meaning of this, of course, is that he ceaselessly calls on the Jewish people and humanity at large to remember this tragedy: "After Auschwitz, everything leads back to Auschwitz."[2] In his case, however, this obsession with the Holocaust gives rise to a theological reflection that begins with a protest at this outrage and continues and ends with an act of faith.

Whereas some, like Richard Rubenstein, have considered atheism the most viable religious option for the Jews of our time, Elie Wiesel's lacerating cry of protest has given a tragic but incontestable expression to the Jewish faith. The singular value of his work is that it objectively puts the question of the impossibility of a faith that is not seared and traumatized by the catastrophe. He shows us that the *Shoah* forces us to reconsider the human being's relationship to God. Despite the darkness and silence, the remembrance of Auschwitz brings us the theological memory that reminds Israel, because of the Election and Covenant, of God's presence among His people.

In this respect, Elie Wiesel's testimony expresses, in a typical and particularly suggestive way for our time, the fundamental attitude of the Jewish people before God throughout its history.

Memory and History in Jewish Consciousness

Liskor velolishkoah, "Remember and do not forget." This is the motto of Yad Vashem, the memorial on Mount Herzel in Jerusalem to the martyrs of the death camps. It is an invitation to future generations to keep the Holocaust alive in their memories. But this act of memory is essentially different from and more profound than the simple remembering of a past event. In this call to remember, Jewish consciousness appeals to that dimension of its being that could certainly be said to characterize its spiritual attitude: namely, memory. This people who rightly has been called "the builder of time"[3] could just as well be called "the people of memory."

Here, however, we are concerned with something very different from the preservation and transmission of past events. At a deeper level than that of the psychological or historical faculty of recalling, there is what could be called the *ontological memory*, the *act of presence* to oneself or to God that Augustine describes in his wonderful summary. Israel's consciousness of itself lies at the permanent source of its identity and development.

At every stage of its journey through time, on every page of the Bible, this call to remember is found: "Hear, O Israel," "Remember, Israel." All the mighty works of God were thus confided to the memory of His people. In the language of the Bible, *zachor*, "to remember", does not mean to preserve or reproduce an image, but to call forth, to re-present, to make present a hidden reality that is always operative, always present. This is verified in a very special way in the commemoration of Passover and of the alliance. It gives to the seder of Pesah its absolutely original and essential value; it makes the Jewish people, the "people of memory." The sentence recited by Jews every year from the Haggadah, "In every single generation it is a sacred duty for each man to consider himself as personally brought out of Egypt," gives to Passover night a present and permanent meaning. Pesah is not just the memorial or figure of a grandiose but far-off historical event; it is the re-presentation, that is to say the present and existential manifestation of a mighty work whose actuality remains contemporary. God appeals to the memory of His people. Through the rite of the paschal meal and the reading of the Haggadah, each son of Israel is in a situation where he is effectively united with the decisive event of Israel's history, an event that is not past but present. All Jews are invited to make their own the adventure of their ancestors whom God brought out of Egypt. Every Jew is invited to live this history personally and in the present.

So the historical commemoration is the occasion and the sign of a deeper remembrance. When Israel recalls this past event, she encounters it as God sees it in the present and in eternity. She becomes aware of her identity as it appears in the revelation of God's choice. "To remember oneself is to remember God." It is evident that for the Jewish people such remembrance is at the same time a source of renewal and a means of discovering and realizing its identity. This is because it presents in its permanent and eternal value what was mysteriously present in the original event.

Liskor velolishkoah, this invitation of Yad Vashem must be understood at the level where Jewish memory and Jewish identity meet and merge. Each new event, each new period of Israel's history, each experience of her destiny is inscribed on the scroll of this original consciousness. As long as time lasts there is endless possibility of understanding events in its light and of integrating them in a living way into the profound and indefinable reality of Jewish experience. In his book *God's Presence in History*, Emil Fackenheim makes a distinction that seems to refer to this intuition and to confirm it. He calls upon his readers to discern in Israel's history *root-experiences* and *epoch-making events;* the latter are, as it were, in continual confrontation with the former. The root-experiences are those in which God revealed Himself to Israel and made her a people, His people, as in the crossing of the Red Sea, and the gift of the Torah. The epoch-making events differ from these clear manifestations of the divine Presence which intervenes to save or to command, in that they do not create a new faith. They appear as challenges to faith through new situations.

But what happens if the event appears to be a radical annulment of the original experience? It is here that the Holocaust suddenly erupts as a scandal that confronts the conscience of Jews—and, indeed, all believers—with a question whose implications are particularly grave. Is it really possible to hear an echo of the voice of Sinai in the clamor that rises from the gas chambers of Auschwitz? Did not the silence of God defeat forever the remembrance of his Word?

Singularity of the Holocaust in the Destiny of the Jewish People

It is important to understand correctly what our Jewish brothers and sisters mean when they speak of the absolutely unique character of the Holocaust. The *Shoah* is, in the first place, a unique event in the very destiny of Israel because it stands out as a tragedy unparalleled in the whole of her history and, for this reason, is beyond all possibility of comparison and measurement. At a much deeper level the event is unique because of its background, which is still more decisively unique: the Election of Israel.

The Holocaust constitutes a scandal for the Jew because of its very nature. In all of Israel's personal destiny, it is absolutely novel, unforeseen, and unforeseeable. It seems to the Jew irreducibly and scandalously unique because of its relationship to its own history. This should be all the more obvious because throughout its thousands of years of existence, Israel has known other trials, other perils, and other catastrophes. By comparison with all the tragedies of the past, the Holocaust and the remembrance of it seem eternally irremediable. It differs from the commemoration of Tishah B'Av in that the mourning is absolute and the hope annihilated. Indeed, for the first time in its history, the Jewish people felt totally abandoned: abandoned by human beings, but above all by God. Indeed, for the Jew, the most terrible torment of the Holocaust was the temptation to think that for the first time in the history of Israel the very covenant of God with His people had been broken.

In this perspective, it is easier to understand the terrifying uniqueness of the Holocaust. It lies in-the fact that the agreement implicit in the covenant does not seem to have been honored. There was nobody to turn to because God Himself was silent. If in face of this silence Jewish consciousness experienced such a sense of dereliction, and if the event was so incomprehensible, it was because it seemed to contradict the entire history of the Jewish people and to make their whole vocation a failure. Thus it was fundamentally the Election that made Israel experience what can truly be called the scandalous uniqueness of the Holocaust.

Paradoxically, the Election helps us to make the Holocaust a sign of contradiction and scandal for the Jewish consciousness. Yet who could fail to see that once again it confers on the event itself another dimension of uniqueness? This new uniqueness is as imposing and as mysterious as the Election itself. It has its source in a certitude that the history of Israel, as presented to our faith by the Bible, suffices to establish and to confirm. Viewed in this light, the Holocaust is a unique event because the destiny is, by the very fact of the Election, unique. It can therefore be affirmed that the ability to understand the unique character of the Holocaust is proportionate to the degree of faith in the Election. As the Election is understood, so is the Holocaust understood.

The Jewish people were confronted, in the very name of its faith and of its memory, with what Martin Buber rightly called "the eclipse of God" and experienced a terrible dilemma, a dilemma expressed by Richard Rubenstein in a form so pessimistic that it bears the accent of despair: "Either a cruel God or none!" For the Jewish conscience, the Holocaust was a paradigm of the ever-recurring problem of evil and injustice whose perpetual presence in the world seems to deny the existence of a God who is good. Against this stumbling block, many Jews fell. Some became disoriented. For them, the immeasurable monstrosity of the Nazi crimes definitely destroyed all possibility of belief in the presence and action of God in history.

And yet, there was a very different response from those Jews who, in the very abyss of anguish and of night, seemingly abandoned, turned their desperate hope to God. Far from evading the bewilderment of the contradiction, they found in their faith the strength to cry out to God from "out of the depths" of their despair and dismay. The Jewish people throughout the ages had confronted and denounced the apparent absurdity of existence, the insolent victory of injustice and of evil. From the story of Abraham in Genesis to the interpolations of the prophets and the psalms, the Bible is full of this daring contestation. Israel calls God to account in the name of His past promises, His mercy, and His justice. The Book of Job will forever be the compendium of this protestation of humankind against the incomprehensible injustice and the wickedness of human beings, and the most striking thing about it is that God, far from being offended, praises His servant Job for his ruthless honesty (42:7). There the very anguish becomes, in the name of faith, a warrant to challenge the Almighty. Hasidim such as Rabbi Levi-Yitzhak of Berditchev showed the same realism and the same audacity, finding in the destitution and the suffering of their people authorization to enter into contestation with God. The more the Jew trusts, the more vehemently does his soul cry out to God.

✓ Nothing Is as Whole as a Shattered Faith

Elie Wiesel's testimony is part of this living tradition: that of a contestation that reaches the point of revolt and despair, but that is expressed within the framework of an unshakable fidelity. One could say that he is the heir to this tradition in our time, the period of history that follows the *Shoah*.

He gave a clear description of this paradoxical attitude in his dialogue with Philippe de Saint-Cheron. The constant return to a remembrance of the Holocaust is the occasion for a vehement protest, but this contestation takes place within the context of the Jewish faith. Genuine protestation, in his opinion, is inseparable from fidelity to the Torah: "I can protest against God, but not outside the Covenant."[4]

Here Elie Wiesel adapted the words of Rabbi Nahman of Bratzlav: "Nothing is as whole as a broken heart." He commented:

I would say that, in our epoch, nothing is as whole as a shattered faith. Faith has to be tested, but then it must not remain a rupture or a laceration. One must continue while facing what is happening in the world today and what has happened yesterday. We can no longer accept faith just as it is. We must pass through a period of anguish and then a period of respite in order that in the end we may find or regain the faith of our Masters. Because, without faith, we could not survive. Without faith, our world would be empty.[5]

Elie Wiesel could only acquiesce in the description that his interlocutor gave regarding the paradox of his position: "Recently, you told me: 'What has been shaken is my faith, my confidence in God and His promises.' On the other hand, you observed that 'if you are sometimes on God's side and often against God, you are never without Him.' " Wiesel's answer was enlightening: "It is exactly in this way that I situate myself in relation to this faith that is mine. I have never abandoned my faith and it has never abandoned me. This upheaval I spoke of was an upheaval within my faith, because it was always there."[6] He admitted, however, that this paradoxical attitude, although he regarded it as by no means contradictory, was not without a sense of tearing. He feels this particularly in prayer, to the point that certain liturgical formulas stick in his throat: "I know, today, that the laceration is there, and that prayer is connected with this laceration."[7]

This condition of permanent testing is characteristic of Judaism and is linked with the Jewish identity. It is impossible to get out of it: "For a Jew, the only way to realize himself is his Jewishness. On that, there is no choice. Either one is Jewish or one isn't. Either one rejects the Covenant or one accepts it. But if we do accept it, it is within that that we have to define ourselves." The conclusion is clear, and Elie Wiesel endorses it resolutely: "We can say anything to God, providing it is within Judaism."[8]

All this enables us to understand how Elie Wiesel's testimony brings together the two different layers of memory. The remembrance of the *Shoah* becomes the occasion, or rather the necessary precondition, for an awakening of the memory of Jewish identity: something that can only be apprehended within the context of faith, sometimes almost involving a contradiction, under the gaze that God directs at His people.

Remembrance of Childhood and Memory of the Source

Elie Wiesel is haunted by the child he once was, or perhaps it would be truer to say, by the child who remains within him. One feels his presence throughout his work. The necessity for this return to childhood was obviously made all the more serious and urgent by the circumstances that marked the destiny of the child Elie Wiesel. This little boy experienced the *Shoah*, discovering Jewish existence through the horror of the camps and the hatred of the Nazi murderers.

And yet, in retrospect, the purest and most spontaneous reference to this childhood was the one in which he joined the little Jewish child who discovered the singular vocation of his people and gravely prepared himself to assume the responsibility involved in it.

In my little town, somewhere in the Carpathians, I knew why I existed. I existed in order to glorify God and to sanctify His Word. . . . I knew that I belonged to His chosen people: the people chosen to serve Him through suffering and at the same time through hope. I knew that I was in exile and that the exile was total, cosmic.[9]

The remembrance of his childhood is here an act of memory and personal identity.

Throughout the work of Elie Wiesel, throughout the destiny of the heroes of his novels, one finds this nostalgia for childhood. Thus Raphael, whose story we read in *Le crépuscule au loin*, speaks as follows:

I wait for the child I was. In order to ask him about his life, his death. And to ask his forgiveness for reasons which escape me. I feel guilty towards this ten-year-old boy.[10]

Here, Elie Wiesel is very close to Georges Bernanos. He has acknowledged, moreover, that he admires this French writer because of his clear-headed and courageous conversion to love and understanding of the Jewish people. One finds in both of them the same nostalgia for an authentic childhood which remains present in the life of the self-knowing adult like a hidden source:

Oh, I know how vain this return to the past is. Certainly, my life is already filled with the dead, and the deadest of the dead is the little boy whom I once was. And yet, when the time comes, it is he who will take his place at the head of my life, and will gather together my wretched years up to the last, and, as a young leader gathers his veterans, rallying his disorderly troops, will be the first to enter the House of the Father. . . . My profound conviction is that that part of the world still capable of salvation belongs only to the children, heroes and martyrs.[11]

Children, heroes, martyrs! That, precisely, was the fate in store for the Jewish children of Elie Wiesel's generation. In the written statement of this same Raphael, who recalled his father Aaron's words to his brother Chaim, we can discern the message that the young Elie received from his own father:

Remember, my children. In the days of old, our ancestors were hunted, starved, tortured, in Egypt. But God—blessed be His Name—needed them, their faith, their witness and above all their memory. What was the result? They survived their enemies. Now, too, we shall survive.[12]

One must therefore remain true to childhood, to the identity and authenticity of childhood, in order to find the light in the child's vision of the world and human beings: the light and the strength with which to experience trials while remaining true to oneself. Raphael speaks once again:

What frightens me? It is not that man is a lonely child who makes himself a man in order to defend himself, but that he wants to deny this child, because he considers him as a weakness, while actually it is his real strength and his vital force. Oh, Enemy, there are two ways of looking: an absent look and an offering one, the look of the hunter and the look of the child. Pedro and I had one unique look, the look of the hunted child.[13]

Testimony Through Remembrance

These children driven out of everywhere and condemned to death, whose voice Elie Wiesel is conscious of being, were the victims and witnesses of a tragedy that left humanity with an ineffaceable wound. This being so, they were endowed with a terrible responsibility: that of being the memory and conscience of a world that is in danger of forgetting the evil that it bears within itself. In this respect, their witness transcends their own history: it concerns not only the history of Israel, but that of the entire world. It is a protestation on behalf of justice and the honor of humankind. In *A Beggar in Jerusalem*, Elie Wiesel relates the prophetic cry of the rabbi, in front of the pit, before the mass shooting that was about to wipe out his community:

Should one of us manage to escape, I want him to look, listen and remember. I rely on him more than on the patriarchs, because he will have the courage to go further than they. I want him to become a vessel of truth, a carrier of eternity and fire. And if he too must perish with us, I appeal to heaven, and the winds and the clouds, and the ants burrowing in the ground beneath our feet: let them bear witness for us; perhaps the world deserves no other witnesses.[14]

This is the vocation that Elie Wiesel has taken upon himself, and whose demands are constantly recalled by his characters. Thus Aaron told his son Chaim in *Le crépuscule au loin:* "My son, you have survived, it is your duty to bear witness. Even if people refuse to believe you, you are bound to speak."[15]

This testimony through remembrance is an obligation of conscience for those who have been through hell. As Pedro says to Raphael: "Perhaps, it is not given to man to obliterate evil, but he can be the awareness of it. It is not given to him to forge the glory of the night, but he can attain it and give account of it."[16]

To tell the story is a victory, first of all, over forgetfulness. In this respect, as Pinchas Reichmann the bookseller says in order to justify his passion for the documents of the past: "The historian is a fighter, his weapon is memory, if he knows how to use it he will win."[17] A victory over time, a victory over forgetfulness, a victory over death. Raphael, searching for his parents in his hometown where he returned after the catastrophe, heard a voice that said:

You shall look and you shall not forget . . . Promise me to survive. Thus you will await the return of the absent ones. And you will welcome them in your memory. And they will have a refuge in you, if not even a burial-place.[18]

In reality, as Raphael assures his friend Pedro, it is not a matter of a burial but rather of perpetuating a life, for, by their presence at the heart of our memory, it is the dead who carry us:

One must remember everything. Perhaps a day will come and you will speak. Then the heart of your children will quiver because you have not forgotten. Our dead have no graves. We are their graves, he said after a long silence. We carry our dead with us, but, perhaps, this is not true? It may be that they carry us.[19]

Thus, the remembrance of the Holocaust is the precondition and the means for the survival of Israel in what might be called the memory of eternity.

In the peculiar perspective which is that of Israel as the people of God, this reference via remembrance to the terrible trials the European Jews have passed through is not merely some chronicle of a painful past; it is an act that is as serious and solemn as that of any liturgy of the Word. To remember, to speak, to relate is a vocation whose requirements the witnesses, the Jews of our time, have to recognize and respect. This is what the Maggid states in *A Beggar in Jerusalem:*

One day your turn will come to tell tales. Remember that according to the Scriptures we are supposed to be a nation of priests. What does that mean? Remember, once upon a time the High Priest prepared and purified himself all year long to pronounce one single word—God's name—just once, in just one place: in the inner sanctum of the Temple, on the day of Atonement. He who wishes to follow in his footsteps must learn to say the right word at the right time and in the right place.[20]

It is therefore not surprising if, in the very singularity of its existence, as it appears in its history and memory, as in its remembrance of its tragic history, the Jewish people appears before the world as a symbol of contradiction that ceaselessly questions humanity. This is what Kalman the Kabbalist declares on one Tisha B'Av in *A Beggar in Jerusalem:*

The Jews are God's memory and the heart of mankind. We do not always know this, but the others do, and that is why they treat us with suspicion and cruelty. Memory frightens them. Through us they are linked to the beginning and the end. By eliminating us they hope to gain immortality. But in truth, it is not given to us to die, not even if we wanted to. Why? Perhaps because the heart, by its nature, by its vocation too, cannot but question memory. We cannot die, because we are the question.[21]

Indeed, the testimony of remembrance consists in inviting Israel first, and, then every human consciousness, to pay attention through memory to the presence of God in the history of humankind.

In this connection, it might be said that God needs the testimony of human beings, a testimony for which Israel has been made responsible. Elie Wiesel expresses this certitude in an admirable summation from which one can learn, in addition, the meaning that he attaches to his own work: "Let's say He also needs witnesses. In the beginning there was the word; the word is the tale of man; and man is the tale of God."[22]

The Memory of God in Darkness and Conflict

If the memory of self implied in the remembrance of the Holocaust is for Israel the opportunity and way to commemorate God, it is in a totally contradictory and, in truth, painfully mysterious manner. The Augustinian *memoria* opens out into a sense of wonder that derives from the discovery of a presence. The memory to which the survivors of the death camps bear witness opens into the darkness of a presence that is shadowy and veiled. God is present in the Jewish memory, but as the object of questioning or accusation.

Here one comes upon the main point of Elie Wiesel's message. At the heart of the tragedy, in the depths of the outrage, threatened by doubt, Israel bears witness to its God even in confrontation and contestation. A new version of the struggle with the angel in the night. Indictment and protestation, for the Jewish people, are ways of affirming the existence and presence of God. Is He not, for the heart of Jewish faith, above any kind of appearing contradiction? Elie Wiesel relates the dialogue between a child and his grandfather. The little boy asks the question: "It is written that the Shekhinah, the divine Presence, never leaves Jerusalem; but it is also written that it follows the Jews, all the Jews, into exile: isn't a contradiction in that?" The answer of the grandfather is admirable and gives a key to understanding the paradox of Jewish faith in the depth of contradiction: "That proves the Shekhinah is present even within the contradiction."[23]

Commenting on the work of Elie Wiesel, André Neher once said that the Book of Job was, for the survivor of Auschwitz, the breviary of revolt. Job, "that man betrayed by God," was the symbol of those six million people, all named Job. The Book of Job was one that every survivor of the Holocaust could have written. The attitude of Job is a perpetual model of justification for every person under trial, and in particular for every son and daughter of Israel. This man did not hesitate to declare his distress, to rise up against God, to call Him to account, to insult and accuse Him.

In Wiesel's first book, *Night*, the one closest to a personal confession, the young believing and practicing Jewish deportee quite naturally identifies with Job:

Some talked of God, of his mysterious ways, of the sins of the Jewish people, and of the future deliverance. But I had ceased to pray. How I sympathised with Job! I did not deny God's existence, but I doubted His absolute justice.[24]

At Rosh Hashanah, in the haunting atmosphere of the religious services in a death camp, Eliezer refuses to pray: "This day I had ceased to plead. I was no longer capable of lamentation. On the contrary, I felt very strong. I was the accuser, and God the accused."[25]

On Yom Kippur he refuses to fast: "I no longer accepted God's silence. As I swallowed my bowl of soup, I saw in the gesture an act of rebellion and protest against Him. And I nibbled my crust of bread."[26]

God remained present, certainly, but He was sided against and His justice was contested. This, too, after Auschwitz, was the attitude of Michael, the hero of *The Town Beyond the Wall*, an Auschwitz survivor who found it difficult to reinstate himself in the world of human beings. He reproaches Job with not having gone far enough in protestation and revolt:

> He was seeking his God, tracking him down. He would find Him yet. And then He won't get off as lightly as He did with Job. He won't win out so quickly. I'll be a match for Him. I'm not afraid of Him, not intimidated.
>
> Michael never ceased resenting Job. That biblical rebel should never have given in. At the last moment he should have reared up, shaken a fist, and with a resounding bellow defied that transcendent, inhuman Justice in which suffering has no weight in the balance.
>
> I won't be had so easily, Michael thought. I'll ask Him, why do You play hide-and-seek with Your own image? You'll tell me that You created man in order to put him to the test—which explains nothing. The contest is too unequal; and anyway it isn't an explanation I need, but a clear, concise answer in human terms![27]

Here Michael expresses the fundamental theme of Elie Wiesel's work: the drama of a Job who bitterly and violently called God to account for the absurdity of the Holocaust. It was the tragedy of an eminently religious consciousness that the scandal of evil, grown inordinate, had set against God. It was the rebellion of a son against his father, demanding justification for an incomprehensible attitude, and divided between anger due to disappointment and an immense anguish at having been abandoned.

And yet, however bitter and vehement the protestation was, it was expressed in the consciousness of God's presence. Thus, we have the reaction of Pinchas in *Le chant des morts*. After having decided not to fast, he nevertheless refrains from eating:

> Yes, I have fasted. Like the others. But not for the same reasons. Not by submission but by defiance . . . Here, it is in fasting that a possibility is given to us to claim our indignant protest. Yes, my disciple and my master,

know that I have fasted, not for the love of God, but against Him . . . Here and now, the only way of arguing against Him is to praise Him.[28]

As we have recalled it, quoting the words of Elie Wiesel himself: "Genuine protestation is inseparable from fidelity to the Torah. I can protest against God but not outside the Covenant . . . We can say anything to God, providing it is within Judaism."[29]

Truly, if the remembrance of Auschwitz is the occasion for an altercation with the God of Israel, the certitude of His presence is part of the very existence of His people. The awareness of the God of Sinai within the Jewish identity is vitally and logically anterior to doubt and questioning.

Memory and Hope

If the remembrance of the Holocaust is always present to the Jewish soul as an obsessive challenge, this victory of faith over the absurdity of evil henceforth provides him with the means of confronting it. It is true to say that it is forever integrated into the memory of Israel as a phase of her consciousness, a part of her continuing existence, a confirmation of her destiny. Thus, the witness given by the martyrs has reversed the value sign of the Holocaust. Annihilation and death have become sources of life. The temptation to despair has been transformed into an invitation to hope.

Emil Fackenheim goes so far as to say that in the form of a tragic challenge the Holocaust has revealed a new commandment to the Jewish conscience: the commandment to survive. The manner in which Jews understand the threefold exigency of this commandment seems to resume the new condition of their existence after the Holocaust: survive as a Jew, or the Jewish people will perish; remember the martyrs, or their memory will die; do not deny God, do not lose hope in Him, whatever struggle or revolt this may involve, or Judaism will cease to exist.

However, as Elie Wiesel has so often said in his own overpowering way: for the Jew to transcend the trial of the Holocaust, he or she has to make sense of an event that defies understanding. The Jew must find an outlet to God from the stagnation of anguish that has no name and no recourse. This victory over the absurdity of a senseless evil is very different from the kind of desperate heroism described by Camus that obliges a person at whatever the cost to create happiness by revolting against a joyless and purposeless world. Here the victory is not by revolt but by hope; the *af al pi chen* that Elie Wiesel sings is not so much a wager on the future as an act of faith in the God of Israel. The victory of the Jewish people over the Holocaust is finally accomplished by fidelity to its vocation: the sanctification of the Name.

The remembrance of Auschwitz. The memory of Israel. The memory of God. This, for Elie Wiesel, is the permanent source of hope. One could summarize the spirit that informs all his work with the admirable saying of the Baal Shem Tov: "Memory is the gateway to Geoula [redemption]."

Notes

1. Augustine *De Trinitate* 14. xii, 15.
2. "Elie Wiesel n'est-il pas particuliérement le héraut de la mémoire de la Shoah" in *Le mal et l'exil: Dialogue avec Philippe de Saint-Cheron*, ed. Philippe de Saint-Cheron (Paris: Nouvelle-Cite-Rencontres, 1988), 10.
3. This is the title of the admirable book by Abraham Heschel.
4. *Le mal et l'exil*, 42.   *The Builder of Time*
5. Ibid., 51–52.
6. Ibid., 53.
7. Ibid.
8. Ibid., 56.
9. Ibid., 67.
10. Elie Wiesel, *Le crépuscule au loin* (Paris: Grasset, 1987), 40.
11. Georges Bernanos, *Les grands cimetières sous la lune*, trans. J. M. D. (Paris: Plon, 1947), preface.
12. Wiesel, *Le crépuscule au loin*, 50.
13. Ibid., 254.
14. Elie Wiesel, *A Beggar in Jerusalem* (New York: Random House, 1970), 73.

15. *Le crépuscule au loin,* 137.
16. Ibid., 145.
17. Ibid., 73.
18. Ibid., 162.
19. Ibid., 231.
20. Wiesel, *A Beggar in Jerusalem,* 83.
21. Ibid., 113.
22. Ibid., 135.
23. Ibid., 207.
24. Elie Wiesel, *Night* (New York: Hill and Wang, 1960), 53.
25. Ibid., 75.
26. Ibid., 76.
27. Elie Wiesel, *The Town Beyond the Wall* (New York: Atheneum, 1964), 52; cf. A. Neher, *The Exile and the Word,* trans. David Maisel (Philadelphia: The Jewish Publication Society of America, 1981), 220.
28. Elie Wiesel, *Le chant des morts* (Paris: Editions du Seuil, 1966), 48.
29. *Le mal et l'exil,* 51–56.

8

Elie Wiesel's Challenge to Christianity

John K. Roth

Whoever listens to Sarah and doesn't change, whoever enters Sarah's world and doesn't invent new gods and new religions, deserves death and destruction.

— ELIE WIESEL, *The Accident*

My reading of Elie Wiesel began in July 1972, just a few days after my second child was born. My wife and I named her Sarah. In more ways than one, my entry into Sarah's world coincided with my entry into Elie Wiesel's. For in the latter I would meet another Sarah, the one named in the quotation from *The Accident* that serves as this essay's epigraph. Tensions created by the contrast between my joy as Sarah's father and the despair of "Sarah's world" portrayed in that early novel by Wiesel—these were among the catalysts that ever since have compelled me to respond to his words in writing of my own.

The first essay I published in that vein was called "Tears and Elie Wiesel." It began with a reflection: "Lately something has been puzzling me. I do not regard myself as an emotional person, so why do I sometimes find myself about to weep? Nobody notices, but why is it that especially in church on Sunday mornings tears well up in my eyes?"[1] This experience has continued; it is one reason why I still go to church. In writing that initial article more than fifteen years ago, I began to understand that my tears were partly a response to Elie Wiesel's challenge to Christianity. Today, after studying the

78

Holocaust and its legacy for nearly twenty years, that awareness is all the more poignant. So, what is Elie Wiesel's challenge to Christianity? How can we Christians best respond to it? How does a dedicated Jew like Wiesel help to show us the way? Those questions govern these pages. They do so by taking us back to Sarah's world and beyond.

Speaking of *Night*, that classic recounting of his "exodus" into Auschwitz and beyond, Wiesel has said that "all my subsequent books are built around it."[2] Spare and lean, it starts with a boy who "believed profoundly" and ends with a reflection: "From the depths of the mirror, a corpse gazed back at me. The look in his eyes, as they stared into mine, has never left me."[3] In *l'univers concentrationnaire*, as David Rousset, another Holocaust survivor, named it, assumptions treasured and persons loved were stripped away. But the dead left Wiesel to wonder and thereby to encounter the living.

That fate could hardly be a happy one. *The Accident* testifies to that. In this story, despite the fact that he has friends and a woman who loves him, another survivor, Eliezer, steps in front of a moving car in New York City. This "accident" is no accident, and so the victim's artist-friend, Gyula, whose name means "redemption," has a formidable task as he urges Eliezer to choose life and to put the past behind him.

Part of Gyula's strategy is to paint Eliezer's portrait. Its eyes are searing, since "they belonged to a man who had seen God commit the most unforgivable crime: to kill without a reason." After showing Eliezer the portrait, Gyula symbolizes the end of the past by setting fire to the canvas. Eliezer is moved by Gyula's caring, but he will not be fully healed by it: the novel's final line states that Gyula departed and forgot "to take along the ashes."[4]

Included among the ashes are visions that Eliezer's eyes did not see directly—"Sarah's world," for example—but he has glimpsed more than enough of them as well. Though she is the namesake of the Jewish people's mother, Sarah knows too much has happened between their biblical genesis and their post-Holocaust survival. In *The Accident*, Sarah's world is that of a Paris prostitute. As Eliezer relives his encounter with her, however, he and Sarah are taken back to an earlier time and place. Thus it becomes clear that the foundation of Sarah's world is a question: "Did you ever sleep with a twelve-year-old woman?"[5]

That question was asked and answered with a vengeance in special barracks of Nazi concentration camps, erected for the camp officers' diversion. The despair of Sarah's world intensifies that of Eliezer's even more when Sarah discloses that her purity as a victim is forever compromised. Sometimes, Sarah recalls, she felt pleasure in those barracks and probably survived because of it.

Who created Sarah's world? God had much—too much—to do with it. Elie Wiesel never shies away from that insistence and its tortuous implications. Human beings had much—too much—to do with it, too. Wiesel never uses God's responsibility to excuse humankind. On the contrary, his insistence on human responsibility and its tortuous implications requires him to move from the general to the specific. Nazi perpetrators, bystanders (whose neutrality, indifference, and passivity aided the killers far more than the victims), even some of the victims themselves—all have a share of responsibility to bear. No apportioning of responsibility, however, can approach completeness without giving the Christian tradition and its adherents the attention they deserve. One way to put Elie Wiesel's point in this regard is to argue, as he has rightly done, that "there would have been no Auschwitz if the way had not been prepared by Christian theology."[6]

Christianity was not a sufficient condition for the Holocaust, but it was a necessary one. Remove Christianity and Sarah's world would not have been. That is a specific, concrete way to encapsulate Elie Wiesel's challenge to Christianity. The challenge, however, is not just about the past. It involves judgment about the present and the future as well: "Whoever listens to Sarah and doesn't change, whoever enters Sarah's world and doesn't invent new gods and new religions, deserves death and destruction."[7] With the help of Elie Wiesel and several moments from his books, we Christians can focus where those words ought to take us.

A Problem for Christians

To the extent that they are good, all religious traditions should celebrate their own existence. On that basis, we Christians have reasons to rejoice—but not too much. We can begin to become rightfully, painfully, aware of the "not too much" by considering a moment in Wiesel's book, *A Jew Today*. It begins by reflecting on his initial awareness of Christianity as a boy growing up in Sighet, Romania. Early on he understood that his Jewishness made him a minority in such a way that "everything alien frightened me."[8] In his circumstances, Wiesel emphasizes, "alien" was synonymous with "Christian." Thus, for this young Jew, and he speaks for millions before and after, Christmas and Easter were hardly holidays. On the contrary, "they imposed a climate of terror upon our frightened community."[9]

As Wiesel recounts these early relationships with Christianity, the account becomes even more telling. It does so because he underscores that their effect was not to breed within him curiosity about Christianity or even animosity toward it. "We seemed to intrigue them," he observes, "but they left me indifferent."[10] Powerful though Christians might be, dependent on them though the Jews surely were, the effect that Christianity had on the young Wiesel was to render that tradition so utterly incredible that it was not to be taken seriously as a religious faith.

Before we finish, it will be clear that Wiesel has a different appraisal of some Christians and of some aspects of the Christian tradition. If we Christians are to find ourselves within that affirmation, however, we need to start with Wiesel's boyhood impression, which was empirically grounded in his experience with Christians and churches. That impression convinced him that Jews should be wary of Christian power, but by virtue of the same fact this tradition showed itself to contain little if anything that was worth spiritual inquiry.

For anyone like myself who has lived within the Christian tradition and found it rich and meaningful, Wiesel's challenge is nothing less than shocking. The shock, it must be emphasized, is *not* that of receiving an undeserved affront—it is far from and much deeper than that. Rather, the shock is one of recognition. Rooted in historical awareness, such recognition produces understanding that Elie Wiesel's Jewish boyhood appraisal of Christianity is precisely what it should have been—not in the sense that his appraisal is what Christians ought to desire but, on the contrary, in the sense that his appraisal is what Jewish honesty could rightly produce, given the relations Christians have too often sustained with Jews.

Wiesel's boyhood appraisal of Christianity existed before the Holocaust. With good reason, it intensified after Auschwitz: "For we had been struck by a harsh truth: in Auschwitz all the Jews were victims, all the killers were Christian. . . . It is a painful statement to make, but we cannot ignore it: as surely as the victims are a problem for the Jews, the killers are a problem for the Christians."[11] Wiesel has long opposed theories of collective guilt, and, one must stress, his intent is not to heap guilt on Christians. He does want, however, to encourage Christian responsibility. Thus, he would be the first to distinguish between Christians who are genuinely faithful and those who are not. Apparently the problem for Christians, however, is that it took the Holocaust to drive home much of what that distinction entails.

After Auschwitz, Wiesel helps us Christians to see that the genuine Christian must give priority not to imposing a climate of terror on Jews but to mending the world and Christian-Jewish relations in particular. Before and during the Holocaust that same priority should have existed. The fact that it did not goes far toward explaining how and why Auschwitz scars the earth. Those who destroyed the European Jews, and also those who stood by while the process of destruction occurred, were products of and even baptized within a Western civilization that remains indelibly Christian to this day. If the perpetrators and bystanders did not practice their Christianity as they should have done, that fact is a problem for Christians. If they practiced genocide instead, or observed it without protest, that is a problem for Christians even more so. At least it must be for those of us who are persuaded that Christianity—in spite of, and even in some ways because of, its shortcomings—still has valuable contributions to make.

"You Betrayed the Son of God!"

What a story!

In his novel *The Gates of the Forest*, Elie Wiesel invites his readers to enter Gregor's world. Related to Sarah's, it belongs to another Jewish survivor of the Holocaust who has found his way to New York. During the Holocaust, Gregor obtained refuge in Nazi-occupied Europe with Maria, a Christian who was once a servant for his now-annihilated family. The price for Gregor's safety was silence. Pretending to be a deaf-mute nephew who had come to live with his aunt, Gregor walked safely the streets of a town in which no Jew was safe. The disguise, however, did not last. Cast in the role of Judas for the town's passion play, Gregor found that appearance was reality. As the citizen-actors delivered their lines—"You betrayed the Son of God!"—they also enacted them and began to beat Gregor to death. [12]

To fend off the blows, Gregor broke his silence. Brought to their senses only momentarily, the townspeople went beyond them and thought a miracle had occurred. They took Gregor to be a saint. But when Gregor rejected that identity by proclaiming his Jewishness, the townspeople cried "Betrayal!" all over again. They would have done their worst, but Gregor managed an escape into the forest where he joined a group of resistance fighters.

A Christian reading of Wiesel's novel will drive home the point that we Christians need to be resistance fighters, too. That resistance should include protest against those parts of our tradition that nearly took Gregor's life and did doom countless of his brothers and sisters. Taken together, Wiesel challenges us to see that those parts form what has come to be called a "teaching of contempt." It has caricatured the Judaism of Jesus' day as being degenerate and thereby cast aspersions on contemporary Jewish life as well. It has held, too, that the Jews were responsible collectively for killing Jesus—hence the symbolic significance of Judas in Christian lore—and thus for rejecting God through deicide. And it also has advanced belief that the dispersion of the Jews from Israel late in the first century C.E. —and perhaps all their subsequent difficulties—was God's punishment for the crucifixion.

After the Holocaust, all Christian triumphalism is rightly found wanting. Prayer books, religious pronouncements, commentaries on Scripture, sermons—many of these have been revised to improve Christian images of Jewishness. Interfaith dialogues are held, and at least it can be said that Christian persuasion rarely authorizes persecutions and pogroms any longer. And yet . . . vestiges of the "teaching of contempt" remain in the Christian tradition even after the Holocaust. Unless resistance against them continues, the line that epitomizes the threat against Gregor's life—"You betrayed the Son of God!"—will more aptly advance instead the toll it has already taken on Christianity.

A Meeting with Yeoshua

It is 1967. Israel is under threat again; the death of Jews is still desired. This time, however, there is a difference: the Jews win. The Wall in Jerusalem is recovered, washed with Jewish tears new and old, rebuilt with joy and laughter, even reestablished with prayers.

Elie Wiesel's response to the Six-Day War was a novel called *A Beggar in Jerusalem*. David, the novel's narrator-beggar, was in the struggle. In David's world, Jerusalem has been secured by Israeli troops, but the net result does not add up to satisfaction, for David cannot forget the prices paid—particularly the loss of his friend, Katriel, and the repeated "destructions of Jerusalem elsewhere than in Jerusalem." [13] In joy and sadness, David finds companionship with penetrating spirits who gather at the Wall. They are waiting—some for understanding, some for lost friends, and all in their own ways for God. They also swap stories. One of them, told by Shlomo, involves a meeting with Yeoshua.

Christians call him Jesus, but his Hebrew name, Yeoshua, is used in Shlomo's tale of a conversation between two Jews. By Shlomo's reckoning, Yeoshua was an "innocent preacher who had only one word on his lips: love." [14] The other tried to convince him that he ought not to let himself be killed—or at the very least that he ought not to think that his suffering and dying would be redemptive.

Misunderstanding and perversion of that message of love would dominate, partly because the message was so simple that it was complex,
so clear that it would become obscure in practice.

To make this point, the protesting Jew described the horrors that
would be visited upon all Jews because of the death of another Jew
on a cross. Then it was Yeoshua's turn to protest back. No, things
would not be that way. His heritage, said Yeoshua, would "be a gift
of compassion and hope, not a punishment in blood!"[15] Yeoshua's
heart was breaking more than ever. It was too late, though—the
conversation occurred on Friday.

Traditional Christianity holds that the Messiah has come in the
person of Jesus Christ. But the Jewish challenge to Christianity, and
Wiesel's version of it in particular, is as follows: "One thing is clear
to me as a Jew—he [the Messiah] hasn't come yet."[16] Wiesel's
reason for saying this is simply that the world is unmended, to say
nothing of unredeemed. The redemption of the world and the arrival
of the Messiah go together, but, if the world has been transformed,
the movement has been more in the direction of Auschwitz than
toward redemption. A decisive factor in that reality is that the cross
of Christendom, intended though it may have been to be a sign of
love, has too often been an evil presence instead.

Wiesel's challenge to Christianity is not simply to say that Christian judgment about Yeoshua is wrong. The challenge is more profound than that because it looks toward the future. As a Jew, Wiesel
waits for the Messiah, and it is an open question when or whether the
Messiah will come. This is true for him because the determination of
that question depends on what men and women do. What Wiesel
suggests most strongly, then, is not a criticism from outside Christianity that says "Christians are wrong—period." Rather he provides
an opportunity for us Christians to open a question that has been
closed too long: Who, in fact, is Jesus? The point of opening this
question-closed-too-long is precisely to see that Jesus' identity depends on who his followers are and on what they do. Wiesel's
challenge provides a corrective that can make better Christians. By
observing that Jesus cannot be the Messiah until his followers are
committed to mend the world—a task they cannot begin to accom-

plish apart from solidarity with others, including Yeoshua's own
people—Wiesel rightly gives us Christians pause to reflect on our
meetings with Jesus.

More than twenty years after *A Beggar in Jerusalem,* Elie Wiesel
is still waiting for the Messiah. He does so because "destructions of
Jerusalem" continue—this time in part from within Israel itself. At
the time of this writing, in October 1988, some critics, Jewish as
well as Christian, have taken Wiesel to task—especially in the light
of his being the 1986 recipient of the Nobel Peace Prize—for openly
criticizing Israel's current Palestinian policies too little and too late.
Whether this criticism is deserved is a question with which Wiesel
must grapple. Time's passage will reveal the quality of his doing so.
A similar dilemma faces us Christians as we consider Israel today.
What to say and how to say it? What to do and how to do it? As all of
us, Jew and Christian alike, wrestle with these agonizing questions,
which are crucial aspects of the Holocaust's legacy, some others from
A Beggar in Jerusalem are worth contemplating as well: "And you,
men and women, who sit in judgment, do you understand now that
love, no matter how personal or universal, is not a solution? And that
outside of love there is no solution?"[17]

God's Defenders?

Christian women named Maria appear more than once in Elie Wiesel's writings. In a drama entitled *The Trial of God,*[18] Maria, for
example, keeps house for Berish, a Jewish innkeeper in Shamgorod,
which was ravaged by a murderous pogrom in 1647. Berish is one of
only two survivors. He had to watch while his daughter was unspeak-
ably abused on her wedding night. She now lives mercifully out of
touch with the world.

The play is set at the season of Purim, a joyous festival replete
with masks and reenactments that celebrate an ancient moment in
Jewish history when oppressors were outmaneuvered and Jews were
saved. Three Jewish actors have lost their way. They arrive in the
village, but they will discover that Shamgorod is hardly a place for
festivity. In the region anti-Jewish hatred festers once again, and it

is not unthinkable that a new pogrom may break out to finish work left undone two years before.

Purim, however, cannot be Purim without a play, and so a *Purim-spiel* must be given, but with a difference urged by Berish. At Purim people can speak openly. This time, therefore, the play will enact the trial of God. As the characters in Wiesel's drama begin to organize their play-within-a-play, one problem looms large. The defendant, God, is silent, and on this Purim night no one in Shamgorod wants to speak for God. But just when it seems that the defense attorney's role will go unfilled, a stranger who has entered the inn— his name is Sam—volunteers to act the part. Apparently Maria has seen this man before, and she advises the others to have nothing to do with him. Her warning, unfortunately, goes unheeded.

Berish contends with God, prosecutes God. His protest is as real as his despair. Neither denies God's reality; both affirm it by calling God to account. Sam's style is different. He has an answer for every charge, and he cautions that emotion is no substitute for evidence. In short, he defends God brilliantly. Sam's performance dazzles the visiting actors who have formed the court. Despite their curiosity, Sam will not tell them who he is, but his identity and the verdict implicit in *The Trial of God* do not remain moot. As the play's final scene unfolds, a mob approaches to pillage the inn at Shamgorod once more.

Sensing that the end is near, the Jewish actors choose to die with their Purim masks in place. Sam dons one, too, and as he does so, Maria's premonitions are corroborated. Sam's mask is worthy of his namesake, Samael. Both signify Satan. As a final candle is extinguished, Sam lifts his arm as if to give a signal, and the inn's doors open to the sound of deafening and murderous roars. Satan's laughter is among them.

In the Christian New Testament, the Gospel according to John puts volatile words into Jesus' mouth. On one occasion, for example, Jesus is described as identifying his Jewish listeners as follows: "You are of your father the devil, and your will is to do your father's desires" (John 8:44). Elie Wiesel knows all too well the tragedies that such attributions have produced. He has no intention of asserting them in reverse in *The Trial of God*. His target instead is language abused, which in turn heaps abuse on others. Sam's defense of God legitimates evil by being for God at the expense of humankind. That same defense, Wiesel suggests, makes it fitting that Sam is the one who gives the signal for the repetition of a pogrom in Shamgorod.

After Auschwitz, how does Christian language fare, including that of Scripture itself? That question is another facet of Wiesel's challenge to Christianity. Just as Berish challenged God, a Christian reading of Wiesel's play suggests that we Christians should challenge our own sense of being God's defenders, particularly as it is expressed in New Testament statements and interpretations that vilify the Jews and thereby "defend" God at humankind's expense. Not only Sarah's world but Maria's as well demand changes as fundamental as quarreling with sacred texts. The testimony of those texts, Wiesel can help us Christians to see, must be evaluated by their highest standards of love and justice, which rightly call into question other things they say.

Friendship

Elie Wiesel's challenge to Christianity emerges not only from a profound sense of injustice that this tradition has done to his. It emerges even more from a yearning based on the hope of friendship. The friendship Wiesel has in mind accents honesty, deplores domination, and encourages mutual trust and esteem. Such friendship is what he contemplates when he writes, "I believe that no religion, people or nation is inferior or superior to another; I dislike facile triumphalism, for us and for others. I dislike self-righteousness. And I feel closer to certain Christians—as long as they do not try to convert me to their faith—than to certain Jews . . . I have more in common with an authentic and tolerant Christian than with a Jew who is neither authentic nor tolerant."[19]

Suggestions about what Wiesel can admire as authentic and tolerant in Christianity appear throughout his writings. Maria in *The Gates of the Forest* protects a Jewish refugee at her own risk, and her counterpart in *The Trial of God* warns against Sam, who is a father of lies. Another novel, *The Fifth Son*, includes "some good honest people" who are willing to hide a Jewish child from the Angel of Death in Hitler's Europe. [20] The examples could be multiplied. They even include a recollection in *Night* of a Hungarian police inspector who had promised to alert the Wiesel family about Nazi danger in Sighet. After the war, Wiesel learned that the policeman had acted on his promise by trying to give them a warning. [21] The policeman did not succeed, nor did the honest people in *The Fifth Son* who tried to save a Jewish child. Nonetheless, the fact that they tried, when so many others did not, gives them a special place in Wiesel's memory. Often these caring non-Jews are not specifically identified as Christians in Wiesel's writings. Whether they were or not, they provide examples that we Christians need.

The first three books that Elie Wiesel published were *Night* and two brief novels, *Dawn*, and *The Accident*. If the title of the latter were translated literally from French, *Le Jour*, it would be *Day* instead. These early works travel through the destruction of a supportive universe into a post-Holocaust world of ambiguity and nothingness in which life almost succeeds in fulfilling a desire to cancel itself. Plumbing such depths had to be the prelude to Wiesel's hard-won insistence that friendship is essential if despair is to be kept at bay.

Although it speaks less about Jewish-Christian relationships than some of his other writings, Wiesel's 1988 novel, *Twilight*, speaks to the issue of friendship in a way that can round out helpfully this reflection on Wiesel's challenge to Christianity. For this story shows how friendship—especially when it is courageous enough to defy suspicion, mistrust, fear, and the violence they generate—is a resource for mending the world that has no substitute. The novel stresses this insight by probing "the domain of madness," a realm never far from the center of Wiesel's consciousness, and by illuminating, in particular, Maimonides' conviction—it serves as the novel's epigraph—that "the world couldn't exist without madmen." [22]

Arguably Wiesel's most complex novel, *Twilight* defies simple summary, but its emphasis on friendship emerges when Raphael Lipkin's telephone rings at midnight. This survivor of the Holocaust, now a university scholar, hears an anonymous voice denouncing Pedro: "Professor, let me tell you about your friend Pedro. He is totally amoral. A sadist. He made me suffer. And not just me, there were many others."[23] Pedro is Raphael's friend indeed. More than once he has saved Raphael from the despair that repeatedly threatens to engulf him.

They met first in September 1945. Raphael, saved by two "honest peasants and good Christians," had returned to Rovidok, the Eastern European town that had once been his home. Before World War II, Rovidok was a colorful place. Its inhabitants were diverse religiously and ethnically, but they "had endured the centuries with an unusual grace. Rarely affected by external events other than the occasional war or epidemic, Jews and Christians had coexisted harmoniously. A harmony barely disrupted by the anti-Semitic incidents that predictably occurred at Easter and Christmas." That harmony would not last. Even if not in Rovidok, there were still far too many Christians —significantly Wiesel describes them here as "not necessarily followers of Christ"—who persecuted Jews and thereby helped to pave the twisted road that would pass through that "pretty town in Galicia" on its way to the Nazi death camps.[24]

On Shabbat afternoons in Rovidok, well before Pedro entered his life, Raphael first encountered madness. He would go to the town's asylum to visit an old man who had become his friend. Although Raphael did not understand all the old man had to say, his friend's impassioned vision never left him. Some time later, an encounter with madness of another kind—it, too, never left him—invaded Raphael's Rovidok. Germans occupied that place in September 1939. Raphael was among those who had to watch them hang an old Jew— it seems the victim was Raphael's friend from the asylum—for resisting the occupation.

This death was but the first of many losses Raphael experienced in Rovidok and elsewhere. All too soon nothing remained for him there. That town could never be his home again. So Raphael left with Pedro, who worked for a clandestine Jewish organization that helped survivors. Pedro's help was more than physical. Akin to Raphael's old friend from the asylum, he taught the young Lipkin: "It may not be in man's power to erase society's evil, but he must become its conscience; it may not be in his power to create the glories of the night, but he must wait for them and describe their beauty."[25]

Much later, the midnight calls keep coming. What's more, the caller seems to know too much. Eventually suggesting where the "truth" about Pedro can be found, the calls lure Raphael to upstate New York. There a Dr. Benedictus—only gradually does Raphael sense that, in spite of his name and calling, this "healer" may be the malevolent caller—administers the Mountain Clinic. It "caters to patients, men and women—mostly men—whose schizophrenia is linked, in some mysterious way, to Ancient History, to Biblical times."[26]

Raphael seeks the truth about Pedro as he encounters persons who think they are biblical characters such as Adam, Cain, the Messiah, and even God. Their madness, which is rooted in an inability to come to terms with humanity or God after Auschwitz, is compounded for Raphael by the attempt that is under way to discredit Pedro. Thus, Raphael edges toward the abyss that awaits him: "What am I to do?" Raphael asks a Pedro who is both there and not there. "To whom shall I turn for a little light, a little warmth? Madness is lying in wait for me and I am alone."[27]

The madness that lies in wait for Raphael would destroy him, and, if he were truly left alone, Raphael might succumb to it. Perhaps that is what the telephone voice intended by calling Pedro into question and Raphael toward despair. Recognition of that possibility, recollection that "Pedro taught me to love mankind and celebrate its humanity despite its flaws," a renewed realization that Pedro's "enemy is my enemy"—such forces rally Raphael's resistance.[28]

By reaffirming a summons to save, Raphael's battle against madness that destroys does not ensure a tranquil equilibrium. A different kind of madness, the moral madness without which the world could not exist, is the prospect instead. "The caller tried to drive you out of my life," Raphael tells the absent Pedro. "He failed. Does that mean I've won? Hardly. I cry into the night and the night does not answer. Never mind, I will shout and shout until I go deaf, until I go mad."[29]

Twilight is not the first time a man named Pedro has appeared in Wiesel's novels and provided saving inspiration. Differing from his namesake in *Twilight* because he is not Jewish, another Pedro is a decisive presence in *The Town Beyond the Wall*. This book, Wiesel's fourth and fittingly the one most closely linked to *Twilight,* begins with an epigraph from Dostoevsky: "I have a plan—to go mad."[30] It also starts at twilight and under circumstances that can drive one to madness that destroys.

Once Michael's home, Szerencseváros ("the city of luck") is now in the vise of Communist victors over Nazi tyrants. Secretly returning to see whether anyone can be found, Michael stands before his former home. Ages ago a face watched silently there while Jews were sent away. The face, seeking a hatred from Michael to match its own hidden guilt, informs the police. Michael finds himself imprisoned in walls within his past, tortured to tell a story that cannot be told: there is no political plot to reveal; his captors would never accept the simple truth of his desire to see his hometown once more; his friend, Pedro, who returned with him, must be protected.

Michael holds out. He resists an escape into one kind of madness by opening himself to another. His cellmate, Eliezer, dwells in catatonic silence. But Michael hears and heeds the advice that he knows his friend Pedro would give him: "That's exactly what I want you to do: re-create the universe. Restore that boy's sanity. Cure him. He'll save you."[31]

What of such a plan? *Twilight,* as well as *The Town Beyond the Wall* and some thirty more of Wiesel's books, follows *Night.* All of *Night's* sequels, in one way or another, explore ways in which the world might be mended. Nonetheless we know that in the order of things, dawn, day, and especially twilight leave night close by. Yet even if, as Wiesel contends, "everything to do with Auschwitz must, in the end, lead into darkness," questions remain concerning what that darkness might be and whether the leading into darkness is indeed the end."[32] For if *The Town Beyond the Wall* concludes with Michael's coming "to the end of his strength," it also ends with "the night . . . receding, as on a mountain before dawn."[33] Similarly, as *Twilight* moves toward night, "from far away, a star appears. Uncommonly brilliant."[34]

Although often regarded as noncanonical, the ancient texts of Tobit and Enoch from the Apocrypha, as well as Kabbalistic writings, refer to an angel named Raphael. Stories about this angel make clear that Raphael has power to conquer demons. The name, significantly, is a compound of the Hebrew *rapha*, meaning "healed," and *el*, which designates God. Raphael, then, is the Angel of Healing or "God's healing."

In *Twilight* Raphael Lipkin finds a healing that can help him to heal others. Friendship with Pedro is its source. The other Pedro's friendship in *The Town Beyond the Wall* also links Raphael with Michael, whose name — meaning "Who is like God?" — stands for another protecting angel. These four are friends — not merely for each other but for all others who fall under the threat of destructive madness. They embody the invitation that Elie Wiesel's challenge to Christianity contains. For their example shows us Christians how to be "necessarily followers of Christ." Such commitment mends the world by encouraging and renewing friendship that refuses to leave alone those who are in need.

Sarah's World Once More

Sarah's world, contends Wiesel, requires new gods and new religions. For Jews as well as Christians, that challenge poses a problem, because both are ancient traditions. Historically, however, each has sources for renewal. The Holocaust aimed to crush Jewish life and targeted its religious vitality in particular. Jewish spirituality after Auschwitz will never be entirely the same as it was before, but its ways have more than survived. With renewed intensity and determination, they reveal new insights about God and about what it does and should mean to be a Jew today.

Can Christianity be renewed after Auschwitz? For those who try authentically to be followers of Jesus, that question is Elie Wiesel's challenge. Presently the answer remains in suspense. Clearly, though, the Holocaust leaves an immense crisis of Christian credibility, one that deserves to doom that tradition's anti-Jewish leanings. What would Christianity be like if those leanings were stripped away as they should be? It might begin to qualify as one of the new religions, with new understandings of God, that Sarah's world needs.

Here I think of Sarah's world in both of the ways alluded to at the beginning of this essay. For me, it is not only that of Elie Wiesel's

Sarah in *The Accident* but also that of my daughter, Sarah, a baptized Christian in the United States. As her father, as one responsible for initiating her into the Christian tradition that we share, I want that tradition to be characterized less by the darkness it has produced and more by the light it can give. Hence, with the hope and confidence that there are other Christians who will understand what I mean, these pages conclude with the final words in that meditation on tears with which my responses to Elie Wiesel began: "After reading Elie Wiesel my faith may be less sure of itself, because no one can read his books without being shaken. On the other hand, I think my faith is also more passionate than before. I am grateful to him for moving me, for setting my soul on fire."[35]

Notes

1. John K. Roth, "Tears and Elie Wiesel," *Princeton Seminary Bulletin* 65 (December 1972): 42.
2. Elie Wiesel, "Talking and Writing and Keeping Silent," in *The German Church Struggle and the Holocaust*, ed. Franklin H. Littell and Hubert G. Locke (Detroit: Wayne State University Press, 1974), 269.
3. Elie Wiesel, *Night*, trans. Stella Rodway (New York: Bantam Books, 1986), 1, 109. This work was published originally as *La Nuit* in 1958. The English translation appeared in 1960.
4. Elie Wiesel, *The Accident*, trans. Anne Borchardt (New York: Avon Books, 1970), 123, 127. This novel was published originally as *Le Jour* (Day) in 1961. The English translation appeared in 1962.
5. Ibid., 97.
6. Elie Wiesel, "A Small Measure of Victory," in *Against Silence: The Voice and Vision of Elie Wiesel*, ed. Irving Abrahamson, 3 vols. (New York: Holocaust Library, 1985), 3: 224. The statement is from an interview with Wiesel by Gene Koppel and Henry Kaufmann, University of Arizona, Tucson, 25 April 1973.
7. Wiesel, *The Accident*, 96.
8. Elie Wiesel, *A Jew Today*, trans. Marion Wiesel (New York: Random House, 1978), 3. This book was published originally as *Un juif aujord'hui* in 1977. The English translation appeared in 1978.
9. Ibid., 4.

10. Ibid.
11. Ibid., 11–12.
12. Elie Wiesel, *The Gates of the Forest*, trans. Frances Frenaye (New York: Avon Books, 1972), 107. This novel was published originally as *Les portes de la forêt* in 1964. The English translation appeared in 1966.
13. Elie Wiesel, *A Beggar in Jerusalem*, trans. Lily Edelman and the author (New York: Avon Books, 1971), 82. This novel was published originally as *Le mendiant de Jerusalem* in 1968. The English translation appeared in 1970.
14. Ibid., 67.
15. Ibid., 68.
16. Quoted in Harry James Cargas, *Harry James Cargas in Conversation with Elie Wiesel* (New York: Paulist Press, 1976), 17.
17. Wiesel, *A Beggar in Jerusalem*, 72.
18. Elie Wiesel, *The Trial of God (As It Was Held on February 25, 1649, in Shamgorod): A Play in Three Acts*, trans. Marion Wiesel (New York: Random House, 1979). This play was originally published in French in 1979.
19. Wiesel, *A Jew Today*, 11.
20. Elie Wiesel, *The Fifth Son*, trans. Marion Wiesel (New York: Summit Books, 1985), 184. This novel was published originally as *Le cinquième fils* in 1983. The English translation appeared in 1985.
21. See Wiesel, *Night*, 12.
22. Elie Wiesel, *Twilight*, trans. Marion Wiesel (New York: Summit Books, 1988), 202, 9. This novel was published originally as *Le crépuscule au loin* in 1987. The English translation appeared in 1988.
23. Ibid., 179.
24. Ibid., 124, 17–18.
25. Ibid., 118.
26. Ibid., 37.
27. Ibid., 11.
28. Ibid., 201.
29. Ibid., 202.
30. See Elie Wiesel, *The Town Beyond the Wall*, trans. Stephen Becker (New York: Avon Books, 1970), 3. This novel was published originally as *La ville de la chance* in 1962. The English translation appeared in 1964.
31. Ibid., 182.

32. Elie Wiesel, "Auschwitz—Another Planet," in *Against Silence*, ed. Abrahamson 2: 293. The statement is from Wiesel's review of *Auschwitz* by Bernd Naumann, which appeared in *Hadassah Magazine*, January 1967.

33. Wiesel, *The Town Beyond the Wall*, 189.

34. Wiesel, *Twilight*, 217.

35. Roth, "Tears and Elie Wiesel," 48.

9

Silence and Dialogue:
Reflections on the Work of Elie Wiesel

Eugene J. Fisher

The following reflections are neither a systematic analysis of the portraits of Christians or Christianity in the work of Elie Wiesel nor a comprehensive response to them. Rather they are reflections offered in a spirit intended to open a dialogue with him on these topics. Wiesel does not often depict Christians *as Christians* in his fiction nor does he directly discuss Christianity as a religious tradition in his articles and essays.[1] In the vivid, complex world of darkness and the defiance of darkness in which Wiesel's words of hope struggle against the silence of despair, he has few words either of condemnation or solace to spare for specifically Christian problems or concerns. It is enough for him, and perhaps more than enough for us, simply that he tells his own story, the manifold story of his people.

Wiesel's Challenge to Christians

The words Elie Wiesel does have for Christians are usually both terse and challenging. Irving Abrahamson has collected a representative sampling:

As most historians have stated, Christianity's role in the Holocaust should not be underrated. The Final Solution was rooted in the centuries-old Christian hatred of the Jews . . . Pope John XXIII understood the guilt of the Church—and of Christianity in general. The mass killings took place in a Christian setting. Protestant leaders applauded Hitler—as did their Cath-

olic counterparts. Those who killed . . . felt no tension, no conflict between
their Christian faith and their criminal deeds. (3 June 1974)

Are we, as Christians would say, witnesses to *their* truth? This is what the
Christians usually say—that the Jews should live, but live in suffering for
having rejected Christ. And we Jews all suffered: they made us suffer. But
this is their view, not the Jewish view. We reject suffering. (23 November
1975)

John XXIII, a saint even in my vocabulary, opened the Church and liberal-
ized it not only because he was a friend of the Jewish people but also
because he felt the Catholic Church had failed. It had gone bankrupt. It was
inconceivable to him that the Holocaust could occur within Christianity.
Germany was a Christian nation—devotedly Christian and Catholic. Therefore John XXIII said we must rethink even Catholicism. And he began. (13
April 1987)[2]

Aside from the rather global language here employed (for example,
"the guilt of the Church" and "the Catholic Church had failed . . .
gone bankrupt"), Christians have much to learn from what Wiesel
has to say to us in these passages.[3] I believe we Christians should
not seek to evade, with the historical quibbles to which many of us
are often tempted, Wiesel's moral and spiritual challenges. Pope
John Paul II, in his controversial but powerful Christian meditation
at Mauthausen on the conscience of "Christian Europe" at the end of
what he has called "the century of the *Shoah*," made much the same
point about Christian moral bankruptcy "after Auschwitz . . . after
Mauthausen":

Here, and in so many other places . . . a totalitarian domination existed.
From this, one of the most terrifying experiences in its history, Europe
emerges defeated—defeated in what seemed to be its inheritance and
mission. 'Its ways are blocked' *(Lamentations)*. The burden of doubt has
come down hard on the history of people, nations and continents.[4]

Wiesel, I suspect, is not about to lift from us Christians that
awesome "burden of doubt." In a 1982 interview about his book *A
Jew Today*, he gives his reasons, and they are strong ones:

My background justifies a total suspicion. As a child, I wouldn't even come
close to the church. I changed sidewalks. It wasn't because of me: it was

because of them. Because twice a year they would beat us up. Also we were
afraid of being taken into the church by force. I would never go close to it.[5]

Wiesel's reference to *A Jew Today* led me back to that work,
which I first read some years ago. There, Wiesel's portrait of his own,
pre-Auschwitz boyhood attitude toward Christians and Christianity is
laid out in such telling detail that it needs to be cited at length,
uncomfortable as it may make some readers of the present volume:

Once upon a time, in a distant town surrounded by mountains, there lived a
small Jewish boy who believed himself capable of seeing good in evil, of
discovering dawn within dusk and, in general, of deciphering the symbols,
both visible and invisible, lavished upon him by destiny.

To him, all things seemed simple and miraculous: life and death, love
and hatred. On one side were the righteous, on the other the wicked. The
just were always handsome and generous, the miscreants always ugly and
cruel. And God in His heaven kept the accounts in a book only he could
consult. In that book each people had its own page, and the Jewish people
had the most beautiful page of all.

Naturally, this little boy felt at ease only among his own people, in his
own setting. Everything alien frightened me. And alien meant not Moslem
or Hindu, but Christian. The priest dressed in black, the woodcutter and
his ax, the teacher and his ruler, old peasant women crossing themselves as
their husbands uttered oath upon oath, constables looking gruff or merely
preoccupied—all of them exuded a hostility I understood and considered
normal, and therefore without remedy. I *understood* that all these people,
young and old, rich and poor, powerful and oppressed, exploiters and
exploited, should want my undoing, even my death. True, we inhabited the
same landscape, but that was yet another reason for them to hate me. Such
is man's nature: he hates what disturbs him, what eludes him. We depended
on the more or less unselfish tolerance of the "others," yet our life followed
its own course independently of theirs, a fact they clearly resented. Our
determination to maintain and enrich our separate history, our separate
society, confused them as much as did that history itself. A living Jew, a
believing Jew, proud of his faith, was for them a contradiction, a denial, an
aberration. According to their calculations, this chosen and accursed people
should long ago have ceased to haunt a mankind whose salvation was linked
to the bloodstained symbol of the cross. They could not accept the idea of a
Jew celebrating his Holy Days with song, just as they celebrated their own.
That was inadmissible, illogical, even unjust. And the less they understood

us, the more I understood them. I felt no animosity. I did not even hate them at Christmas or Easter time when they imposed a climate of terror upon our frightened community. I told myself: they envy us, they persecute us because they envy us, and rightly so; surely *they* were the ones to be pitied. Their tormenting us was but an admission of weakness, of inner insecurity. If God's truth subsists on earth in the hearts of mortals, it is our doing. It is through us that God has chosen to manifest His will and outline His designs, and it is through us that He has chosen to sanctify His name. Were I in their place I, too, would feel rejected. How could they not be envious? In an odd way, the more they hunted me, the more I rationalized their behavior. Today I recognize my feelings for what they were: a mixture of pride, distrust and pity.

Yet I felt no curiosity. Not of any kind, or at any moment. We seemed to intrigue them, but they left me indifferent. I knew nothing of their catechism, and cared less. I made no attempt to comprehend the rites and canons of their faith. Their rituals held no interest for me; quite the contrary, I turned away from them. Whenever I met a priest I would avert my gaze and think of something else. Rather than walk in front of a church with its pointed and threatening belfry, I would cross the street. To see was as frightening as to be seen; I worried that a visual, physical link might somehow be created between us. So ignorant was I of their world that I had no idea that Judaism and Christianity claimed the same roots. Nor did I know that Christians who believe in the eternity and in the divinity of Christ also believe in those of God, *our* God. Though our universes existed side by side, I avoided penetrating theirs, whereas they sought to dominate ours by force. I had heard enough tales about the Crusades and the pogroms, and I had repeated enough litanies dedicated to their victims, to know where I stood. I had read and reread descriptions of what inquisitors, grand and small, had inflicted on Jews in Catholic kingdoms; how they had preached God's love to them even as they were leading them to the stake. All I knew of Christianity was its hate for my people. Christians were more present in my imagination than in my life. What did a Christian do when he was alone? What were his dreams made of? How did he use his time when he was not engaged in plotting against us? But none of this really troubled me. Beyond our immediate contact, our public and hereditary confrontations, he simply did not exist.[6]

Most chilling in this description of a long-past worldview is not its essentially accurate portrayal of the ancient Christian "teaching of contempt" or even its generalizations about the inner mentality of so

large a portion of humanity as Christians make up. The latter is, after
all, described by Wiesel as a boyhood image, a simplification of
reality to grow out of as one reaches maturity and begins to encounter
the complex ambiguities of oneself and other human beings. What is
chilling is the deep honesty of the final line, that for such a youthful
mentality Christians as persons "simply did not exist."

The Christian as Bystander

One major role of Christians in Wiesel's works is that of the Christian
as spectator or bystander. On reflection, the implicit challenge to the
Christian conscience may be as deep in considering this passive
Christian role as is that of the Christian as persecutor or even
executioner of Jews. It was at least quantitatively more typical of the
situation of far more Christians before and during the Holocaust than
any other role. As Christians, we can and must acknowledge the evil
acts of those of our tradition who willingly participated in or cooper-
ated with the twisted Nazi machinery of mass murder. Although sin
is not an unknown in our traditional theological categories, nor
sinners a new phenomenon in our history, the sinful deeds of Christians both before and during the Holocaust can and must be straightforwardly condemned in the present without hesitation or moral
ambiguity.

The paradigm presented to us by the bystander, however, is some-
what more difficult to categorize. Quantitatively, it described the
large majority of Christians of that enormously complex period, themselves sometimes powerless before the Nazi onslaught. In this sense,
they might be said to be among its victims as were all Jews. Many,
however, could have done something, at some point, no matter how
minor, to ameliorate or confront the growing tide of evil, which, after
all, took almost a decade to reach its genocidal crescendo. In retrospect, we know now that more was generally known then than most
people afterward wanted to admit.[7] The concentration camp of Da-
chau, for example, was in the town itself, the trains rolled on tracks
amid its pleasant homes, conveying thousands of people into an area
far too small to maintain them. Incessant volleys of gunfire must have

been heard. And few came out. So, too, the smells of the crematoria would have been unmistakable in the town. Yet people seemingly denied, even to themselves, what their senses and simple logic had to have told them.

This denial response was true in America as well as in Europe.[8] So it is perhaps with the bystanders that most American Christians today will tend to identify. Wiesel is aware of the moral ambiguities involved, of the desperate human urge to survive cataclysmic events at whatever cost. Knowing this, he does not hesitate to indict the bystanders for their silence and inaction. Nor should he.

In *The Town Beyond the Wall*, the central character returns to his hometown after the war. He meets a Christian whom he remembers as having watched silently as the Jews were herded into the trains to be deported. The survivor cannot restrain a heartfelt accusation against his former neighbor:

You're a shameful coward. You haven't got the courage to do either good or evil! The role of the spectator suited you to perfection. They killed? You had nothing to do with it. They looted houses like vultures? You had nothing to do with it. Your conscience is clear . . . "Not guilty, your honor!" You're a disgusting coward![9]

Silence, of course, is a central theme in Wiesel's work. The silence of the murdered victims of the death camps is reciprocal to the silence of the watching world: the one the silent witness of the martyr, the other the silent shame of the bystander. Wiesel returns to this theme again and again:

If someone suffers and keeps silent, it can be a good silence. If someone suffers and *I* keep silent, then it is a destructive silence. If we envisage literature and human destiny as endeavors by humanity to redeem itself, then we must admit the obsession, the overall dominating theme of responsibility, that we are responsible for one another. I am responsible for his or her suffering, for his or her destiny. If not, we are condemned by our solitude forever and it has no meaning. This solitude is a negative, destructive solitude, a self-defeating solitude.[10]

Out of the solitude of the past, a solitude that played such a large role in making possible the Holocaust, there must come today the healing words of dialogue. The key word for our generation, too young during or born after the *Shoah*, however, is the one used here by Wiesel. It is not guilt so much as responsibility, responsibility for forging a future of reconciliation that alone can respond to that past and to all the evil of its calculated, technological horror.

Christian Responsibility and Historical Guilt

Wiesel speaks powerfully and unflinchingly of the world's and especially Christianity's betrayal of the Jewish people. He speaks with surgical precision:

Munich taught us that civilization betrayed. Munich was a bankruptcy for mankind. Christianity failed. Christianity killed itself when it killed Jews in Treblinka . . . No, there would have been no Auschwitz had it not been for one thousand years of Christian teachings. Christian preachers and fanatics prepared the ground for the dehumanization and the atrocities at Treblinka. There would have been no massacre, there would have been no dehumanization on that scale had it not been for what they—they, the Christians— have done to us for so many centuries.[11]

The language here is both strong and very precise. The ancient Christian "teaching of contempt" did prepare the soil in which the seeds of Nazi race hatred grew. Without that Christian teaching, there would have been no Holocaust.

Yet that centuries-long Christian teaching and practice of contempt is not in itself, I believe, the whole story that needs to be told about modern anti-Semitism and genocide. It was a sine qua non for genocide but not its sole cause. To employ the perhaps dry but still useful distinctions of scholastic philosophy, Christian teaching was a necessary cause, but not a sufficient one. Otherwise, as many historians of anti-Semitism have pointed out, the *Shoah* would have happened much sooner in the two-millennia history of the Jewish-Christian encounter in Europe—perhaps as early as the fifth century of the common era, with the consolidation of Church power in the Roman Empire, and certainly by the sixteenth century, when the churches still wielded enormous political power and the specifically *Christian* polemic against Judaism had already reached its peak.[12]

The Holocaust, which is not possible to explain or understand *without* the centuries of negative Christian teaching, was, it is also true to say, not possible without the dissolution of that teaching in the modern era. Something new had happened.

Elie Wiesel, if I am not presuming to infer too much from his words, pinpoints that "something" for us. Speaking of the dilemmas facing the teacher struggling to communicate at once the evil of the Holocaust and a sense of hope for the future, Wiesel states:

Something happened there [in the confrontation between killer and victim], something theological, metaphysical, something trans-historical and historical. . . . How do you teach events that defy knowledge . . . How do you unveil horrors without offering at the same time some measure of hope? Hope in what? In whom? In progress, in science and literature and God? In the viability of human endeavors? And what if man were but a spasm of history, a smile, a sneer. . . ? The Holocaust was preceded not by medievalism but by emancipation and enlightenment, by generations of humanists and liberal revolutionaries who preached their gospels, advocated their faith in universal brotherhood and ultimate justice. [13]

Those secular "enlightened" who rejected so much of the understanding of the world and of society offered by the Church may have rejected along with it crucial elements of its moral restraints. One cannot, as Abrahamson seems to do in summarizing Wiesel on "Christian responsibility," [14] simply *equate* the world with the Church as if no further distinctions were necessary. Even as between two Catholic countries such as Italy and Vichy France, both "allied" with Hitler during the war, for example, the actual experiences of the respective Jewish communities with their Christian neighbors differed radically.

This said—and the distinction above is my own, not Wiesel's— what Wiesel has to say to us as Christians today remains a simple and essential truth. It is a truth that can only be acknowledged in humility and wholehearted repentance by the Church, not caveated away in historical distinctions, however valid and important they may be. For each member of the Church, baptized into communion with its spiritual riches, is also baptized into communion with its sinners. When one limb ails, St. Paul reminds us, the whole body of the Church aches. Spiritually, we can only say "amen" to Wiesel's charge that "the history of Christianity is full of anti-Semitism. More than that—there would have been no Auschwitz if the way had not been prepared by Christian theology."[15] Repentance on the Christian side is the bottom line, the necessary beginning point of dialogue for Jewish-Christian reconciliation after Auschwitz. It is that simple— and that humanly complex. Anti-Semitism is a sin. One does not explain or explain away sin. One repents.

Repentance and the actions presumed in repentance to ensure that the sin is never again repeated are thus necessary even on the part of those Christians today who bear no personal guilt for the Holocaust. Again, Wiesel puts it well: "We [Jews] do not blame the Christians of today for crimes perpetrated by their ancestors against the Jewish people. We have suffered too much from the collective guilt imposed upon us."[16]

If reconciliation, properly understood, is a valid goal for our Christian endeavors in the dialogue after the Holocaust, it will have to be embodied concretely in Christian liturgy. An important step in this direction has now been taken by the Bishops' Committee for the Liturgy of the National Conference of Catholic Bishops. In their recently approved liturgical guidelines for homilists, the bishops recommend "joint memorial services" for the victims of the Holocaust and the recitation of prayers for them at all masses on the Sunday closest to the Jewish observance of Yom Hashoah:

Also encouraged are joint memorial services commemorating the victims of the Shoah (Holocaust). These should be prepared for with catechetical and adult education programming to ensure a proper spirit of shared reverence. Addressing the Jewish community of Warsaw, Pope John Paul II stressed the uniqueness and significance of Jewish memory of the Shoah (Holocaust): "More than anyone else, it is precisely you who have become this saving warning. I think that in this sense you continue your particular vocation, showing yourselves to be still the heirs of that election to which God is faithful. This is your mission in the contemporary world before . . . all of humanity" [Pope John Paul II, Warsaw, 14 June 1987]. On the Sunday closest to Yom Hashoah Catholics should pray for the victims of the Holocaust and their survivors. The following serve as examples of petitions for the general intercessions at Mass:

— For the victims of the Holocaust, their families, and all our Jewish brothers and sisters, that the violence and hatred they experienced may never again be repeated, we pray to the Lord.
— For the Church, that the Holocaust may be a reminder to us that we can never be indifferent to the sufferings of others, we pray to the Lord.[17]

On Jesus the Jew

The fact that Jesus was a Jew and a faithful adherent of the Judaism of his times in continuity with biblical Israel is not, for Christians, a happenstance. Rather, it is an essential element of the divine design for the salvation of humanity. But if the Jewishness of Jesus is a fact and a theological datum that inevitably draws the Church toward the Jewish people, for the Jews over the centuries the Christian embrace has been a highly problematic one. Wiesel's response to Christian claims is vivid and clarifying for Christian understanding of Jewish reactions to our approaches to them:

A messiah who divides the Jewish people is a false messiah. I often quote this definition when I speak to Christians: Jesus, more than anyone else in history, provoked dissension and division in the world. Can that be the Messiah? How could he have been the redeemer?[18]

Jesus' Jewishness, and the Jewishness of Jesus' death at Roman hands, however, is acknowledged by Wiesel, and forcefully applied to the *Shoah*. For example, to those who would question the Jewish preoccupation with the Holocaust, Wiesel has responded:

Two thousand years ago a Jew died in Jerusalem, and out of his death a religion was born. Two thousand years ago *one* Jew died, and hundreds of millions of people all over the world are still talking about this death. So why shouldn't we of today try to talk and try to remember, in words or in art, the death of six million Jews?[19]

Like all truly useful questions, this one answers itself in the asking, and yet leads to many more.

The theme of the one and the many occurs also in other contexts in Wiesel's thought, sometimes with bemusement, at other times with a trace of bitterness, always with a sense of irony and paradox:

For two thousand years the Jewish people lived on the edge of destruction; somewhere Jews were always being killed. For what? For no reason. Because one person died two thousand years ago in Jerusalem, every single Jew everywhere, in every country, in every generation, was involved. One act. One death in Jerusalem then, involved us nineteen centuries later.[20]

Why, Wiesel seems to be asking us, do Christians make so much of the death of one Jew and so little of the deaths of millions? Our reasons for the former are religious, foundational, and, for us, paradigmatic of the human condition itself. Regarding the latter, Wiesel's critique is incisive. His trenchant challenge to us should make us hesitate very seriously before, as is our natural Christian tendency, we speak of Auschwitz as "another Calvary" or as "the crucifixion of the Jews." I do not mean to reject such images, but only, drawing upon Wiesel, to urge extreme caution in their use.[21] Powerful, visceral symbolism redolent of all the history that stands between our two communities is immediately triggered by such language and must be respected and approached in awe and trembling. The very heart of our respective faith traditions is radically involved and not to be lightly taken.

Finally, Wiesel meditates, for us and with us as Christians, on a way of approaching the mystery of the pervading significance of the death of one Jew: Where, he asks would Jesus have been during the *Shoah?* Citing the great Hebrew poet, Uri Zvi Greenberg, Wiesel tells a story about Jesus' return to a town in Eastern Europe. Jesus is searching for his people:

"Where are my brothers?" "Where are the Jews?" Killed. "Where are the teachers?" Killed. "Where are the children?" Killed. "Where are the synagogues?" Burned. "Where are the Jewish homes?" Looted. So Jesus begins to cry, and suddenly the townspeople realize that he too looks Jewish. And they begin shouting, "Look! Another Jew!" And they kill him too. When they killed Jews, they killed themselves.[22]

Wiesel carried this theme a step further in response to a student's question at the University of Oregon in 1975. This response, I believe, strips away yet another layer of Christian defensiveness. Here, Wiesel offers us as Christians a great gift, the gift of self-understanding:

I am convinced that had Jesus Christ lived during the Holocaust, he would not have done anything about it because he would have been a victim. And who knows? I wonder whether deep down the killers did not try to kill Jesus by killing the Jews.[23]

In confronting the Holocaust, are we Christians forced, among other challenges, to confront our own religious insecurities? Our own rejection of God's call to us in Christ? Our very fear of redemption? Each of us needs to answer this on his or her own. It would, however, be worth devoting several Lents to the effort.

The Encounter Today: Hope and Ambiguity

Many of the difficulties and dilemmas of the current, very delicate state of the dialogue may at this stage of reflection begin to become a little clearer. In most places of the world even today, most Christians and Jews are still not "real" to one another. We see each other as embodiments of the past, symbols of our historical fears and hurts.

The deeply ensconced, mutually reinforcing stereotypes, fantasies, and projections (though differently motivated and acted out on the two "sides" of the relationship) have created vast walls of mistrust between our communities, walls that must be scaled or broken down if we are to meet, face to face, and be at last fully *present* to one another. In the words so favored by Rabbi Leon Klenicki, one of the great pioneers of the art of interreligious dialogue in our time, we must begin to become "subjects" of encounter for one another, rather than mere "objects" of religious judgment over each other.

Elie Wiesel, being who he is and having suffered what he has suffered, can neither entirely lay aside his boyhood perspective, confirmed as it undoubtedly was for him by the stark horrors of Auschwitz, nor remain in the deceptive comfort of its simplistic dualities. And so he will say, almost immediately after declaring that his experience "justified a total suspicion," that:

Today I have changed my view. Today I do believe there is a possibility of coexistence between Judaism and Christianity, provided, again, it is built on respect, that they will not do what their ancestors did. I do not say that the Christian of today is responsible or guilty for the Inquisition. No. We measure a person by whatever he is doing today.[24]

Rev. Theodore M. Hesburgh, C.S.C., former president of the University of Notre Dame, recounted in tribute his recollection of the beginning of a series of lectures given by Elie Wiesel at the University of Notre Dame. The day was *Yom ha-Atzmauth* (Israeli Independence Day), the year 5737 of the Jewish calendar:

All too little in the sad history of the twentieth century can help to convince Elie Wiesel that the search of Christian and Jew is in fact the same search, and there are nightmares which seem sometimes irreversibly to demand the opposite conclusion. Only an unyielding faith, a faith that functions even in the face of despair itself, could go on to throw a bridge over that chasm of so much horror. No one who saw Elie after his first lecture at Notre Dame could doubt the anguish or the significance of his action.[25]

Since that time, Wiesel has addressed Christian audiences on numerous occasions, including the National Workshop on Christian-Jewish Relations in St. Louis in 1984.[26] From all accounts these experiences have been positive ones, certainly for his audiences and perhaps also for Wiesel himself, enabling him to see and experience Christians sincerely striving to hear what he has to say, listening to and grappling with its significance for them.

While there exists evidence of a change of heart among Christian theologians[27] and in Church practice[28] to nourish Wiesel's spark of hope with regard to Christians, it must be admitted that the Jewish community has not been receiving unambiguous signals from us over the years since the Second Vatican Council. Despite a steady stream of excellent official statements, in my view, from Protestant and Catholic bodies on all levels,[29] the Jewish community in general and Elie Wiesel in particular remain uncertain as to the ultimate Christian intent in the dialogue.[30] The underlying issue, I believe, is one of repentance and commitment on the one side (Christian) and the slow, painful opening to trust on the other.

What we Christians at times forget is that opening oneself to trust, after such a wound to the body and the spirit of the Jewish people as the *Shoah*, is by no means an easy or painless process. The trauma endured by the Jewish people, we must remember, was so profound (one-third of the entire Jewish population of the world killed in a few short years), that as a people they are still and inevitably in the very early stages of communal bereavement, sitting *shiva* over their lost mothers and fathers, sisters and brothers, one million children, an entire generation. It is too early, perhaps generations too early, to ask for simple trust, though that must be asked (and, first, earned). For Jews to risk trust in us is to risk opening scars that have, in truth, not yet fully formed, much less healed.

We Christians too easily say "Forgive!" to Jews, when it is certainly not ours to forgive, perhaps not even the Jewish community's, to forgive. Only God and the murdered victims themselves can do that. Not even the living survivors can, in fact, do it for their deceased families and friends. So in asking, we may be asking not only the difficult of Jews, but perhaps the morally impossible. It is ours to repent and to change, as it is the task of Jews to witness and to remember. These are compatible tasks and vital ones for both communities. But they are not reciprocal tasks.

In our efforts to renew the Church, we do not seek nor expect gratitude from Jews. Cardinal Johannes Willebrands, president of the Holy See's Commission on Religious Relations with the Jews, speaking extemporaneously on 10 September 1987 to over four hundred American Jewish leaders assembled in Miami for a meeting the next day with the Pope, spoke of the setbacks that the Church's task, our task of renewal and reconciliation, will inevitably suffer as it progresses. "It is a difficult thing for us [Christians] to do," he said with the authority of one who has devoted over twenty-five years to it. "But it is the right thing to do. And we will do it." Given Cardinal Willebrands's stature, integrity and vision, no one in the room doubted his words, nor that they represented an "irreversible" (a word he used several times) commitment on the part of the Holy See that is institutional and not merely personal. The record thus far, I believe, confirms the cardinal's sense of the irreversibility of the renewal begun by the Second Vatican Council with respect to Judaism. It does not, it should be duly noted, however, indicate that the conciliar promise will be fulfilled overnight. Too much remains to be done for Catholics today to be satisfied with "a glass half full." Elie Wiesel's continuing reminder of its relative emptiness remains a necessary one for us. The challenge to the Christian conscience is not in the distant past, but exists now, in the painfulness of the present formed by the past.

Toward a Dialogue of Silence

Instead of defensive apologetics toward a deeply concerned and still traumatized Jewish community, Christians need silence. Not the silence of the bystander, but the engaged silence of the listener, the expansive silence of compassion. The silence that, above all, is the beginning of a dialogue, when words bring forth, not more words, but tears and ultimately the smile of understanding. In the beginning, even before the creative word was spoken, we are reminded in Genesis, there was the Silence of the *rucah*, the divine wind of God's spirit hovering over the primal waters (Gen. 1:2).

In our age, it may be said, this creative silence of the divine *ruah* has been threatened as perhaps never before by a destructive wind, the devastating, diabolic wind of the *Shoah* that scoured the earth of life, leaving chaos and death in its wake.[31] It was out of a silence of dialogue with a Christian, François Mauriac, that Wiesel himself found the encouragement to break his own self-imposed, ten-year silence after his release from Auschwitz. Wiesel's moving account of that meeting provides a fitting conclusion to this personal reflection, as well as a compelling model for Jewish-Christian dialogue in the years to come.

He received me in his home.

To put me at ease, he began speaking to me of his feelings toward Israel: a chosen people in more ways than one, a people of witnesses, a people of martyrs. From that he went on to discuss the greatness and the divinity of the Jew Jesus. An impassioned, fascinating monologue on a single theme: the son of man and son of god, who, unable to save Israel, ended up saving mankind . . .

"Sir," I said, "you speak of Christ. Christians love to speak of him. The passion of Christ, the agony of Christ, the death of Christ. In your religion, that is all you speak of. Well, I want you to know that ten years ago, not very far from here, I knew Jewish children every one of whom suffered a thousand times more, six million times more, than Christ on the cross. And we don't speak about them. Can you understand that, sir? We don't speak about them."[32]

Mauriac, a man who Wiesel correctly describes as having exhibited "exemplary behavior" during the German Occupation of France, did not react defensively, but rather,

Motionless, his hands knotted over his crossed legs, a fixed smile on his lips, wordlessly, never taking his eyes off me, he wept and wept. The tears were streaming down his face, and he did nothing to stop them, to wipe them away . . . [33]

Wiesel narrates that he lost his own composure at Mauriac's vulnerable openness and rose to leave. But "with an infinitely humble gesture the old writer" touched his arm and began to ask Wiesel the details of his tragedy:

I shook my head: "I cannot, I cannot speak of it, please don't insist." He wanted to know the reason. Again I shook my head. He wanted to know why I had not written *all that*. I answered that I had taken a vow not to. Again he wanted to know why. I told him. I shall never forget that first meeting. Others followed, but that one left its mark on me. It was brought to a close by Mauriac's escorting me to the door, to the elevator. There, after embracing me, he assumed a grave, almost solemn mien. "I think that you are wrong. You are wrong not to speak . . . Listen to the old man that I am: one must speak out—one must *also* speak out."

One year later I sent him the manuscript of *Night*, written under the seal of memory and silence.[34]

Notes

1. In the comprehensive three-volume collection of hundreds of Wiesel's "occasional" pieces edited by Irving Abrahamson, *Against Silence: The Voice and Vision of Elie Wiesel* (New York: Holocaust Library, 1985), I found several entries dealing with Christians and Christianity. Some were negative, e.g., on Pope John Paul II's 1979 visit to Auschwitz (1:172–73) and on Pius XII and Paul VI (3:299). Pope John XXIII and François Mauriac (3:109), on the other hand, are treated positively.

Rescuers, such as the Danes (1:100) and Raoul Wallenberg (1:111) are acknowledged, but not specifically as Christians. There are six references to Jesus listed in the index. Wiesel's views on Jesus are discussed later in this paper.

2. Ibid. 3:299.
3. Briefly, I understand Wiesel's collective nouns in this context to be symbolic rather than historical, as one might use the word *Washington* meaning not the actual city and its citizens, but rather a particular administration, and at times only a particular group within a given administration.
4. John Paul II at Mauthausen Concentration Camp, Austria, 24 June 1988, in *Origins* 18, no. 8 (7 July 1988):124.
5. Abrahamson, *Against Silence* 3:110. This statement inevitably recalls Father Edward H. Flannery's original introduction to his now-classic study of the history of anti-Semitism, *The Anguish of the Jews* (New York: Macmillan, 1965); see p. xi.
6. Elie Wiesel, *A Jew Today* (New York: Vintage Books, 1978), 3–6.
7. See Michael D. Ryan, ed., *Human Responses to the Holocaust: Perpetrators and Victims, Bystanders and Resisters* (New York: Edwin Mellin, 1981).
8. Deborah Lipstadt, *Beyond Belief* (New York: Free Press, 1986) and A. O. Morse, *While Six Million Died* (New York: Overlook Press, 1983).
9. Cited in Harry James Cargas, "The Spectator," *Face to Face: An Interreligious Bulletin* 6 (Spring 1979):27.
10. Ibid., 27.
11. Elie Wiesel, "The Meaning of Munich" (Address delivered to United Jewish Appeal, New York, 14 December 1972), in *Against Silence*, ed. Abrahamson 1:134.
12. The literature on the development of anti-Semitism is vast, and growing exponentially. My article "Anti-Semitism and Christianity: Theories and Revisions of Theories," in *Persistent Prejudice: Perspectives on Anti-Semitism*, ed. H. Hirsch and J. D. Spiro (Fairfax, Va.: George Mason University Press, 1988), 11–30, seeks to summarize its major trends today. While they have invectives and practices in common, Nazi ideology and the polemics of Chrysostom and Luther are not the same. They are historically related, but not identical.
13. Cited in Abrahamson, *Against Silence* 1:35.
14. Ibid. 1:150–51.

15. Ibid. 1:33.
16. Ibid. 1:377.
17. Bishops' Committee on the Liturgy, *God's Mercy Endures Forever: Guidelines on the Presentation of Jews and Judaism in Catholic Preaching* (Washington, D.C.: U.S. Catholic Conference, 1988), 29.
18. Abrahamson, *Against Silence* 1:131.
19. Ibid., 49.
20. Ibid., 255.
21. See Franklin H. Littell, *The Crucifixion of the Jews* (New York: Harper and Row, 1975), who uses the analogy, I believe, both respectfully and properly.
22. Abrahamson, *Against Silence* 1:334.
23. Ibid. 3:228.
24. Ibid. 3:110–11.
25. Theodore M. Hesburgh, "Tribute and Response," *Face to Face: An Interreligious Bulletin* 6 (Spring 1979):32.
26. Incorrectly identified in Abrahamson *Against Silence* 1:211 as "The National Conference of Christians and Jews," which was only one among many sponsors.
27. For surveys of Christian theological reactions to the Holocaust, see, among others, Michael McGarry, *Christology After Auschwitz* (New York: Paulist, 1977); John Pawlikowski, *The Challenge of the Holocaust for Christians* (New York: ADL, 1978); John Pawlikowski, *What Are They Saying About Christian-Jewish Relations?* (New York: Paulist, 1980); and Eugene Fisher, "Covenant Theology and Jewish-Christian Dialogue," *American Journal of Theology and Philosophy* 9, nos. 1–2 (1988):5–40.
28. See Eugene Fisher, J. Rudin, and M. Tanenbaum, eds., *Twenty Years of Catholic-Jewish Relations* (New York: Paulist, 1986).
29. Conveniently collected by Helga Croner in the two volumes of *Stepping Stones to Further Jewish-Christian Relations* (London: Stimulus Books, 1977; New York: Paulist Press, 1985). See also *Fifteen Years of Catholic-Jewish Dialogue, 1970–1985*, selected papers of the International Catholic-Jewish Liaison Committee (Rome: Libreria Editrice Lateranense and Libreria Editrice Vaticana, 1988).
30. E.g., Elie Wiesel, "Pope John Paul II and His Jewish Problem," *New York Post*, 28 June 1988, 27. This article, because of its strong language and inaccuracies, caused profound pain and confusion to many of those Catholics most deeply involved in the dialogue. It therefore

requires more extensive treatment than can be given in the context of this paper. It was responded to publicly by the editors of *America*, 16 July 1988, 27, and by me personally in conversation with Mr. Wiesel. Our common goal, as it must be, remains a meeting of minds and hearts in dialogue.

31. Eugene Fisher and Leon Klenicki, *From Death to Hope: Liturgical Reflections on the Holocaust* (New York: Stimulus Foundation, 1983).
32. Wiesel, *A Jew Today*, 22.
33. Ibid.
34. Ibid., 23.

10

Mauriac's Preface to *Night* — Thirty Years Later

Eva Fleischner

Whenever I use *Night* in my classes I tell my students: "Be sure to read François Mauriac's preface. Not all prefaces deserve to be read, but this one does. It will give you a key to the book." All these years *Night* has remained linked to Mauriac's name. This had always seemed quite normal to me, even fitting. After all, it was he who, in Elie Wiesel's own words, launched him as a writer. I can imagine that it had been an honor for Wiesel—at the time a young, unknown Jewish journalist—to have the famous French writer and member of the Académie Française introduce his first book, introduce him to the world.

But thirty years have gone by. Wiesel no longer needs Mauriac to introduce him to the world. The world knows Elie Wiesel well; he has written many other books, each new book eagerly awaited; he has received the Nobel Peace Prize. Mauriac is dead. And yet, Elie Wiesel has kept his preface as prelude to *Night,* and thereby as prelude to his entire work. What may have been grateful acceptance on Wiesel's part thirty years ago has long since become a deliberate choice.

Could this choice have had its moments of difficulty for him? I wonder about this because of all that Mauriac represents: not only in literature—fame and success—but also in religion—Catholicism. Given the profoundly tragic history of the relationship between Wie-

This chapter appeared originally in *America* Magazine, 19 November, 1988, in the form of a letter addressed to Elie Wiesel. Hence the personal tone.

sel's faith and Mauriac's (and mine), was it really so easy for Wiesel to accept the endorsement of his work by France's leading Catholic writer? Was it perhaps even more difficult than one might suppose, given Mauriac's approach to Judaism? At least initially, Mauriac's approach to Judaism was cast, quite understandably, in the mold common to Catholics, even those Catholics who, although sympathetic to Judaism saw it as no more than a prelude to Christianity, as the setting for Jesus:

> Every reference led back to him. Jerusalem? The eternal city, where Jesus turned his disciples into apostles. The Bible? The Old Testament, which, thanks to Jesus of Nazareth, succeeded in enriching itself with a New Testament. Mendès-France? A Jew, both brave and hated, not unlike Jesus long ago . . . [1]

Wiesel leaves no doubt in the reader's mind how deeply these words offended the Jew in him, offended him to the point where, for the first time in his life, he "exhibited bad manners." So great was his anger that it overcame his shyness. He wounded the old man with his words, and François Mauriac began to weep.

Wiesel allowed himself to be angry, and Mauriac allowed himself to weep. Each had the courage to be in touch with who they truly were at that moment. It was this that broke down the wall between them. There is no downplaying the moment of harshness. Mauriac's humanity made him weep over his insensitivity to Wiesel as a Jew. Wiesel's humanity caused him to be deeply troubled because he had hurt an upright and profoundly moral man.

Elie Wiesel's humanity has seemed to me to be the constant in his life. No matter how much has changed *for* Wiesel and *in* Wiesel these past thirty years—he is no longer homeless and alone, he has a beloved wife and son, he is revered the world over—Wiesel's humanity has not changed. If, at times, his judgment of Christianity has seemed harsh to me, in his personal interactions, whether with me, or with my students, or with the many Christian friends who admire and love him, there has never been anything but gentleness and graciousness.

And is it any wonder that Wiesel should judge Christianity harshly? Even as a child, he would cross the street out of fear whenever he passed a church. No, it is no wonder; it is, alas, all too understand-able. For Christians have incurred much guilt toward the Jewish people. What is surprising, what is extraordinary, is that Elie Wiesel has been able to distinguish between the tradition as a whole, and individual Christians. For this I have long been grateful to him.

Recently, since reading Wiesel's newest book, *Twilight*, I am grateful in yet another way. For I sense in *Twilight* a change in his attitude. Not only is the hero, Raphael, saved by two peasants "who are good Christians," but in describing the age-old pogroms that used to break out during Holy Week in Rovidok (as in so many other villages and towns of eastern Europe) Wiesel speaks of the perpetra-tors as "Christians who were not necessarily followers of Christ."[2]

Why do these few words move me so? At times for us Christians the sense of guilt at our corporate history of persecution of Jews becomes almost too heavy to bear. The burden is lightened when we discover, or remember, that there have been, through the centuries, Christian women and men who did not run with the mob. That even during that darkest of times, which will forever be known as the Holocaust, there were a few "good Christians" who tried to help Jews, who had the courage to care about what was happening to them.

Because of the weight his words carry for millions of people, non-Jews as well as Jews, the text I have quoted can, I believe, make a crucial contribution to the reconciliation of Christians and Jews. Thus, more than ever will Elie Wiesel have become the "messenger of peace" he is called in the Nobel Peace Prize citation.

And perhaps, also, Wiesel's relationship with his old friend Fran-çois Mauriac will have entered a new phase. Were Wiesel and Mauriac to talk once more face to face today, thirty years later, yet another barrier between them would have fallen. Perhaps, indeed, the dialogue continues. After all, both Jews and Christians worship a "God who raises the dead."

I conclude these reflections with a wish. In *A Jew Today*, Elie Wiesel promised someday to publish his conversations with François Mauriac. My hope is that the day is not far off when that promise becomes reality. We then would know a little more of the relationship between these two men, a little more of what enabled both to transcend their religious and political disagreements and to enter into a dialogue. Only the publication of those conversations between Elie Wiesel and François Mauriac can give us the answers and, thereby, shed further light on one of the most remarkable friendships of this century.

Notes

1. Elie Wiesel, *A Jew Today* (New York: Random House, 1978), 17–18.
2. Elie Wiesel, *Twilight* (New York: Summit Books, 1988), 18.

11

Historical Horror and the
Shape of *Night*

Lea Hamaoui

What follows is an attempt to study the ways in which a traumatic historical experience shapes narrative in a powerful example of this genre, Elie Wiesel's *Night*.[1] It is my conviction that in groping toward formal and literary understanding of such texts, we move closer to the human meanings that the violent world we live in has all but erased.

To render historical horror is to render, by definition, that which exceeds rendering; it projects pain for which there is no solace, no larger consolation, no redemptive possibility. The implications, both formal and aesthetic, for such a rendering are critical. The great tragedies negotiate exactly such a balance. King Lear's terrible journey from blindness to insight brings him reunion with loyal Cordelia even as he loses her and the restoration of the Kingdom is not far behind. The young Eliezer staring into the mirror upon his liberation from Buchenwald has also gained knowledge, but this knowledge in no way justifies the sufferings that preceded it. It is not a sign of positive spiritual development. Nor is it linked to restorative changes in the moral and political realm. *Night* is not about a moral political order violated and restored, but about the shattering of the idea of such an order.

It is clear enough that in comparing *King Lear* and Wiesel's *Night* we do violence to both. But the juxtaposition throws light on a crucial aesthetic issue. It helps us define the experience of a work like *Night* and moves our inquiry in the direction of the specific means by which the writer shapes that experience.

120

Lear's death is the death of an old man, flawed like ourselves, vulnerable like ourselves, a character with whom a powerful emotional transaction and bonds of identification have been established over the course of the play. In Lear's death we reexperience the tragic dimensions of our own experience. The play articulates, in symbolic form, an existential pain we could hardly afford to articulate ourselves. But it is pain that, no matter how great, is contained, since the very act of its symbolic articulation also gives form, and therefore limits or boundaries, to that pain.

Night proceeds from experience that is not universal. It does not expand from kernels of the familiar but from the unfamiliar, from data in historical reality. The deaths of Eliezer's father, of Akiva Drummer, of Juliek the violinist and of Meir Katz are different because, after all of the pain, there is nothing to be extracted by way of compensation. They are not symbolic but very real, and we experience, not a purging of feelings tapped but the fear of the unpredictable in life to which we, like the Jews of *Night*, are subject.

If symbol is something that stands in place of something else, the historical narrative does not stand in place of our experience, but alongside it. We experience historical narrative much the way we experience a neighbor's report of his or her visit to a place we have not ourselves visited. The report is informational—it is "adjacent" to our experience, neither interpretive nor metaphorical nor symbolic. It is "other" than our experience but also part of the same historical matrix within which we experience the flow of our own lives. *Night* threatens and disturbs in a way that symbolic narrative does not.

Night is Wiesel's attempt to bring word of the death camps back to humanity in such a form that his message, unlike that of Moshe the Beadle to Eliezer and to the Jews of Sighet, will not be rejected. The word I wish to stress here is *form*. The work, which is eyewitness account, is also much more than eyewitness account. In its rhetorical and aesthetic design, *Night* is shaped by the problematic of historical horror and by the resistances, both psychic and formal, to the knowledge Wiesel would convey.

When the narrator, Eliezer, sees a lorry filled with children who are dumped into a fiery ditch, he cannot believe what he has seen: "I pinched my face. Was I alive? Was I awake? I could not believe it. How could it be possible for them to burn people, children, and for the world to keep silent? No, none of this could be true. It was a nightmare"(42).

Eliezer cannot believe what is before his eyes. His disbelief seems to numb him physically—he pinches his face to ascertain that the medium of that vision, his body, is alive, perceiving, present. So fundamental is the horror to which he is an eyewitness that seeing comes at the expense of his bodily awareness of himself as a vital and perceiving entity. What Eliezer witnesses contradicts psychic underpinnings of existence so thoroughly that his very awareness brings with it feelings of deadness.

It is precisely this moment, this confrontation with data that negates the human impulses and ideas that structure our lives, with which Wiesel is concerned. We cannot know that which we cannot know. In order to bring the fact of Auschwitz to us, Wiesel must deal with the inherent difficulty of assimilating the truth he would portray.

His method is simple, brilliant and depends upon a series of repetitions in which what is at stake is a breakdown of critical illusions. At this level, the experience of the reader reading the narrative is structurally parallel to his experience of life, at least as Karl Popper describes it. Life, in Popper's view,

resembles the experience of a blind person who runs into an obstacle and thereby experiences its existence. Through the falsification of our assumptions we actually make contact with "reality." The refutation of our errors is the positive experience we gain from reality.[2]

Eliezer's tale is the story of a series of shattered expectations, his and our own. The repetition of this "disappointment," of optimism proven hollow and warnings rejected, becomes the crucial aesthetic fact or condition within which we then experience the narrator's account of his experiences in Auschwitz, in Buna, in Gleiwitz, and in Buchenwald. In this way we come to experience the account of the death camps as an account cleansed of past illusion, pristine in its terrible truth.

The quest for this truth is established at the outset of the narrative in the figure of Moshe the Beadle. Eliezer is devoted to his studies of

Talmud. His decision to study Kabbalah with Moshe focuses the narrative on the problematic of reality and imbues it with the spiritual longings of this quest.

There are a thousand and one gates leading into the orchard of mystical truth. Every human being has his own gate . . .
    And Moshe the Beadle, the poor barefoot of Sighet, talked to me for long hours of the revelations and mysteries of the cabbala. It was with him that my initiation began. We would read together, ten times over, the same page of the Zohar. Not to learn it by heart, but to extract the divine essence from it.
    And throughout those evenings a conviction grew in me that Moshe the Beadle would draw me with him into eternity, into that time where question and answer would become *one*. (14)

The book, which begins with Eliezer's search for a teacher of mystical knowledge and ends with Eliezer's contemplating his image in a mirror after his liberation from Buchenwald, proposes a search for ultimate knowledge in terms that are traditional, while the knowledge it offers consists of data that is historical, radical, and subversive.

If directionality of the narrative is established early, a counterdirection makes itself felt very quickly. Following Eliezer's dream of a formal harmony, eternity and oneness toward which Moshe would take him, Eliezer's initiation into the "real" begins:

Then one day they expelled all the foreign Jews from Sighet. And Moshe the Beadle was a foreigner.
    Crammed into cattle trains by Hungarian police, they wept bitterly. We stood on the platform and wept too. (15)

Moshe is shot but escapes from a mass grave in one of the Galician forests of Poland near Kolomaye and returns to Sighet in order to warn the Jews there. He describes children used as targets for machine guns and the fate of a neighbor, Malka, and of Tobias the tailor.

From this point onward in the narrative, a powerful counter direction of flight away from truth, knowledge, reality, and history is set into motion. Moshe is not believed, not even by his disciple, Eliezer. The Jews of Sighet resist the news Moshe has brought them:

I wanted to come back to Sighet to tell you the story of my death . . . And see how it is, no one will listen to me . . . (16)

And we, the Jews of Sighet, were waiting for better days, which would not be long in coming now.
Yes, we even doubted that he [Hitler] wanted to exterminate us.
Was he going to wipe out a whole people? Could he exterminate a population scattered throughout so many countries? So many millions! What method could he use? And in the middle of the twentieth century? (17)

Optimism persists with the arrival of the Germans. After Sighet is divided into a big and little ghetto, Wiesel writes, "little by little life returned to normal. The barbed wire which fenced us in did not cause us any real fear" (21).

While the narrative presses simultaneously toward and away from the "real," the real events befalling the Jews of Sighet are perceived as unreal:

On everyone's back was a pack . . . Here came the Rabbi, his back bent, his face shaved, his pack on his back. His mere presence among the deportees added a touch of unreality to the scene. It was like a page torn from some story book, from some historical novel about the captivity of Babylon or the Spanish Inquisition. (26)

The intensity of the resistance peaks in the boxcar in which Eliezer and his family are taken to the death camp. Madame Schächter, distraught by the separation from her pious husband and two older sons, has visions of fire: "Jews, listen to me! I can see a fire! There are huge flames! It is a furnace!" (35). Her words prey on nerves, fan fears, dispel illusion: "We felt that an abyss was about to open beneath our bodies." She is gagged and beaten. As her cries are silenced the chimneys of Auschwitz come into view:

We had forgotten the existence of Madame Schächter. Suddenly we heard terrible screams: Jews, look! Look through the window! Flames! Look!
And as the train stopped, we saw this time that flames were gushing out of a tall chimney into the black sky. (38)

The movement toward and away from the knowledge of historical horror that Moshe the Beadle brings back from the mass grave and the violence that erupts when precious illusions are disturbed, shapes the narrative of *Night*. The portrait and analysis of the resistances to knowing help situate the reader in relation to the historical narrative and imbue the narrative with the felt historicity of the world outside the book. Eliezer's rejection of the knowledge that Moshe brings back, literally, from the grave, predicts our own rejection of that knowledge. His failure to believe the witness prepares the reader for the reception of Eliezer's own story of his experience in Auschwitz by first examining the defenses that Eliezer, and, thereby, implicitly, the reader, would bring to descriptions of Auschwitz. The rejection of Moshe strips the reader of his own deafness in advance of the arrival at Auschwitz.

Once stripped of his defenses, the reader moves from a fortified, to an open, undefended position vis-à-vis the impact of the narrative. Because the lines between narrative art and life have been erased, Wiesel brings the reader into an existential relationship to the historical experience recounted in *Night*. By virtue of that relationship, the reader is transformed into a witness. The act of witnessing is ongoing for most of the narrative, a narrative that is rife with horror and with the formal dissonances that historically experienced horror must inflict upon language.

Human extremity challenges all formal representation of it. It brings the world of language and the world outside language into the uncomfortable position of two adjacent notes on a piano keyboard that are simultaneously pressed and held. The sounds they produce jar the ear. In a work of historical horror, language and life, expression and experience are perceived as separate opaque structures, each of which is inadequate to encompass the abyss that separates them.

The most powerful passages in *Night* are those that mark Eliezer's arrival in Auschwitz. The family is separated. Eliezer and his father go through a selection and manage to stay together. Eliezer watches a truck drop living children into a ditch full of flames. He and his father conclude that this is to be Eliezer's fate as well. Eliezer decides he will run into an electrified wire fence and electrocute himself rather than face an excruciating death in the flaming ditch.

The moment is extraordinary and extreme beyond the wildest of human imaginings. Hearing his fellow Jews murmur the Kaddish, a formula of praise of the Almighty that is the traditional prayer for the dead, Eliezer revolts: "For the first time, I felt revolt rise up in me. Why should I bless His name? The Eternal Lord of the Universe, the All-Powerful and Terrible, was silent. What had I to thank Him for?" (43). The Jews continue their march and Eliezer begins to count the steps before he will jump at the wire:

Ten steps still. Eight. Seven. We marched slowly on, as though following a hearse at our own funeral . . . There it was now, right in front of us, the pit and its flames. I gathered all that was left of my strength, so that I could break from the ranks and throw myself upon the barbed wire. In the depths of my heart, I bade farewell to my father, to the whole universe. (44)

And the words of the Kaddish, hallowed by centuries and disavowed only moments before, words of praise and of affirmation of divine oneness, spring unbidden to his lips: "and in spite of myself, the words formed themselves and issued in a whisper from my lips: *Yitgadal veyitkadach shme raba* . . . May His name be blessed and magnified" (44). Eliezer does not run to the wire. The entire group turns left and enters a barracks.

The question of formal dissonance in *Night* is revealing. The narrative that would represent historical horror works, finally, against the grain of the reader and of the psychic structures that demand the acknowledgments, resolutions, closure, equivalence, and balances that are enacted in Lear. When Cordelia is killed in Shakespeare's play, Lear's sanity gives way and, finally, his life as well. Holding her lifeless body in his arms Lear cries out against heaven, "Howl, howl, howl! O you men of stone. / Had I your tongues and eyes, I'd use them / That heaven's vault should break."[3] The scene, terrible as it is, formally restores the balance disturbed by Cordelia's murder by virtue of the linguistic energies and dramatic consequences it sets in motion. Those consequences are a terrible acknowledgment of a terrible event. The adequacy of the acknowledgment reconstructs a formal balance even while taking account of the terrible in life.

The words of the Kaddish in *Night* do not express the horror to which Eliezer is a witness. They flow from an inner necessity and do not reflect but deflect that horror. They project the sacredness of life in the face of its most wrenching desecration. They affirm life at the necessary price of disaffirming the surrounding reality. The world of experience and the world of language could not, at this moment, be further apart. Experience is entirely beyond words. Words are utterly inadequate to convey experience.

The dissonance makes itself felt stylistically as well. Eliezer sums up his response to these first shattering hours of his arrival at Auschwitz in the most famous passages of *Night* and, perhaps, of all of Wiesel's writing: "Never shall I forget that night, the first night in camp, which has turned my life into one long night, seven times cursed and seven times sealed" (44). The passage takes the form of an oath never to forget this night of his arrival. The oath, the recourse to metaphorical language ("which has turned my life into one long night"), the reference to curses and phraseology ("seven times cursed") echo the biblical language in which Eliezer was so steeped. He continues: "Never shall I forget that smoke. Never shall I forget the little faces of the children, whose bodies I saw turned into wreaths of smoke beneath a silent blue sky" (44). The oath is an oath of protest, the "silent blue sky," an accusation: "Never shall I forget those flames which consumed my faith forever" (44). Here and in the sentences that follow, Wiesel uses the rhythms, the verbal energy, imagery, and conventions of the Bible to challenge, accuse, and deny God:

Never shall I forget that nocturnal silence which deprived me, for all eternity, of the desire to live. Never shall I forget those moments which murdered my God and my soul and turned my dreams to dust. Never shall I forget these things, even if I am condemned to live as long as God Himself. Never. (44)

The elaborate oath of remembrance recalls the stern biblical admonitions of remembrance. The negative formulation of the oath and the incremental repetition of the word "never" register defiance and anger even as the eight repetitions circumscribing the passage give it rhythmic structure and ceremonial shape. Ironically, these repetitions seem to implicate mystical notions of God's covenant with the Jews, a covenant associated with the number eight because the ceremony of entrance into the convenant by way of circumcision takes place on the eighth day after birth. The passage uses the poetry and language of faith to affirm a shattering of faith.

The passage is a tour de force of contradiction, paradox, and formal dissonances that are not reconciled, but juxtaposed and held up for inspection. In a sparely written, tightly constructed narrative, it is the only extended poetic moment. It is a climactic moment, and, strangely, for a work that privileges a world outside words altogether, a rhetorical moment: a moment constructed out of words and the special effects and properties of their combinations, a moment that hovers above the abyss of human extremity in uncertain relationship to it.

Like the taste of bread to a man who has not eaten, the effect of so poetic a passage lies in what preceded it. Extremity fills words with special and different meanings. Eliezer reacts to the words of one particular SS officer: "But his clipped words made us tremble. Here the word 'furnace' was not a word empty of meaning; it floated on the air, mingling with the smoke. It was perhaps the only word which did have any real meaning here" (49).

Wiesel's narrative changes our conventional sense of the word "night" in the course of our reading. Night, which as a metaphor for evil always projects, however subliminally, the larger rhythm and structure within which the damages of evil are mitigated, comes to stand for another possibility altogether. The word comes to be filled with the historical flames and data for which there are no metaphors, no ameliorating or sublimating structures. It acquires the almost-tactile feel of the existential, opaque world that is the world of the narrative and also the world in which we live.

Perhaps the finest tribute to *Nigh'* is to be found in the prologue of Terrence Des Pres's book on poetry and politics, *Praises and Dispraises*. Des Pres is speaking of Czeslaw Milosz and of other poets who have lived through extremity and writes: "If we should wonder why their voices are valued so highly, it's that they are acquainted with the night, the nightmare spectacle of politics especially."[4] Des Pres uses the word "night" and the reader immediately understands it in exactly Wiesel's revised sense of it.

To be acquainted with the night, in this sense, and to bring that knowledge to a readership is to bring the world we live in into sharper focus. The necessary job of making a better world cannot possibly begin from anywhere else.

Notes

1. Elie Wiesel, *Night*, trans. Stella Rodway (New York: Avon Books, 1958). All references to this work will refer to this edition and page references will be included in the body of the Chapter.
2. Cited in Hans Robert Jauss, *Toward an Aesthetic of Reception* (Minneapolis: University of Minnesota Press, 1982), 40. Translated from the German by Timothy Bahti.
3. *The Complete Works of Shakespeare*, ed. G. L. Kittredge (New York: Ginn, 1936), 1238.
4. Terrence Des Pres, *Praises and Dispraises* (New York: Viking Penguin, 1988), xiv.

12

Elie Wiesel's Poetics of Madness

Rosette C. Lamont

A tradition as ancient as recorded thought connects two polar states of being: the illumination of sainthood and the flaming darkness of madness. The dazzlement of wonder and the deep night of the soul belong initially to the formlessness of mystical experience. Though an abyss seems to separate their apprehensions, both the holy man and the fool are bringers of a message received from a zone beyond the workings of the rational mind. Light and Night are the two faces of a single knowledge, that imparted to "the wise heart."[1]

In "Religious Authority and Mysticism," the initial chapter of Gershom G. Scholem's *On the Kabbalah and Its Symbolism*, the great scholar delineates the mystic's perilous spiritual voyage, from the initial illumination, which takes him away from the accepted tradition of things divine, toward a personal redefinition of transcendence. Because "the mystical quest for the divine takes place almost exclusively within a prescribed tradition,"[2] the individual who has received a particular illumination comes in conflict with the authority developed over a period of historical evolution by a community. As Scholem points out, an important aspect of Jewish mysticism favors the "hidden saint" *(nistar)*, but the history of religions is not concerned with "mute, anonymous saints,"[3] though they may be the thirty-six righteous men who, in every generation, constitute the foundation of the world. The moment a mystic formulates and communicates his apprehension by elaborating specific structures based on conventional symbols culled from his society, he comes in conflict with the keepers of the tradition, specifically, in the Jewish society, with the rabbinate. Often the mystic is not aware, at least initially, of the revolutionary quality of his vision and interpretation. [The nature of his experience, incommunicable, indistinct, defies translation, unlike that of the prophet, who conveys a clear message. The *unio mystica* is a profoundly personal emotion, but once felt it can no longer be forgotten or denied. To the outsider, however, the result of this radical transformation appears akin to madness.] The mystic claims to be above authority, he seeks to establish his own system based on this revelation.

One of the strengths of the Jewish religion lies in its ability to incorporate various stages of mystical evolution, bringing them into the canon, or reshaping the tradition. Thus, when Kabbalistic mysticism developed from rabbinical Judaism, "a number of different revelations were recognized as authentic and each in its own way authoritative, namely, the revelations of Moses, of the Prophets, of the Holy Spirit . . . of the receivers of the 'Heavenly Voice' . . . and finally the 'revelation of the Prophet Elijah.' " In fact, Elijah is the prophet who will reconcile all the conflicting messages. To hear his voice, to claim that one's vision stems directly from him, meant that a mystical experience could be incorporated into the tradition. Such was the conservative basis of the first Kabbalists, Rabbi Abraham of Posquieres and his son Isaac the Blind. Scholem likens the sixteenth-century Jewish mystic, Isaac Luria, to the first Kabbalists in his conservative claim to be part of the established authority while clearly indulging in interpretations of "glaring novelty."[4]

Scholem's central point in this initial chapter is that [the mystic actually sets out "to confirm religious authority by reinterpreting it."[5]] However, in the process of splitting open the symbolic structures, he cannot help but transform them. His private symbolism is the instrument of this transformation.

In a later chapter of the same book, *Kabbalah and Myth*, Scholem explains that although Jewish philosophy disdained popular faith, and the impulses of primitive life, a world of myth arose in the writings of the Kabbalists. He wonders at the phenomenon of a largely aristocratic group of mystics, enjoying "an enormous influence among the common people."[6] Perhaps a reason for this can be found in the fact that, unlike the philosophers, the Kabbalists opened themselves to the problem of evil and the presence of the demonic.

They resurrected mythic thinking and feeling in the very realm which monotheism had "wrested from myth."[7] Modern man is well aware that the repression of fears is as dangerous, as lethal to the psyche's health, as preventing individuals from deep sleep, from dreaming. Scholem states that "the demonization of life was one of the most effective and dangerous factors in the development of the Kabbalah."[8] The Kabbalists echoed the sacred awe of the common people before an infinite, beginningless God, and their terror of the evil spirit.

With the later Kabbalists, such as Isaac Luria, a new myth is elaborated as "a response to the expulsion of the Jews from Spain."[9] This catastrophic event "gave urgency to the question: why the exile of the Jews and what is their vocation in the world?"[10] The Lurianic Kabbalah, according to Scholem, wove a bond between the myth of exile/redemption and the historical experience of the Jewish people. Symbols specific to Jewish life acquired universal meaning. Thus, Israel's exile was no longer viewed as punishment, but as a necessary step in the Jewish mission in the world. Scholem states that every Jew, in fact every person, participates in "the process of *tikkun*," a harmonious mending following the crisis of creation, "the Breaking of the Vessels."[11] This mending unites the members of the Jewish community, and melds them to God. It allows for transmission to take place.

Orderly transmission is one of the community's safeguards against uncontrollable deviations. For this process to occur one needs spiritual guides and their written works. Scholem offers two examples, one a manual of Catholic mysticism (the *Spiritual Exercises* of Ignatius de Loyola), the other a treatise from the Habad School of White Russian Hasidism (*Kuntras ha-Hithpa'aluth* by Rabbi Baer). The latter "provides the traditional Kabbalistic symbols with which this path of the Jewish mystic toward the experience of the divine can be described and interpreted, thus making sure that the path will conform, especially at its most dangerous turning points, to the dictates of authority."[12] As Wiesel states: "To be a Jew is to insert oneself within a tradition in order to transmit it."[13] Communication is one of the key Jewish obsessions. That is why it is fundamental to Jewish culture to listen to storytellers, to become a teller of stories in turn. As Wiesel writes: "You say something about yourself as you recount a tale." [14]

Elie Wiesel is the spinner of tales par excellence. The roots of his poetics must be sought in Hasidic lay mysticism. He is the spiritual heir of Israel Baal-Shem, the founder of Polish Hasidism, and his great followers Rabbi Levi-Yitzhak of Berdichev, Rabbi Elimelekh and Rabbi Zousia, Rabbi Israel of Rizhin, Rabbi Nahman of Bratzlav. Through his grandfather, Dodye Feig, the Hasid of Wizhnitz who perished in a concentration camp, Wiesel is profoundly connected to this line of scholars, mediators, and innovators. Like the Maggid of Mezeritch, he knows that a fine orator "must become one with his words." [15] Going back to the origins of this movement, one could see that he may in fact have derived his own belief in the importance of the creative act from the teachings of the Baal-Shem. For him, as for the Bescht, creation transcends common sense.

Unlike the lay mystics, Wiesel is well versed in rabbinical knowledge, but his own approach to writing is instinctive and poetic. He has drawn into his being the Baal-Shem's principal theme: "Man owes it to himself to reject despair; better to put faith in miracles than to accept resignation. By changing himself, man can alter the world." [16]

Much has been said about Wiesel's prevalent image of the witness. However, the more one peruses the complex body of his writings, the more another haunting theme emerges. It appears almost in every one of his books, although it is most clearly expressed in two works: *The Oath* and, more recently, *Twilight*. It is the image of the mad seer, the visionary, the holy martyr. He is the conscience of his people, their memory of the future. [In a world gone mad, the holy madman may be the only clear-seeing member of the community.]

Wiesel's first madman appears on the first page of *Night*; he is Moshe the Beadle, who becomes Eliezer's Master in Sighet, a town devoid of Kabbalists. Moshe teaches the boy that man questions God, and God answers. However, these answers, rising from the depths of the soul, are not easily decipherable. The only answer lies within oneself.

In his essay, "Midrashic Existence after the Holocaust," Emil L. Fackenheim addresses the question of "Midrashic madness." He writes:

> What is this madness? Not insanity, if insanity is flight from reality. It is just because it dare not flee from *its* reality that this Midrash is mad. This madness is obliged—condemned?—to be sane . . . Midrashic madness . . . *knows*, in some cases has known all along. Its discernment is informed by a Truth transcending the world of which it is a victim. Irrational by the standards of lesser rationalities, its rationality is ultimate.[17]

The second mad person in *Night* is a Madam Schächter, who is being deported with her ten-year-old son. Her husband and two older sons left with the first transport. This brutal separation has unhinged her mind. From the start of the journey she keeps on moaning, but, on the third night, she utters a piercing cry: "Fire! I see fire! I see fire!"[18] She points to something outside the train. Her companions peer through the bars, unable to see anything but the darkness. They treat the unhappy woman with kindness, trying to assuage her fears. She, however, continues to proclaim: "Jews, listen to me! . . . I see fire! What flames! A conflagration!"[19] As she continues to shout, kindness yields to rage. People hit her over her head. Finally, the train reaches its station: Auschwitz. The train comes to a standstill. Two of the prisoners are allowed to go down to fetch water. They return with the reassuring news that there will be work at the camp, that families will not be separated. In the evening, however, the madwoman begins to shout again. The train lurches forward, moves toward its final destination. When it stops, everyone sees the flames issuing from a high chimney: the crematorium of Birkenau.

Published in 1973, *Le serment de Kolvillàg (The Oath)* is the story of a pre-Holocaust holocaust, a progrom wipes out the Jewish population of a small town of central Europe. We are told that this town does not exist on any map, in any history book. It lives in the memory of an old man who has taken the oath of never revealing the events he witnessed. There is also a book, the *Pinkas*, started in 1851 by Itzhak, son of Israel, and continued through the generations. It is the sum of Jewish meditation, a collective *oeuvre* that testifies to a lucid confrontation with injustice and violence. In a sense, the author of *The Oath* is the last scribe of the *Pinkas*.

The *Oath* is a polyphonic structure, a tone poem recited by many voices. Basically it is a conversation between Azriel, the sole survivor of Kolvillàg and a very young man, born after the Holocaust, whose horror with life inspires him with a suicidal urge. How will the old man keep the young one from carrying out his dreadful purpose? He will have to tell him the story of the city's destruction, a story he is sworn not to reveal.

Haunted by his story, Azriel does not know what to do. He is alone in the world, having lost his entire family, in fact the whole community. He comes to seek the counsel of a famous sage, Rabbi Zousia of Kolomey. The latter warns him that he will not offer any solution; all he will do is listen. His silence is so eloquent that any visitor able to catch his attention will acquire a clarity of vision, a perception of his own inner depths.

Azriel's presence among the faithful and the disciples grouped around Rabbi Zousia is so full of somber despair that it infects the atmosphere. The bearer of the secret wants to know whether he should break his oath, whether he ought to tell the tale. Zousia will not let him speak, but he will listen to his silent confession, and, though no words will have been uttered, the holy man's inner ear will hear it. However, once this horrifying message has been delivered, it is obvious that Azriel is not relieved of his burden. The learned rabbi then orders him to leave. He will become an eternal wanderer, a stranger among strangers, the *Na-venadnik*. He will have only one aim in life: to keep the book open. Although he will not be free to talk, he will have the freedom of keeping silent. Wiesel offers a philosophical redefinition of freedom: One continues to do what one did before, but one does it freely. Freedom is not an objective fact; it is an inner sentiment, a spiritual experience.

Behind the disquieting character of Azriel another face appears, its features showing from under those of the wanderer, as in a photographic montage. It is that of Moshe, the mad saint of Kolvillàg, who, when the city is threatened with a pogrom, will take upon himself the irrational guilt of which the Jews are being accused. He *actually Shoah*

is a Christlike figure who offers his life in vain, as a holocaust, a supreme sacrifice to save the city. It is Moshe's voice that Azriel hears in his ceaseless wanderings. He remembers Moshe in prison, Moshe tortured, beaten, and humiliated. Yet nothing could break the madman's faith, the strength of his belief in God. Moshe's voice whispers to Azriel that one can never escape from Kolvillàg, that in fact, in the heavens above, a Platonic city burns like a sacred flame, the twin of all the persecuted communities on earth. God walks among the sages, telling them the story of the Jewish victims. Only there, in God's heaven, can this tale be told.

Moshe, the mad saint, is not the only insane person in *The Oath*. Azriel fears for his mind, thinking that he is going to die in the state of insanity. There is, he says, deep in his being, a madman who says *I* in his place. He and Kolvillàg are one. [Not only does the flaming city live on in his subconscious, but he continues to inhabit a city that no longer exists.] Its image, the rhythm of its life, are caught in the amber of his memory. The dead rise again, walk the streets, go about their daily occupations. For how can one accept the unacceptable: the annihilation of a people, a way of life, an ancient, noble, gentle culture? Azriel's apprehension is that of most survivors. Yet, by having shifted the familiar Holocaust story to an earlier time, Wiesel not only universalized the motif of Jewish persecution and destruction, but suggested that [the plight of the Jews is not confined to a precise historical moment, that it is an ever-repeated scandal, a perennial catastrophe.]

Indeed, it is not surprising that the youngest character in Wiesel's novel/poem/meditation should wish to die, unable to face a world of boundless, endless cruelty. Although he himself has not lived through the Holocaust, he knows that his mother lost a first child in a death camp. Azriel's interlocutor feels that he has no right to live, that he has taken someone else's place on earth. Thus, he is also a survivor, albeit after the fact. As to Azriel, who keeps him from taking his life by the power of a mysterious, untold story, then, eventually, by telling the shattering tale, he is more than his savior, he gives him a second chance, a new life. We recognize in the young would-be suicide the archetypal figure of "the Twice-Born."

In opposition to the holy inspiration of Moshe and the incipient insanity of right-thinking men and women, *The Oath* presents the evil madness of the gentile community of Kolvillàg. An insignificant event, at least at the start, unleashes the apocalyptic destruction that constitutes the core of the novel's weltanschauung. A lazy, cruel, fourteen-year-old boy, utterly devoid of conscience, Yancsi, the son of a stableman, disappears with some of his father's horses. Universally disliked, he is not missed, not even by his parents. Yet, gradually, the air begins to thicken with suspicion. Yancsi seems to have vanished without a trace. Soon a phrase begins to be tossed about: "the Jews!" An ancient, recurrent myth rises from the swampy atmosphere that engulfs the town, that of the paschal murder of a Christian boy. Despite the fact that the events are taking place in October, the irrational hatred of the gentile community is awakened. Yancsi is the messenger of evil, a creature of destiny called upon to light the all-consuming fires, or bring about a flood. Slowly, irrevocably, the forces of destruction set to work. Neither the civil authorities, in the person of a reasonable prefect, nor the moral authority of the region's lord of the manor will stop them. It is at this point that it is suggested to the Jews that they themselves identify a culprit. Perhaps this sacrifice might check the disaster. This is when Moshe, the madman, offers himself for this office.

Moshe's sacrifice will not save the Jewish community. In jail, he will be tortured and asked to name his accomplices. No one believes that this mad beggar could be the boy's assassin. In the face of the uselessness of his supremely noble gesture, Moshe reacts in an unexpected way: He bursts out laughing. This is no ordinary laugh. It has nothing to do with merriment, amusement, or humor. It is in fact a metaphysical, transcendent laughter, such as that attributed by Homer to the Greek gods, or, perhaps the philosophical laugh beyond bitterness analyzed by Charles Baudelaire in his essay "De L'essence du rire."

In his fine book on this subject, *Le rire dans l'univers tragique d'Elie Wiesel*, Joel Friedmann points to the filiation between Wiesel's "grimace of madness" and Erasmus's *In Praise of Folly*.[20] In Erasmus also, Folly, at first a wild apparition, emerges as an inspired figure, one that seems to have greater discernment than the so-called wise men. Metaphysical laughter, Friedmann points out, is rooted in the

Bible, the Talmud and the Midrash. For Wiesel, Isaac is the first survivor. He emerges from the experience of death with the ability to dream, to continue to trust, and to laugh. Wiesel says: "In my tales I try to convey and to transmit Isaac's laughter."[21]

The mystery of the metaphysical laugh appears in Wiesel's chapter on "Levi-Yitzhak of Berditchev" in *Souls on Fire*. This is how it is reported:

A disciple of Moshe-Leib of Sassov, a certain Avraham-David, future Rebbe of Bucsacs, planned to spend Shabbat in Berditchev. The Tzaddik of Sassov asked him: "Will you be able to resist laughter?"—"Yes, Rebbe." But Avraham-David had overestimated his strength. Delirium struck him during the Shabbat meal. Without apparent reason, he burst into laughter and could not stop for thirty days and thirty nights. Rebbe Moshe-Leib then wrote to his Berditchev friend: "I sent you a whole vase and you gave it back to me shattered into a thousand pieces." . . . The disciple recovered. But why had he laughed in the presence of the Master and the entire audience? . . . What did he see, discover or understand in Berditchev to make him laugh at the holiest moment of the week, in front of one of the most exalted and exalting figures of Hasidism? We shall never know.

Wiesel adds his commentary: "Levi-Yitzhak admired King Solomon, the wisest of our sovereigns. Why? Because, according to the Midrash, he mastered all languages? Because he knew how to speak to birds? No. Because he understood the language of madmen."[22]

One of the Hasidic masters Wiesel admires the most is Nahman of Bratzlav, the great-grandson of the Bescht. Wiesel likens his tales to those of Kafka. Separated by more than a century, the two writers "seem to have shared the themes of obsession that lend their work its realistic yet dreamlike quality. Their heroes live their lives by imagining them, and their deaths by telling them."[23] Not content with being a fine storyteller, Nahman seems to have been a kind of comic actor, a buffoon. He assumed many personalities, put on various masks. Wiesel writes: "To the many people who assailed him with questions, Nahman refused to disclose who he was and where he came from. One day he claimed to be Cohen; the next he chose to be Levi or Israel . . . He flew into a rage over nothing and humiliated all who approached him, provoking people into beating and insulting him. In the end they doubted his reason and thus fulfilled his profound wish."[24]

Who is this "soul on fire" who wishes to be taken for a madman? Why has he chosen this solitary path? Why does he wish to pose as "comedian, imposter, clown . . . simpleton, escaped lunatic"?[25] He forgoes all the honors of his position, that of esteemed rabbi. He chooses the most humble demeanor: to be the butt of derision. Yet there is nothing derisory about this decision; it is a way of gesturing through the consuming fire. [His single-minded aim, to make himself "into a caricature,"[26] is undoubtedly a way of pointing to the fundamental ridiculousness of the world.] Wiesel speaks of Kafka, but one could also liken Nahman to the more modern creators of the dramatic genre I call the Metaphysical Farce: Samuel Beckett, Eugene Ionesco, and Fernando Arrabal. Wiesel says that one must not apply to this peculiar sage the Hasidic standards, but rather that he must be viewed as one who "places the accent on laughter."

Laughter occupies an astonishingly important place in his work. Here and there, one meets a man who laughs and does nothing else. Also a landscape that laughs. And a man who hears time, and everything he touches, roar with laughter—and hears nothing else.[27]

Moshe the madman is such a man. The laughter he hears in the landscape of his jail, in the flow of time, in the world, rises through him. He is the receptacle and conduit of metaphysical laughter. Within the confines of his cell, he envisions appearing before a supreme tribunal, a jury of prophets and disciples: Rabbi Yohanan ben Zakkai, Rabbi Akiba, Rabbi Yishmael, Rabbi Yehuda, Rabbi Itzhak, the Lion of Safed. Yet, something is missing. There are no madmen on the jury. Of course, the court could proclaim that the madman is not mad, but this is not what Moshe expects. Throughout his life he assumed his madness, dwelled in it. Now it must not be taken away from him. The judge agrees: "Your argument is valid; true madmen are as worthy as true saints."[28]

This is the lesson Moshe conveys to his only student and disciple, Azriel, the son of the community's scribe. Azriel will also be able to burst with laughter at a critical moment, one that could easily have culminated in his being put to death. This is the grotesque episode of the *Na-venadnik*'s encounter with a group of cripples. In the course of his eternal wanderings he enters an inn where a demented old woman thinks she recognizes in him a holy man, a healer. The woman's identification is contagious. Azriel is lifted up, carried by the villagers to the hospice. There, he is surrounded by a grimacing band of amputees. From neighboring villages other cripples converge upon this place. One hundred twenty legless, armless adolescents, bony women, and horribly deformed girls expect him to perform a miracle. This is a scene worthy of Goya's *pintura negra*, a fresco from the "house of the deaf man." As the crowd thickens and its expectations rise, there seems to be no escape. It is at this moment that Azriel begins to laugh. Recalling this moment, the principal narrator of *The Oath* says: "I was laughing and did not know it; I could not hear myself laughing . . . Unconsciously I chose escape into laughter."[29] This is Moshe's laughter issuing from the disciple's lips. "I am dreaming your dream, Moshe. It is you who are laughing."[30] This transcendent laugh, a laugh beyond laughter, captures Azriel's audience. [The audience begins to shout that the gates of heaven will open at the sound of the saint's laugh.] A chorus of voices rises toward God: "Pity, pity!" Hearing their imploration, the *Na-venadnik* realizes that one last recourse remains in this vale of tears. The chapter ends with a statement that brings Azriel close to Nahman of Bratzlav:

Brave, Moshe . . . I will laugh like you. I am laughing louder and louder, louder than the noise of the mob and of the valley below, the noise of life and of heaven, I laugh with all my strength and I know that this time it is not your doing, it is mine. With my laughter I drive the living to life, the dead to oblivion. With my laughter I bring together earth and sea, hell and redemption, enigma and light, my self and its shell.[31]

The double figure of Moshe/Azriel, master and disciple, both inspired madmen and saints, is able to perform the miracle of saving the would-be-suicide. By telling the story of Kolvillàg's annihilation, Azriel does not violate the sacred oath; instead, he enters in the Hasidic process of transmission. Now that the desperate boy has received the sacred oral text of the town's destruction, he must live on to insure the continuity of its communication. As to Elie Wiesel, the reader receives his words as though they came directly from

Azriel's father, the community's scribe. The latter sums up his particular task when he whispers to Moshe, on the occasion of visiting him in jail: "Aren't we the people of memory?"[32]

Elie Wiesel's latest poem/meditation—one hesitates to call it a novel, a piece of fiction—is the culmination of the writer's poetics of madness. *Twilight* opens with a striking epigraph taken from Maimonides: "The world couldn't exist without madmen." The book is set in an insane asylum in upstate New York, the Mountain Clinic. The hero, Raphael, has traveled to this quiet, remote place to track down the whereabouts of his friend Pedro, who has disappeared without a trace. A night caller has been pursuing the young refugee, college professor with bizarre stories about Pedro, insinuating that someone at Dr. Benedictus's clinic might enlighten him. Could the caller be Dr. Benedictus himself? As often in Wiesel's work there are many questions but no easy answers. Life's mystery is given its due.

The most ambitious and skillfully composed Wieselian piece of writing, *Twilight* does not yield at once the facts that make up the various strands of the plot. The book is like a complex puzzle: the reader is handed evocative, brightly colored bits and pieces of information that gradually form a total picture. The technique is modern, cinematic, with quick cuts, closeups, flashbacks, and a sound track that does not always coincide with the flow of events. However, as always in Wiesel, the subject transcends time and literary fashions.

The central theme of madness is given from the start, like the opening notes of a Beethoven symphony: "I am going mad, Pedro."[33] In tone and mood *Twilight* forms a diptych with *The Oath*. Even typographically there are similarities, with the alternation of italicized sections. Both novels move constantly through time and consciousness.

The paradox of Wiesel's apprehension lies in the fact that although his novels are grounded in history, they are animated by what Mircea Eliade calls "a primitive ontology."[34] As for archaic man, "an object or an act becomes real only insofar as it imitates or repeats an archetype."[35] Thus, Wiesel's protagonists exist simultaneously in profane and mythical time. He "tolerates history with difficulty and attempts periodically to abolish it,"[36] an attitude shaped by the religious community in which he came of age. Eliade explains:

The . . . transfiguration of history into myth . . . is found in the visions of the Hebrew poets. In order to "tolerate history," that is, to endure their military defeats and political humiliations, the Hebrews interpreted contemporary events by means of the very ancient cosmogonic-heroic myth, which, though it . . . admitted the provisional victory of the dragon, implied the dragon's final extinction through a King-Messiah.[37]

The madman-saint of Wiesel's novels is able to transcend history, to move through cosmogonic timelessness. However, he is still the heir of the messianic vision that announces the end of Yahweh's personal intervention by closing once and for all the cycle of becoming. In the meanwhile, this ambiguous character prefigures the Messiah; he might even be an unrecognized Christ. Like the madman "with veiled eyes"[38] of *Twilight*, who saves Raphael when the boy is dying of typhus, these holy men appear and reappear, benevolent ghosts who mingle with the living. Through their intercession "the historical event becomes a theophany."[39]

The above weltanschauung, which stems from Wiesel's growing up in a tightly knit religious community, also dictates the form of his more recent novels. They evolve on more than one plane, moving simultaneously through historical time and spiritual timelessness. They cannot be presented as a linear development. Thus, the modernity of *Twilight*'s form has less to do with contemporary aesthetics than with the inner necessity to reflect strata of consciousness.

Twilight is written in two narrative voices. The story unfolds in the third person, shifting from one character to the next, moving back and forth in time and space. Interspersed through the text, another text seeps in, written in the first person and printed in italics. The italicized text reproduces the flow of the main character's thoughts, forming an interior monologue. It is like a continuous letter, or dramatic soliloquy addressed to the absent Pedro, Raphael's friend, mentor, and savior. In all likelihood Pedro is dead, or "at best wasting in a Soviet prison."[40] His trip beyond the Iron Curtain, occasioned by his desire to rescue Raphael's only surviving brother, a captive of the Russians, ends in his own arrest.

One of the leaders of the Briha, the Jewish organization established to help survivors and bring them to Palestine, Pedro acquired his name in 1936, when he fought in the International Brigades. However, this foe of fascism never joined the Communist party. When questioned by Raphael, he answers with an ironic, self-deprecating smile that he was "an idealist."[41] There is something of the young Malraux—one of Wiesel's French literary ancestors, together with Albert Camus—about Pedro. The theme of virile fraternity, of a close partnership of heroes struggling together for a better future, issues directly from *Man's Fate*. After Franco's victory, Pedro seeks refuge in France, together with numerous political expatriates. When France enters the war he is interned. We can only guess at his escape during France's occupation by the Germans. He has to move fast: to London, Egypt, and Palestine. Recruited by the Haganah, Pedro is subsequently assigned to the Briha. With his whole family "reduced to ashes"[42] he makes of the young Jews he has rescued his only kith and kin.

However, much about Pedro is unclear. The man who emerges gradually from the "obscene nocturnal calls"[43] of an unidentified foreigner might be an "amoral . . . sadist,"[44] an "*agent provacateur*,"[45] "a rat."[46] Could he have been a Soviet collaborator who betrayed his friends? The voice claims to have shared a cell with him and fifteen other men at the Butyrka in 1948. Pedro, the informer claims, was taken out three times for interrogation; all three times he returned smiling. Each time one of the fifteen men was taken out for interrogation and torture: Boris Genchov, a carpenter from Kazan, Yossif Pomosh from Kiev, and Piotr Volokhov a famous physician. Did Pedro denounce his companions? What game was he playing? There will be no answer, but the voice advises Raphael to seek the truth at the upstate New York asylum. In the "bewitched world of the *Klipot* where no light penetrates,"[47] Raphael will not find an answer, but he will come in contact with eleven patients whose delusions are based on the Bible. As to Pedro, he might have been "a madman in his own way. He was forever telling Raphael that one must not seek to understand, that one must understand without seeking, that it is sometimes necessary to seek in order not to understand."[48] The encounters with eleven mad patients constitute one of *Twilight*'s basic structures. They are Adam, Cain, the Prophet, Abraham, the Man in Flames, the Dead Man, the Scapegoat, Joseph, Zelig, who sees the dead in the heavens, the Messiah, and the Man who thinks he is God.

Adam, the first patient Raphael meets, converses only with God. He is trying to persuade the Lord to "reverse"[49] himself, giving up his project of creating man. This former scholar, who looks "like a clown begging for laughter,"[50] wants to escape the curse of having been born. Creation, he maintains, will be far more resplendent in the absence of the paltry creature. For "Adam" God is perhaps another patient.

Indeed, the last patient Raphael is to meet before leaving the clinic is "the Man who thinks he is God." The Mountain Clinic sojourn is framed by these two meetings. From the last patient Raphael hears that there are various degrees of suffering. One should not only "cry for others,"[51] one ought to cry for God. Raphael's master of the Midrash, with whom he studied Ecclesiastes, left him with this thought: "We must pity God, who cannot help but be God, who cannot help but be."[52] The patient, "madman of God or God of madmen,"[53] sees "his" creation as supreme mockery. Sitting next to him on a bench, Raphael sees in his mind's eye his dead father teaching his dead students, his dead mother shielding her dead children. Could the past be reinvented, history altered, the clock turned back? This is the ultimate temptation, one that brings the visitor to the brink of madness. In Dr. Benedictus's clinic, Raphael has discovered that "madness could be contagious."[54]

Between the first and last encounter there are nine others. All of them take the visitor through "a dark wood / Where the right road was wholly lost and gone."[55] Like the traveler of the *Inferno*'s canto 2, he witnesses the coming of dusk, "Loosing from labor every living thing,"[56] save him. "Twilight is the domain of madness,"[57] he cries out to his Virgil, the absent Pedro. Dante also feared falling "into some folly."[58]

Raphael's confrontations with mystical madmen is a form of meditation, an encounter with the self *in extremis.* There is Cain, the only son of a Cleveland industrialist, full of murderous rage at the world's injustice. This Cain, suffering from "pathological kindness,"[59] may never have killed, or even had a brother. His wrath is turned against the Lord himself. He shouts: "Any fool knows that whoever kills, kills God."[60] Next comes the bald "Prophet," tossing his invisible long curls. Having opted for silence he is an antiprophet. Yet Raphael feels close to this seer without a message; his refusal to speak parallels the choice of many a survivor. The visitor is also reminded of a statement Pedro made in Paris: "The path to enlightenment leads through the ravaged landscape of death."[61]

This is the landscape that rises from the discourse of the mad "Abraham," a survivor from the village of Zhitomir where his only son perished. As the boy's Bible teacher, he feels that he failed the boy fatally. When the Germans invaded their province, capturing and jailing the Jews, he had to witness his son's incapacity to scale walls, jump fences, run faster than a hare, feed on herbs and roots, drink the dew. These precepts for survival have been proffered by the peasant who sheltered father and son for a while. However, the scholar Abraham can only pass on the Word. Unwittingly, by being true to his people's tradition, he has caused the boy's death. Although he can in no way be faulted, his sense of guilt has driven him insane. Is Wiesel questioning here the basis of Jewish education? Is he indicting a God who allowed his people to be led to slaughter?

God's justice is also questioned in the episode of the fifth madman, Nadav, one of the sons of Moses' brother, the high priest Aaron. Culled from chapter 10 of Leviticus, it is the mysterious story of the priest's two sons, Nadab and Abihu, devoured by the fires they lit in the censers. The Nadav of *Twilight* is alive and dead at the same time. In a voice as melodious as "the ethereal sound of a harp,"[62] he proclaims that he is "nothing but a handful of ashes."[63] His everlasting burning could be seen as a symbol of the Holocaust, the everlasting burning of the Jewish people sealed in its memory, consigned to history and literature. This may be the reason for Nadav's being "song personified."[64]   *Music & Madness*

Forty days after his arrival at the clinic (the number is biblical), Raphael meets with "the Dead Man." This episode, located at the core of the novel, and central to the sequence of the mad patients, constitutes a richly poetic separate tale within the work. It echoes the fables Wiesel heard from his Hasidic masters.

The patient, who seems to recognize Raphael (Did they meet during the war? In Paris?) is eager to recount the story of his death. He describes with wry humor the senseless agitation of the living, first around his corpse, then his coffin. His own senses have grown keener with death so that he is able to hear "the sound the earth makes as it spins."[65] Also his sense of time has altered. "That is the real victory of death: it stops time."[66] However, sleep and dreaming continue. What is the nature of these dreams? The ironic answer is not long in coming: "Our nightmares, do you know what they are? Your reality, the reality of the living."[67] However, this lucid cadaver is trapped in a nightmare of his own: he cannot speak his own name. When the Angel of Death comes knocking at his grave, his lips are sealed. The concluding image evokes a terrifying limbo: "I found myself in the *Kaf Hakela*, the space outside space, outside time, far from God, far from everything. And, just as you see me today, that is where I have remained."[68]

This is the ultimate suffering, to be one of the living dead, to have consciousness and yet to be nowhere. The Dead Man has reached the deepest pit of madness and despair. To choose silence like the Prophet, to become a statue of ashes like Nadav can only lead to the sealed lips of the self-exile, the exiled from self. In this tale, Wiesel becomes our master and guide; he instructs us in the dangers of dissolution, assists us in skirting the abyss.

Boris Galperin, "the Scapegoat," imagines he has been the prisoner of the Soviet police. His story—the only form of madness in *Twilight* unrelated to the Bible—parallels that of Raphael's brother, Yoel. A sympathizer of the clandestine Communist movement in Poland, Yoel is arrested by a Soviet officer in the Moscow train station after his evacuation from Lvov. He finds himself a prisoner of Stalin's penal system accused of being a spy. After repeated torture sessions, the young man has a vision of himself as mad. He reaches a logical decision: "Since they want me to go mad, I'll oblige them. I'll say anything that comes to my mind."[69] Assuming the rhetoric of Jeremiah addressing King Zedekiah, or witnessing the plunder of the

Temple, he exclaims: "God forced my hand. I am his emissary . . . the end of time is approaching."[70] From that time on, Yoel perfects his act; his life hangs on this mask of prophetic madness.

The Scapegoat also speaks of confessing to acts he never committed. He provided his interrogators with outrageous lists of conspirators, going so far as to include the name of Lavrenti Beria, the chief of the Soviet police. Thus, the regime's schizophrenia is matched by Galperin's fake delirium and Yoel's mock prophecies. When Raphael asks the patient whether he might not have met with Pedro in the Soviet jails, the Scapegoat readily admits: "Of course I knew him. I knew everybody, for everybody was guilty. I am the guilty God."[71]

With "Joseph," the eighth patient, Raphael finds himself back once more in the biblical universe. This Joseph, however, is not the beloved son of Jacob's old age. His coat of many colors may be the court fool's garb. He suffers from an overwhelming feeling of horror: "My father sent me to my death."[72]

Is there any truth to this delusion? A careful reading of chapter 37 of Genesis yields an answer. As Wiesel himself writes in the "Joseph" chapter of *Messengers of God*, it is Jacob who sent Joseph to Shechem to see whether his brothers and their flocks were well. Wiesel suggests: "At that crucial moment, while his brothers were binding him and throwing him to the ground, Joseph tried to understand, to remember. And suddenly a searing, terrifying thought crossed his mind: Was it possible that his father knew, and had sent him there because he *wanted* this to happen? Because he wanted him to be killed?"[73] For Wiesel, Joseph, like Isaac is a sacrificial victim. He is also "the forerunner of a Messiah, an unhappy, unlucky Messiah."[74] And yet, his is the supreme success story: a poor shepherd becomes the first Jewish prince, a ruler second only to his master, the pharaoh.

What is the meaning of the old man's dream in the "Joseph" episode in *Twilight?* Jacob dreams that he inhabits a strange land peopled by demons. These hellish spirits would like to feel pity, but they are unable to weep. One of the demons is his own "lost son."[75] Were the old man to reveal the story of his son, he could go free, but he keeps silent for fear of harming Joseph.

Is this inimical land the hell on earth of the Jewish Diaspora, foreshadowed by Joseph's exile in Egypt? As the governor of that land, did he in fact become one of the demons? There is no ready answer for this question, yet the question keeps on puzzling the mind. So many Jews gained power and prestige in the Diaspora, only to perish in the Holocaust. Does the father of the mad Joseph envision the future danger to his son, to his nation? Does he know that one cannot live among the enemy forever? In Egypt, Joseph "adopted Egyptian customs and tradition to the point that his brothers did not recognize him . . . In their eyes he was a foreigner, a man who had left his people, repudiated his roots." [76] Although he was the first Jew "to bridge two nations, two histories," [77] the price he paid was a life away from the tender presence of his community, the visitation of God. Wiesel calls him "the most misunderstood man in the Bible." [78]

As to the silence of the mad patient's father, it parallels that of the biblical Jacob. Wiesel writes in *Messengers of God*: "From the day that Joseph was taken away from him, he [Jacob] led a solitary, almost secret life. For twenty years he did not speak . . . He lived outside language, beyond hope." [79] His silence is only matched by that of God.

Neither a prophet, nor a mystic sage, the ninth patient, Zelig, nevertheless does not live on this planet. He walks with his head "tilted skyward," [80] so that he may catch a glimpse in the heavens of the Jews who have been wiped out by the Holocaust. Raphael feels very close to this man. Both have sought the dead in the mass graves of Europe and waited for them to return to their empty homes. Now, the only place where they may be found is above. Raphael shudders when Zelig identifies him as one of the ghosts, "up there, with them." [81]

Raphael's penultimate station of the cross on the via dolorosa of his pilgrimage, is his encounter with the "Messiah of the Wicked." This son of a Protestant minister is said to have experimented with a hallucinogenic drug shortly before his graduation from the Princeton school of theology. The ensuing delirium took the form of a Black Mass figure. The "Messiah" has not lost interest in philosophic inquiry. The conversation he holds with Raphael is strangely reminiscent of those of Hans Castorp with his mentors, or Leo Naphta, an

Austrian Jew converted to the Catholic faith, and the Italian free-
thinker, Settembrini. It is in this passage that *Twilight*'s literary
model clearly appears. Indeed, Dr. Benedictus's clinic is not unlike
Thomas Mann's sanatorium for the tubercular. Like Castorp, Raphael
must develop the "ability to maintain a precarious balance between
the forces of unity and dissolution."[82]

If *The Magic Mountain* is Mann's "World War I novel,"[83] despite
its prewar setting, then *Twilight* may be considered Wiesel's deepest
statement on World War II, the fascisms of the West and the East,
and the Holocaust, despite its postwar, North American setting. The
madness of the Nazi death camps, Russian jails and slave labor
gulags, is reflected in the ravings of the Mountain Clinic's inmates.
Perhaps the most terrifying question raised in this poem/meditation
is framed by the philosophic exchange between Raphael and Pedro.
When the survivor asks his "savior" whether he also thinks that one
must be mad to continue to believe in God, the latter answers: "I can
think of another explanation. What if it is God who is mad?"[84]

In such a universe, what is the place of the mystic? What happens to
the man of faith? In Ruth R. Wisse's review of Lawrence Rudner's
novel, *The Magic We Do Here*, written for the Sunday *New York Times*
(7 August 1988), the critic makes the following statement: "At the
novel's center is the legend of the emergence of the artist in place of
the Talmudic scholar as one of the Jewish accommodations to modernity." In his personal statement, "Why I Write," Wiesel opens with
a short paragraph: "Why do I write? Perhaps in order not to go mad.
Or, on the contrary, to touch the bottom of madness."[85] He might
also have said, like the Maggid of Mezeritch: "Man is the language
of God."[86]

For Wiesel, the poet in prose, it is through language that humanity
will make its way toward survival. In *Twilight*, the mad "Abraham"
tries to explain to the illiterate peasant who has been sheltering him
and his only son that the Jewish people live by the Word. He quotes
from a Hasidic commentary on Noah: "When God ordered him to
build an ark, he used the word *teva* which in Hebrew means both *ark*
and *word*. It is by building words that you will survive the flood."[87]

⌈Could writing constitute an act of mad faith? No more so than the
building of a ship on dry land.⌋The modern poet's ark is a spaceship
whereon he must lure his dead to ferry them from heaven onto this
earth so that they may "vanquish death."[88]

Notes

1. This term can be found in a parable from the *Zohar* reproduced by
   Gershom G. Scholem in his book *On the Kabbalah and Its Symbolism*,
   trans. Ralph Manheim (New York: Schocken Books, 1969), 55.
2. Scholem, *On the Kabbalah*, 5.
3. Ibid., 19–20.
4. Ibid., 21.
5. Ibid., 22.
6. Ibid., 100.
7. Ibid., 98.
8. Ibid., 99.
9. Ibid., 110.
10. Ibid.
11. Ibid.
12. Ibid., 19.
13. Elie Wiesel, Preface to *Célébration hassidique: Portraits et légendes*
    (Paris: Editions du Seuil, 1982), 11. This preface written for the French
    edition was not reproduced in the English translation, *Souls on Fire*.
    This quote, as well as the one in n. 14, below, have been translated
    from the French by the author of this essay.
14. Ibid., 13.
15. Elie Wiesel, *Souls on Fire: Portraits and Legends of Hasidic Masters*,
    trans. Marion Wiesel (New York: Random House, 1972), 71.
16. Ibid., 35.
17. Emil L. Fackenheim, "Midrashic Existence After the Holocaust," in
    Confronting the Holocaust: The Impact of Elie Wiesel, ed. Alvin Rosen-
    feld and Irving Greenberg (Bloomington: Indiana University Press,
    1978), 111.
18. Elie Wiesel, *Night*, trans. Stella Rodway (New York: Hill and Wang,
    1960), 34.
19. Ibid., 35.

20. Joel Friedmann, *Le rire dans l'univers tragique d'Elie Wiesel* (Paris: Librairie A. G. Nizet, 1981), 57. Translated by the author of this essay.
21. Ibid., 28.
22. Wiesel, *Souls on Fire*, 104–5.
23. Ibid., 172.
24. Ibid., 197.
25. Ibid., 198.
26. Ibid., 199.
27. Ibid., 198.
28. Elie Wiesel, *The Oath*, trans. Marion Wiesel (New York: Avon, 1973), 178.
29. Ibid., 85.
30. Ibid., 86.
31. Ibid.
32. Ibid., 193.
33. Elie Wiesel, *Twilight*, trans. Marion Wiesel (New York: Summit Books, 1988), 11.
34. Mircea Eliade, *Cosmos and History: The Myth of the Eternal Return*, trans. Willard R. Trask (New York: Harper Torchbooks, 1959), 34.
35. Ibid., 35.
36. Ibid., 36.
37. Ibid., 37–38.
38. Wiesel, *Twilight*, 14.
39. Eliade, *Cosmos and History*, 110.
40. Wiesel, *Twilight*, 16.
41. Ibid., 181.
42. Ibid.
43. Ibid., 71.
44. Ibid., 179.
45. Ibid., 198.
46. Ibid., 191.
47. Ibid., 216.
48. Ibid., 100.
49. Ibid., 40.
50. Ibid., 39.
51. Ibid., 213.
52. Ibid., 214.
53. Ibid., 216.

54. Ibid., 102.
55. Dante, *The Divine Comedy*, vol. 1, *Hell*, trans. Dorothy L. Sayers (Baltimore: Penguin Books, 1949), 71.
56. Ibid., canto 2, 78.
57. Wiesel, *Twilight*, 202.
58. Dante, *Divine Comedy* 1:79.
59. Wiesel, *Twilight*, 57.
60. Ibid., 58.
61. Ibid., 75.
62. Ibid., 115.
63. Ibid., 114.
64. Ibid., 115.
65. Ibid., 137.
66. Ibid., 142.
67. Ibid., 139.
68. Ibid., 144.
69. Ibid., 92.
70. Ibid.
71. Ibid., 151.
72. Ibid., 169.
73. Elie Wiesel, *Messengers of God: Biblical Portraits and Legends*, trans. Marion Wiesel (New York: Random House, 1976), 165.
74. Ibid., 168.
75. Wiesel, *Twilight*, 170.
76. Wiesel, *Messengers of God*, 160.
77. Ibid., 144.
78. Ibid., 161.
79. Ibid., 162.
80. Wiesel, *Twilight*, 170.
81. Ibid., 174.
82. Lawrence L. Langer, *The Age of Atrocity: Death in Modern Literature* (Boston: Beacon Press, 1978), 96.
83. Ibid., 69.
84. Wiesel, *Twilight*, 213.
85. Rosenfeld and Greenberg, *Confronting the Holocaust*, 200.
86. Wiesel, *Souls on Fire*, 86.
87. Wiesel, *Twilight*, 97.
88. Rosenfeld and Greenberg, *Confronting the Holocaust*, 206.

13
Drama Reflecting Madness: The Plays of Elie Wiesel

Harry James Cargas

The Holocaust demands unprecedented responses from every disci-✕ pline. In law, for example, new legal territory had to be explored and cultivated when the Allies established procedures governing the Nuremberg Trials. In theology, some Christian leaders have begun to make extraordinary efforts to attempt to comprehend the role their theology played in helping to pave the way that led to the enormous tragedy of World War II death camps for Jews. So, too, in the arts. While a few, like Theodore Adorno, have argued that there can be no poetry after Auschwitz, others have insisted that there must be a new kind of art after the Holocaust—an art that transcends, suggests, teaches, remembers.

Surely, this is a challenge that has been faced by those artists engaged in writing about the *Shoah* for the stage. While some theater critics insist that such productions must be judged according to traditional standards, there is an increased awareness that because the content of Holocaust drama is so unparalleled, extraordinary approaches must be found. As Irving Howe has noted, "There are values that supercede aesthetic ones and situations in which it is unseemly to continue going through the paces of aesthetic judgment."[1]

In my view, Howe's comment applies to the plays written by Elie Wiesel, where art is given to the service of testimony. In a book we wrote together, he observes, "Once upon a time it was possible to write *l'art pour l'art*, art for art's sake. People were looking only for beauty. Now we know that beauty without an ethical dimension cannot exist."[2] Others have recognized this as well. Peter Weiss's use of transcripts of a trial of Auschwitz criminals in *The Investigation* is a unique, if failed, attempt at rendering an aspect of inhumanity. In *The Deputy*, Rolf Hochhuth exaggerates an attack on his one-dimensional figure of Pope Pius XII in order to make the point that the institutional Catholic church failed during the great crisis. A number of dramatists even offer bizarrely comic characters and situations to portray the absurd situations they cannot directly confront. These include *Throne of Straw*, by Harold and Edith Lieberman; Shimon Wincelberg's *Resort 76; The Emigration of Adam Kurtzik*, by Theodore Herstand, and *Laughter!*, by Peter Barnes, a play that includes farce, one-liners, and sight gags to present a message.

Wiesel goes in another direction: that of madness. To be sure, Yankele in *Throne of Straw* is a lunatic, and the peddler Shpunt in Millard Lampell's adaptation of John Hersey's novel *The Wall* is insane, but neither of these plays approach the spiritually prophetic character of Wiesel's creation. In his three plays, a single question recurs: [How can humans confront the heinous evil that has been unleashed in the world? The responses that Wiesel's characters make are manifestations of varying degrees of madness.]

The Covenant that God made with His people is perhaps the most fundamental basis for the Jewish faith. But as the attempted annihilation of Europe's Jews became more complete during World War II, as the obverse side of Sinai became increasingly evident, how were believers to react? Who could have been prepared to cope with such monstrous depravity? In his three plays, Wiesel shows a progression of responses going from a despairing madness to mystical madness to a madness of defiance—a kind of faith in spite of God.

Wiesel's first stage effort is a brief one-act work, *A Black Canopy A Black Sky*.[3] Performed in 1968 to commemorate the twenty-fifth anniversary of the Warsaw Ghetto Uprising, *Canopy* is set in an underground bunker in an unnamed Polish ghetto.

Mendel and Sarah anxiously await the return of Sarah's sister, Chava, the man's fiancée, who has left on a mission of risk. The visiting Maggid (an itinerant preacher in Jewish tradition) offers to perform the wedding immediately, to celebrate love blossoming in this environment of death. But Mendel scolds him for speaking foolishly. When the puzzled Maggid turns to Sarah she becomes very vague about Chava, not even being able to tell him which of them is the older sister. A boy enters, interrupting the discussion to tell the three that despite the lack of weapons, the Jews "hope for the privilege of fighting."[4]

None believe there is any chance to defeat the Nazis. The Maggid prophesies: "I see victorious Jews; but we shall not share their victories."[5] Then he complains that God seems to have abandoned his people. Mendel, insisting that the Maggid not make them all insane, rushes out of the bunker to find his bride-to-be. It is then that Sarah tells the Maggid their secret: Chava does not exist. She, Sarah, is actually Mendel's wife. A few months before, Mendel had been captured and was about to be killed. He survived but erroneously thought that Sarah had been taken prisoner as well. Not being able to face the idea of his wife, Sarah's death, Mendel created Chava as a bride who lived. It was his way of coping. But Mendel's madness resulting from an incomprehensible reality outside the bunker is not without its effect inside the bunker. Sarah becomes seriously disoriented. She begs the Maggid for help. "Is Mendel right? Was I killed? Am I dead? And am *I* out of my mind . . . not he?"[6] The Maggid confesses to being unable to distinguish between reality and dream. All that he can see is a black canopy under a sky of black stars. The short piece ends on a note of total despair.

Perhaps the most constant question in all of Wiesel's literary creations is this: Where is God when His people suffer? Indifferent? Dead? Hiding? Ashamed? Powerless? Also suffering? It is not difficult to see how a person might go mad when asking how God and overwhelming evil inhabit the same universe.

One reaction suggests that God, too, may be mad and the correct human resolution may be to join him in that mystical state. Wiesel's second, and best known play, *Zalmen*,[7] approaches this position. Initially performed to critical acclaim at Washington's Arena Stage and later shown on public television (in a version that was merely a filming of the theater production and, consequently, fared poorly on the screen), the play is subtitled *or, The Madness of God.* What Wiesel suggests through this presentation is that some of us are God's madness. To persevere in faith, with hope, in spite of all the cruelty, is sheer mystical madness.

Word has come to the synagogue that a troupe of foreign actors, including four Jews, will attend Yom Kippur services. The Rabbi and members of the synagogue council are cautioned by Communist authorities not to complain of any lack of religious freedom. Tension is upgraded, however, when the title character, Zalmen, the beadle, strongly encourages the Rabbi to make his protest. He tells the Rabbi that "we are the imagination and madness of the world—we are imagination gone mad. One has to be mad today to believe. One has to be mad to remain human. Be mad, Rabbi, be mad!"[8]

The Rabbi resists: "The things that I would have to say, how can I say them? And who am I to say them? All I can do is pray—I am the shepherd who follows his flock."[9] But Zalmen keeps insisting that God does not want a Rabbi who is "bowed down, begging for punishment and pardon." Be strong, the beadle urges, be "proud in spite of your despair."[10]

Tension mounts as the religious service is in progress and the Rabbi is unable to resist the centuries-long tradition of outspoken Jewish perseverance in faith that Zalmen represents. So the Rabbi proclaims "to any who will listen that the Torah here is in peril and the spirit of a whole people is being crushed . . . If we allow this to continue, if you, our brothers, forsake us, we will be the last of the Jews in this land, the last witnesses, the last of the Jews who in silence bury the Jew within them."[11] Act 1 ends leaving the viewer concerned about the Rabbi's fate.

The second act opens with a Soviet inspector investigating the incident. Cautious Jews convince the authorities that the Rabbi, who sits in silence refusing to defend his initiative, merely behaved eccentrically and meaninglessly; his rebellion would have no impact. Unknown to these characters is the small gesture of comprehension by the Rabbi's young grandson who, we are led to understand, has appreciated his grandfather's defiance and will carry the Jewish tradition forward for his generation.

Wiesel's message in this drama comes from the Rabbi's lips: "God requires of man not that he live, but that he choose to live. What matters is to choose—at the risk of being defeated."[12]

Thus the Rabbi triumphs. Not a momentous victory, no epic conquest, he at least manages to save his own soul and to pass his achievement on to another generation. In *Omni Magazine* Wiesel wrote: "I'm a minimalist. I'm satisfied with small miracles."[13] He claimed that when we protest against injustice, "by amplifying our moral comment and moral commitment," we help others.[14]

Madness through rebellion marks Wiesel's most recent drama, *The Trial of God.*[15] The three-act work is set in Shamgorod in the Ukraine on 25 February 1649, not long after a pogrom has taken place in the area. The date is the eve of Purim, the joyous celebration marking the biblical deliverance of Jews from Haman's intended slaughter. Jews were saved through the intercession of Esther who pleads with the king, her husband Ahasuerus.

The scene is an inn where three Jewish wandering minstrels have stopped. They hope to perform for local Jews on Purim, only to find out that the innkeeper and his mad daughter are the only Jews who were not murdered in the recent butchering. The would-be revelers cannot pay for their drinks but offer to sing and act out a Purim drama. Berish, the angered proprietor, finally agrees not to a festive play but to a mock trial of God, and only if he can be the prosecuting attorney.

Gradually, his story in revealed. The price of his survival from the recent pogrom was seeing his wife killed and being forced to watch his now insane daughter repeatedly raped by the invaders. He wishes to accuse God of infidelity.

Meanwhile, a priest enters, warning that another attempt to destroy all Jews is approaching and offers Berish and the minstrels safety if they will convert to Christianity. Maria, the sympathetic, Christian waitress, suggests they go through a meaningless ritual to save their lives. "Your God will forgive you, I promise you." But the chief minstrel replies: "Perhaps He will. I will not."[16] She then suggests a strategy. "My God does not persecute me. Yours does nothing else. Why not play a trick on Him? Why not turn your back on Him for a day or a week? Just to teach him a lesson!"[17] Maria cannot convince them.

Instead, the trial will take place. They agree, since it is Purim, a time when anything goes. The minstrels take roles as court officials, Berish becomes the prosecutor, Maria is the audience. They cannot proceed, however, because no one wishes to play God's defense attorney. Then a stranger, Sam, enters the inn and volunteers to champion the deity.

Berish charges God with hostility, cruelty, and indifference. Sam insists on the kind of evidence that only dead victims can furnish. Besides, he continues, Jews have suffered all through history without accusing God. Berish responds in incredulity. "And they kept quiet? Too bad—then I'll speak for them, too. For them, too, I'll demand justice."[18] The implied question by Wiesel here is evident. How are victims to respond to the greatest Jewish disaster of all, the Holocaust? *Shoah*

The killers approach as the stranger is revealed to be Satan. The lights go out on stage, the mob is heard "accompanied by deafening and murderous roars."[19]

Wiesel tells how this play came to be. "Its genesis: inside the kingdom of night, I witnessed a strange trial. Three rabbis—all erudite and pious men—decided one winter evening to indict God for allowing his children to be massacred. I remember: I was there, and I felt like crying. But there, nobody cried."[20]

What Wiesel does not mention here he elaborated to me; the rabbis found God guilty; then saw that it was time to pray and did so. This is reflected in Berish's refusal to deny God, to rather affirm Him by accusation, to spurn an opportunity to escape in order to persist in his challenge.

The problem that Wiesel confronts in his dramas appears in much of his oeuvre: Where was God at Auschwitz? Has God betrayed His people? Wiesel wants to know what the Covenant means. How are these questions even to be considered?

Robert McAfee Brown writes that in Wiesel's writings "we discover that the mad people challenge the assumptions of the lucid, and that the mad people communicate the real truth about the human situation."[21]

The way that Wiesel has chosen to encounter these questions of such enormous magnitude is through indirection. Just as Moses was unable to stare at the Burning Bush directly, neither can the *Shoah* be faced head on. We are incapable of gazing at the depth of the tragedy lest we become overwhelmed, paralyzed in despair, unable to act because of unbearable sorrow. Therefore Wiesel, in all of his writings, with the exception of his memoir, *Night*, deals with the Holocaust tangentially. Even in *Night* he is not as direct as might initially appear. When the book was first published, in Argentina— in Yiddish—it was some 800 pages long. Now it is about 110 pages. He told me that "I cut away and I cut away but to the sensitive reader it's all still there."[22] Even *Canopy*, though set during the Holocaust, does not attempt to confront the major questions directly.

To better understand what Wiesel has attempted in his plays, it is useful to compare his efforts with those of other dramatists. The differences will readily appear.

The best known of Holocaust plays is Rolf Hochhuth's *The Deputy*, a seven-hour attack against the Vatican's silence regarding the persecution of Jews by the Nazis and their collaborators, with Pope Pius XII singled out in particular. Complete with long explanatory sections by the German author, this work is more an attempt at docudrama than traditional theater and may be the most controversial play ever staged—if the standards of measure are public outcry plus critical as well as theological and historical responses. The rather vicious, anti-Israeli play of Heinar Kipphardt, *Brother Eichmann*, so sympathetic to its title character, comes to mind regarding style here. Peter Weiss's *The Investigation*, in which he uses transcripts from a trial of Auschwitz war criminals for its text, should perhaps be more correctly considered a kind of documentary rather than a drama. Weiss, however, fails to make his survivors-victims believable and therefore capable of our sympathy.

Unlike Hochhuth, Kipphardt, or Weiss, Wiesel does not render his scenes or plots in such a straightforward way, although each of his plays has its basis in historical fact. His approach is much more imaginative, more condemnatory of God, perhaps, than of humans— thus more challenging than the writings of Hochhuth and Weiss, and certainly less political than either.

Unlike some other creators of Holocaust drama, Wiesel does not attempt to shock the audience. In George Tabori's *Cannibals*, for example, prisoners are ordered to eat parts of the body of a dead fellow prisoner. It is a drama that suggests, at the least, a rejection of God.

Nor is there much humor on Wiesel's stage. There's none of the black comedy of Shimon Wincelberg's *Resort 76*, for example, or the general nonsense that goes on in the one-act plays of Peter Barnes, *Auschwitz* and *Tsar*. Neither does Wiesel attempt the Brechtian stage techniques that critic Robert Skloot ascribes to Harold and Edith Lieberman's *Throne of Straw*. The attempt here, notes the critic, is to force the spectator "to draw back from emotional involvement at strategic moments in the play, to *alienate* the audience by making the familiar strange through some aspect of staging."[23]

Humor and eye-catching staging have no place in the work of Elie Wiesel. He prefers a more methodical approach wherein the bizarre actions do not elicit laughter but rather pity and questions. Wiesel is not about to allow us an Aristotelian catharsis while in the audience. He prefers to keep us troubled so that we do not leave the theater relieved, but rather anxious because we are aware that what we have seen is either happening elsewhere or is capable of recurring. This also, of course, is far removed from the ambiguity of Robert Shaw's *Man in the Glass Booth* where the main character's Jewish identity crisis overshadows the Holocaust theme without itself being resolved in any satisfactory way.

Wiesel's approach to drama is not that of a historian, humorist, technician, or traditionalist. Rather, as in his other writings, his is the role of prophet, one who challenges through madness. As prophet, he is properly incapable of leaving us with a feeling of optimism the way Wincelberg does by ending *Resort 76* with most of his characters still living, or with the hope found in Charlotte Delbo's all-woman play, *Who Will Carry the Word?* wherein feminine qualities of mutual support reflect a more positive universe than is generally accorded the concentration-camp scene. For the prophet, mystical madness is the metier.

In our book of conversations I began with a question: "Why are you not mad?" His reply:

Maybe I am and I don't know it. If I am, I try to know it. When I see the world, the way it is; when I watch the events, the way they unfold; when I think of what is going to happen to our generation, then I have the feeling that I am haunted by that madness—that we all are. Then in order to save myself from that madness, I go back to another madness—a holy madness—the one that became a victim, the one that kept us alive for so many centuries, for thousands of years.[24]

It is in that sense that Wiesel's characters must reflect madness.

Notes

1. Quoted in Robert Skloot, *The Darkness We Carry* (Madison: University of Wisconsin Press, 1988), 94.
2. Harry James Cargas, *Harry James Cargas in Conversation with Elie Wiesel* (New York: Paulist Press, 1976), 86.
3. Elie Wiesel, *A Black Canopy A Black Sky* in *Against Silence: The Voice and Vision of Elie Wiesel*, ed. Irving Abrahamson, 3 vols. (New York: Holocaust Library, 1985), 3:19–28.
4. Ibid., 24.
5. Ibid., 25.
6. Ibid., 27.
7. Elie Wiesel, *Zalmen; or, The Madness of God* (New York: Random House, 1974).
8. Ibid., 79.
9. Ibid., 21.
10. Ibid., 5.
11. Ibid., 82–83.
12. Ibid., 53.
13. In Marion Long, "Paradise Tossed," *Omni*, April 1988, 39.
14. Elie Wiesel, *The Trial of God* (New York: Random House, 1979).
15. Ibid., 47.
16. Ibid., 48.
17. Ibid., 134.
18. Ibid., 161.
19. Ibid., iii.
20. Robert McAfee Brown, *Elie Wiesel: Messenger to All Humanity* (Notre Dame: University of Notre Dame Press, 1983), 208.

21. In a private conversation with me.
22. Robert Skloot, ed., *The Theatre of the Holocaust* (Madison: University of Wisconsin Press, 1982), 25–26.
23. Cargas, *Harry James Cargas in Conversation with Elie Wiesel*, 2.
24. Ibid.

14

And God Was Silent

Irving Abrahamson

T*wilight*[1] is Elie Wiesel's eighth novel. Appearing in various guises, speaking through many voices, in *Twilight* he has created an eerie, complex, elusive work. Its few familiar landmarks have an unnerving tendency to shift position, alter their shape, disappear, leaving one lost and bewildered in a forbidding landscape. Interweaving reality and imagination, while mingling past, present, and future, Wiesel creates questions and ambiguities that will mystify even the wary, experienced traveler. By the simple device of deliberately omitting information he turns *Twilight* into a mystery story. Its clues tantalize without revealing. In a sense its form is perfectly suited to its function—for *Twilight* is a maddening book about madness.

Questions are central to both Wiesel's method and his philosophy —and *Twilight* is a novel dominated by questions. "In general," he has cautioned us, "all my work is a question mark. My work does not contain one single answer. It is always questions, questions I always try to deepen."[2] Interrogation remains for him—as for his readers— a challenge to explore unmarked territory. For Wiesel, most important of all, question leads to quest—to mystical quest.

The mystical quest of *Twilight* derives its suspense and mystery from the many questions that swirl around the life of Raphael Lipkin, a professor of mysticism and a survivor of the Holocaust. Though he is not a mystic himself, Lipkin finds himself intrigued by the messianic implications of mysticism. More than forty years after his liberation, he is still so haunted by his memories, he is still so guilt-ridden by his survival that he feels his sanity is at stake. Prompted by a series of anonymous telephone calls, he takes a summer job at

163

the Mountain Clinic, an asylum in upstate New York maintained exclusively for schizophrenics, where he hopes to obtain information about his friend Pedro, a Polish Jew who has been missing in the Gulag ever since the war. Still wounded by his divorce, troubled by his separation from his daughter, Rachel, unsettled by the anonymous phone calls, and sensing his own fears in the madness of the inmates of the asylum, Lipkin is appalled to find himself on "the edge of the abyss" (72).

In exploring Lipkin's tormented soul, Wiesel raises so many questions that he almost overwhelms his novel. Many of them revolve around the identity of the major characters and their place in the scheme of the story, even as Lipkin himself seeks their meaning in his life. *"What business do I have with these madmen?"* (201), he wonders at the Mountain Clinic. *"And Pedro in all this?"* (204), he asks himself. *"And Rachel in all this?"* (102). The same questions hover over the anonymous caller, his ex-wife Tiara, a mysterious old madman he has known since his childhood, and Dr. Benedictus, the director of the Mountain Clinic. To consider these questions is to have the distinctly uneasy feeling that nothing about these characters, or about *Twilight* itself, is what it seems.

While all these questions trouble Lipkin, at the center of his torment is the question of God's silence during the Holocaust, a question Wiesel has asked from the very beginning of his career. For him all roads eventually lead to the Holocaust. "No matter what we do," he writes, "no matter what the subject, no matter in what direction we go, somehow we end up studying the Holocaust as though all questions and perhaps even all answers are embodied in it —and truly they are."[3] For Wiesel the Holocaust is "the question of questions. It is both man's way of questioning God and God's way of questioning man."[4] In *Twilight* the focus is most emphatically on the questioning of God.

Ever since his experience of the Holocaust, Elie Wiesel has engaged in a quarrel with God—a lover's quarrel, to be sure, but a quarrel nonetheless. It is a quarrel that has long fascinated those who have followed his career. In *Twilight* he accepts, as never before, the challenge and the risk of taking it public. "Whose fault was it?

Whose responsibility?" (211), he asks here. "Only God could vanquish evil, halt the massacres, end the wars. Why didn't He?" (211). Lipkin finds his "head . . . spinning with eternal questions about the Eternal One" (212), and he is all but crushed by them. *"Questions, endless questions. Why so many victims? Why so many children among the victims? Why the indifference of the Allies?"* (197), he wants to know. Always he returns to the ultimate question: *"Why the silence of God?"* (197). Central to the novel, this question offers the most promising approach to its meaning.

Wiesel explores the possibilities inherent in the question of questions, first of all, and most directly, by the emphasis he places upon the strange, improbable inmates of the Mountain Clinic. With few exceptions, each of them is convinced he is a character out of the Bible and tells his story *"with an inspiration that carries him back to the twilight of history"* (202). The very first man Lipkin meets, in fact, thinks he is Adam—he is an Adam, however, who wants nothing less than that God admit the failure of his experiment and put an end to it. Subsequently, he encounters, among others, an angry Cain who believes man "poisons everything he touches" (58), an Abraham who thinks himself responsible for his son's death during the Holocaust, a Joseph convinced his father intended to send him to his death. Unable to come to terms with either God or man in our Holocaust era, these tormented souls have been confined within the walls of the mysterious Mountain Clinic, a strange and improbable asylum, *"the only one of its kind in the world"* (71), it seems. Wiesel places them in the hands of the mysterious Dr. Benedictus and his staff, whose twentieth-century psychiatric techniques are obviously irrelevant to the special madness they seek to cure.

Though Wiesel does not provide enough information to identify either the clinic or its director, clearly the inmates of the clinic are no ordinary schizophrenics. Where once in *Messengers of God* Adam, Cain, Abraham, Jacob, and Joseph were Wiesel's messengers *of* God, in *Twilight* he has transformed them and other biblical figures as well into disappointed and desperate messengers *to* God. Once the outriders for God, adventurers sallying forth from "the twilight of history" (202), burdened with the messianic ideal of redeeming man, today, insulted and injured by twentieth-century history but alive still in the Holocaust era we all now inhabit, they have, according to Wiesel, a very different mission: the redemption of God.

Wiesel probes the question of questions still further through another madman, one even more mysterious than those in the Mountain Clinic. He is the nameless old madman who befriends the young Raphael Lipkin before the Holocaust comes to their hometown. Captured by the Nazis and about to be executed by them, instead of saying the *"Shma* — *'Listen, Israel, God is one God'* " — he cries out, "God of Israel: *Listen to the people Israel!"* a very different thing, "something else, not the opposite but something else" (34). Plea, warning, protest, demand — each of these or all of them or something else — his is a desperate, pure call, filled with immense pain and sorrow. It questions God's role during the Holocaust and, by extension, his role in all the suffering that has characterized Jewish history.

A number of other stories add unexpected and surprising links to Wiesel's exploration of the question of questions, even as they provide clues vital to understanding Lipkin's story.

One is the story that an anonymous inmate of the Mountain Clinic tells about his own death, his wait for three days after his burial for the angel inquisitor to come knocking at his grave and ask his name, and his fear of the consequences of forgetting it. The Dead Man relates how he remembered his name only after his dead father appeared before him, how he found himself unable to speak, how his plea to God to unseal his lips failed, and how, thereupon, the angel inquisitor opened his grave, took him "in the palm of his hand, his icy and fiery hand," and a moment later hurled him into "the *Kaf Hakela,* the space outside space, outside time, far from God, far from everything" (144), where he claims he has been ever since.

Another is Lipkin's "farewell story" to Dr. Benedictus. As he is about to leave the Mountain Clinic, Lipkin tells him the tale of a poor, childless Jew who seeks out the Bescht for a blessing, receives it, and a year later becomes the father of a son. When the boy dies six years later, the father brings his body to the home of the Bescht only to learn that the Bescht has died four years earlier. Taking his son's body to the Bescht's grave, he places it there and says, "Master, I asked you for a living child, not a dead child" (206), then leaves. Then "from his grave," concludes Lipkin, "the *Besht* spoke to the boy: 'Cry out, my child, you must cry out, while your father is still in the cemetery, before he crosses the gate. If you do, he will hear you and take you home. If you don't, he will leave and you will die again' " (206).

Shortly before the Dead Man of the first story begins his narration, he angrily challenges Lipkin. "You ignoramus!" he screams. "You don't know who I am? Do you know who *you* are? Tell me, who are you? What is your name? Your father's name? What are you waiting for? Answer me. Hurry up, the angel will come any minute" (134). And Lipkin recognized that, for the moment, the Dead Man has become the angel inquisitor, awaiting a response from him.

These stories suggest a number of illuminating relationships. The angel inquisitor, for example, calls to the dead man in the grave, just as the Bescht calls to the dead child on his grave. The angel demands that the dead man speak out and give his name; the Bescht urges the dead child to call out to its father. The Dead Man cannot speak out, and the child remains silent. The penalty for the Dead Man is to be hurled into infinity, into eternal, irretrievable exile. The penalty for the child if he should fail to speak is to die again. When the dead patient takes on the role of the angel inquisitor, it is Raphael who, in turn, symbolically becomes a corpse in the grave, a dead man who is being challenged to identify himself, to cry out, and who must face eternal exile if he remains silent.

One more story: Zelig, an inmate of the Mountain Clinic who "does not live in Biblical times" (171), tells how the very magnitude and mystery of the Holocaust have driven him mad, for not only have six million Jews been murdered but the killers have "made the corpses disappear" (173). Unable to find the graves in any cemetery anywhere, he has at last discovered the dead in the sky. And even as he speaks to Lipkin he sees "a procession of adolescents" coming toward them. "I see you. I don't mean here . . . I mean up there. With them . . ." (174), he tells Lipkin.

But how are all these stories connected to Wiesel's exploration of the question of questions? To begin with, we must recognize that *Twilight*, like all Wiesel's work, has its roots in *Night*, and that

Twilight, like *Night,* itself, has its origin in Wiesel's first encounter with François Mauriac.

Described in "An Interview Unlike Any Other," in *A Jew Today,* the encounter proved to be a turning point in Wiesel's life. "I think that you are wrong. You are wrong not to speak," Mauriac told him. "Listen to the old man that I am: one must speak out—one must *also* speak out."[5] Mauriac's insistence that Wiesel end his ten-year silence and tell his story in effect initiated Wiesel's career. Central to Wiesel's work ever since, Mauriac's words provide a key to some of the mysteries of *Twilight.*

From the moment—at the end of *Night*—that a corpse looks back from the mirror into the survivor's eyes, Wiesel's life becomes the story of a divided self: of the child he once was—and of the survivor who has carried that child within himself ever since the fall of night. As he told one interviewer, "When my father died, I died. That means that one 'I' in me died."[6] The child he once was is the same child Zelig has seen walking in the procession of the dead; and the survivor is the one who refused to speak of his own death for ten years after his liberation.

Just as Mauriac urged the young journalist who came to interview him to go beyond his silence, to speak out to the world, so does the Bescht urge the dead child lying on his grave to cry out to its father. To cry out is to live; not to do so is to "die again" (206) or, like the Dead Man in the Mountain Clinic, to be hurled into eternal exile. Just as Mauriac cried out against the silence of Elie Wiesel, Wiesel cried out against the silence of the world in *Night* and cries out against the silence of God in *Twilight.* Just as Wiesel, the survivor is the grave for the child he once was, Lipkin is the grave for his dead.

Moreover, by voicing their disappointments in God, the messengers of God cry out to Him against his silence. The call of the mystical old madman—"God of Israel: *Listen to the people Israel!*" (34)—is likewise a cry to Him against his silence.

Only if the dead child on the grave of the Bescht breaks his silence will his father hear him and take him home. The ambiguities inherent in the words *father* and *home* aside, only if Lipkin cries out against the silence of God will he escape total exile, eternal and irremediable separation from God. And Wiesel the same.

While *Twilight* is clearly a cry against silence—against God's silence and against any acceptance of that silence—the absence of answers to the "question of questions" and other questions inevitably haunts the reader. "Why is it wrong," Wiesel has been asked, "to suppose a question has an answer?" His reply, as applicable to *Twilight* as to his other work, is that answers are dangerous because they satisfy, while "a question dissatisfies."[7] He fears that "what divides people is not the question, it is the answer."[8] As for the specific question of questions, "I am afraid of the answer—that is, of the wrong answer," and so he chooses to "keep the question open."[9]

Wiesel announces the significance of the question to him in his very first book. As Moshe the Beadle explains: "Man raises himself toward God by the questions he asks Him. . . . That is the true dialogue. Man questions God and God answers. But we don't understand His answers. We can't understand them. Because they come from the depths of the soul, and they stay there until death. You will find the true answers, Eliezer, only within yourself!"[10] When Raphael Lipkin says, *"I don't mind feeling the touch of death as long as . . . I can raise myself toward God"* (71), one can hear the echo of the beadle's words. It is of the essence of being a Jew, Wiesel feels, "not to give answers. To be a Jew is to ask questions and to live these questions."[11]

Moreover, from a literary point of view, Wiesel believes it is "in art, particularly in literature," that questions are "allowed to remain unanswered."[12] Nor is catharsis his goal in his writing: "I do not believe in catharsis. Catharsis is much too easy. I believe in inner exploration—to explore your own universe. Every writer has only one universe. He should not have more. I do not want to get relief from this universe. On the contrary, I want to explore it."[13] It is questions—only and always questions—that enable him to engage in the adventure of that exploration.

The question of the silence of God has remained a subject of Wiesel's art from *Night* to *Twilight*. As he told a radio audience, "The more I think about it, and the more I live, and the more I meet myself in my own memories, the deeper the question becomes—and the deeper the mystery."[14] And as he remarked to a university audience, "My disputation with God still goes on. To me it was an injustice on a theological scale, on a universal scale. God was silent, and therefore His silence was unjust." [15] In *Twilight*, Wiesel goes still deeper into the mystery and continues still further with his disputation.

Wiesel sees literature as a "way of correcting injustices." He sees art as "a way of saying no — no to reality, no to God, no to man." [16] In *Twilight* he says no to God's injustice, following a tradition that extends "from Adam to Moses, and Abraham to Job, from all our great sages down to . . . Levi-Yitzhak of Berditchev," the tradition that one may question God and "say no to God on behalf of His Creation, on behalf of one's people, one's community." [17] Nowhere in all his writings does Wiesel consider the question of the silence of God or its injustice with greater intensity than he does in *Twilight*. So great is this intensity that it bears comparison with his achievement in *Night*. Originally written in Yiddish, *Night* was called *Un di Velt Hot Geshvign* (And the world was silent). Had Wiesel written *Twilight* in Yiddish he might well have called it *Un Gott Hot Geshvign* (And God was silent).

The emotional intensity of *Twilight* stems from Raphael Lipkin's spiritual crisis. Lipkin's struggle against insanity parallels the "struggle against melancholy" of the great eighteenth-century Hasidic masters that Wiesel portrays in *Four Hasidic Masters*. He is just as mortally engaged in an existential encounter with nothingness as they were. His struggle is, if anything, more desperate and more despairing, for it includes not only his personal experience of the Holocaust but his postwar knowledge of its magnitude as well.

The encounter begins in the days of the ghetto, when young Raphael's brother brings home his account of a Nazi massacre of the Jews. Raphael understands his brother's words, "but not the enormity of their meaning." Nevertheless, he cannot avoid the question of God's failure to act:

Whose fault was it? Whose responsibility? Horror on this scale implicated not only man but God as well. . . . Could He be on the side of the killers? Raphael rejected that notion. God on the side of evil? Unthinkable. Was He not the opposite of evil? He told himself that he would never accept the idea that God could be cruel. Man could be cruel, not God. He was convinced of it. But then, what about the killings in Kolomey? Yes, that was worse than the concept of a cruel God or an indifferent God. (211)

Not yet having experienced the full force of the Holocaust, young Raphael is able to resolve his initial torment, but the existential questioning has begun.[18] By the time of his liberation, however, when he first learns of the immense scale of the Holocaust, a "monstrous anguish" (211) overtakes him. It is an existential anguish that never leaves him.

Four decades later, in the last few, climactic pages of *Twilight*, Lipkin looks inward yet again and once more confronts "that terrible question: *And what about God in all this?*" (214). He must face a terrifying fear that has grown within him through the years: "Before God, there was God. And after God? After God, there is nothing" (214). In short, Lipkin finds himself in a classic existential encounter with nothingness. His existential lucidity must end in despair and, beyond despair, in insanity. The abyss from which there is no return yawns before him.

But, as always, Wiesel refuses to yield to despair. As always, for Elie Wiesel a tale of despair is a tale against despair. The mysterious, nameless old madman offers something else—something else to fill the vacuum, to replace nothingness. He enters the novel on the first page, leaves it on the last, and appears at crucial points between. A mystical figure, he introduces young Raphael to Kabbala and promises to guide the boy "toward knowledge" (13) and beyond:

"If ever you're afraid to go forward," said the madman, "hold onto me tightly. That way you won't fall. True, the road is treacherous. Satan is full of tricks. . . . But bear in mind that he fears courage, so don't ever close your eyes, my boy. If you wish to accompany me, you must promise to keep your eyes open. Otherwise [Satan] . . . will attack you and all will be lost. Remember: a madman is someone whose eyes are always open." (13–14)

Raphael promises to follow the old madman, and *Twilight* is the story of how he keeps that promise.

From the very beginning of the novel he takes a special interest in the young Raphael's physical health and safety. He imposes upon the boy the obligation of surviving typhus, saves him during the Holocaust (hiding with him in a cemetery grave), foretells his future.

He knows beforehand—because of his "negotiations with heaven" (25–26)—that Raphael will survive the Holocaust. Enigmatically, he tells the boy, "I shall die in your place" (26). But even after his execution he somehow "survives" in the life of both the boy and the man.

The mysterious old madman is equally involved in Lipkin's spiritual survival. He forces Lipkin to recognize that his all-consuming concern with the Holocaust dead is self-destructive. "To refuse to live," the voice of the madman warns him, "is an act of treason not only toward the living, but also toward the dead" (132). Lipkin, he insists, must choose "to live without the dead, to live and remember the dead" (132).

The old madman's preoccupation with life and death heightens the mystery surrounding him. "You see," he tells young Raphael, "whenever one of our people dies, I die for him and with him. Oh, I know: it's difficult to understand. Never mind. It's not necessary to understand everything in life" (34–35). He is a "madman who had been dying so long he claimed to be immortal." And he insists to Raphael that all those "who have carried the Word—and have been carried by it" (132–133), all those who have died in the Holocaust, including Raphael's parents, are alive "in me and in you" (132). In calling out for the God of Israel to listen to the people Israel he becomes the spokesman for the people Israel, a bearer today of Wiesel's no to God. Ubiquitous, defying reality as he does, he would seem to be a deus ex machina. He is not. Ever vital, ever recurrent, the mystical old madman is, rather, a symbol of Jewish survival, of the immortality of the Jewish people.

His mystical power is concentrated in his voice and in his eyes, in a voice that has the power to take Lipkin "back to the beginning of his people's adventure" (133) in history and in eyes that reflect "a distant, mysterious light" (26). "*Since the beginning of history*," Wiesel explains in *The Town Beyond the Wall*, "*madmen have represented the divine presence: the light in their eyes comes bathed in the source.*"[19] In promising to "*follow in the footsteps of a mad old man who died more than once*," Lipkin is determined to "*rediscover his madness*" and to "*return to its source*" (28). "*I will become a madman who dreams of twilight*," he says—that is, of a "*twilight of history*," a twilight that is *"the domain of madness"* (202). The madness that inspires the mad old man, the madness Lipkin is determined to follow, is the madness of the faith of the Jews—a madness derived from their God—a dream that is still alive and must be kept alive despite the silence of the source and, if necessary, instead of that silence. If God has been found wanting, the Jewish people have not. To return to the source is to begin again, to rebuild on the dream of Him, to find inspiration and renewal in the source of the dream, to continue the vision of the Jew in spite of God and man.

When Lipkin says, *"I cry into the night and the night does not answer. Never mind, I will shout and shout until I go deaf, until I go mad. Mad? Yes, I will become a madman who dreams of twilight"* (202). it is as though he has become Wiesel's Just Man of Sodom, whose shouts of warning are also ignored. Asked why he continues to shout, since his shouting seems so hopeless, the Just Man answers, "In the beginning, I thought I could change man. Today, I know I cannot. If I still shout today, if I still scream, it is to prevent man from ultimately changing me."[20] If Lipkin cannot change God, if he still shouts against the silence of God, it is to prevent the silence of God from ultimately changing him. But whatever the meaning of God's silence, as long as Lipkin the madman continues to shout, the dream that has its source in Him is still alive, still potent.

Twilight is a piercing cry against the silence of the grave, against the silence of the six million who cannot speak from the grave because they have no grave, and against the silence of a God who seems unable to hear their silence. *Twilight* is a piercing cry for the six million, a voice given to those who are forever mute. In following the mystic old madman, Lipkin joins in his passionate cry "God of Israel: *Listen to the people Israel!*" It is a cry that—one would think —even God himself must hear. Lipkin's cry is the only way he has to preserve both his sanity and his madness. Through it Elie Wiesel says no to God in *Twilight*—but he does so on behalf of the Jewish people.

"In *Ani Maamin*," Wiesel says, "I tested the absence of faith, just as in *Night* I tested faith."[21] In *Twilight* he tests the madness of faith. For him this madness is an answer to insanity. "In order to save myself from *that* madness," he told an interviewer, "I go back to another madness—a holy madness—the one that became a victim, the one that kept us alive for . . . thousands of years." And he added, "No, I wouldn't say that I am not mad."[22]

In *Twilight* Elie Wiesel shares with us his unshakable vision of the immortality of the Jewish people, the madmen of history, who thousands of years ago embarked upon a great mad adventure, embodied in their concept of God, and remain stubbornly dedicated, despite the denials of history and Holocaust, to the proposition that law and justice, understanding and compassion are still possible, must be possible if men are ever to live in peace. He sees in their mystical madness a people forever renewing itself, forever finding its renewal in its mysterious source. He sees the Jewish people as "haunted by the beginning more than by the end."[23] In their mystical madness he sees their undying commitment "to bring the Messiah. To make evil disappear and bring people together."[24] In Raphael Lipkin's promise to "follow in the footsteps" of the mystical old madman, to "rediscover his madness," and "to return to its source" (28), Wiesel reaffirms the stubborn hope of the Jewish people for the redemption of man and—in spite of God's silence—a rededication to it.

Wiesel refuses to let go of the question of questions, even as it will not let go of him. In *Twilight* he confronts the silence of God in the face of the absolute horror of the Holocaust and once more wrestles in anguish with its awesome mystery. As Lipkin explores the existential dimension of the mystery to the very edge of nothingness —to the very brink of insanity and death—he hears the voice of the old madman telling him *"to walk, to keep walking, even if night is near"* (202). It is a call to life, the call that has inspired the Jewish people from their beginning.

The Talmud, Wiesel tells us, defines the Jew as "someone who walks." A Jew, he explains, is "a wanderer. We are always on a journey."[25] Though Lipkin gains neither an answer to the question of God's silence nor a release from it, he triumphs over insanity and death. "Whoever walks in the night," says Moshe in *The Oath*, "moves against night."[26] Joining the procession not of the dead but of all who give life to the Jewish people, Raphael Lipkin—open eyed—will continue his journey against the night.

In prefacing *Twilight* with Maimonides' statement that "the world couldn't exist without madmen," Elie Wiesel offers us both warning and hope. In affirming the mission of the holy madmen of history to preserve and protect, to renew and continue the Jewish dream, in bringing us once again their transcendent vision, he walks forward — with them — against the night.

Notes

All notes identified only by volume number and page number are references to Irving Abrahamson, ed., *Against Silence: The Voice and Vision of Elie Wiesel*, 3 vols. (New York: Holocaust Publications, 1985).

1. Elie Wiesel, *Twilight*, trans. Marion Wiesel (New York: Summit Books, 1988). All internal page references are to this edition.
2. Elie Wiesel, "The Key to the Mystery" 3:197.
3. Elie Wiesel, "Telling the Tale" 1:235.
4. Elie Wiesel, "The Crisis of Hope" 1:144.
5. Elie Wiesel, *A Jew Today* (New York: Random House, 1978), 19.
6. Harry James Cargas, *Harry James Cargas in Conversation with Elie Wiesel* (New York: Paulist Press, 1976), 110.
7. Elie Wiesel, "The Silence between Question and Answer" 3:227.
8. Cargas, *Conversation*, 105.
9. Elie Wiesel, "The Open Question" 1:387.
10. Elie Wiesel, *Night* (New York: Hill and Wang, 1960), 14.
11. Elie Wiesel, "Questions for *Shabbat*" 1:261.
12. Elie Wiesel, *Messengers of God* (New York: Random House, 1976), 52.
13. Elie Wiesel, "The Writer and His Universe" 2:62.
14. Elie Wiesel, "Question and Quest" 3:93.
15. Elie Wiesel, "Questions and Answers: At the University of Oregon, 1975" 3:229.
16. Elie Wiesel, "To Correct Injustice" 2:85.
17. Wiesel "Question and Quest" 3:93.
18. Compare the published passage to the version that appears in the advance uncorrected proofs of *Twilight* (192):

    Could He be on the side of the killers? Raphael rejected that notion. God on the side of evil? Unthinkable. Was He not the opposite of evil? Getting increasingly agitated, he told himself that he would never accept that God could be cruel. Man could be cruel, not God. He was convinced of it. But then, what about the killings in Kolomey? His body was trembling. Could the trembling be his answer?

But there was worse. Yes, worse than the concept of a cruel God, or an indifferent God. In Jewish history, there is always worse.

Whatever it is in Jewish history that is worse than a cruel or indifferent God, and whatever other questions this version raises, including the decision to exclude it from *Twilight,* young Raphael's reaction is clearly existential fear and trembling.

19. Elie Wiesel, *The Town Beyond the Wall* (New York: Holt, Rinehart and Winston, 1964), 94.
20. Elie Wiesel, *One Generation After* (New York: Random House, 1970), 95.
21. Wiesel, "Questions and Answers," 230.
22. Cargas, *Conversation,* 2.
23. Wiesel, *Messengers of God,* xii.
24. Wiesel, "Questions and Answers," 232.
25. Elie Wiesel, "The Great Adventure" 3:257.
26. Elie Wiesel, *The Oath* (New York: Random House, 1973), 191.

15

Twilight: Madness, Caprice, Friendship, and God

Robert McAfee Brown

Elie Wiesel loves madmen. They people the pages of his novels with relentless consistency, some of them, like Moshe, returning in predictable fashion from book to book. This fascination with madness is not some voyeuristic desire on Wiesel's part to focus on crippled minds or bizarre deeds. On the contrary, it is part of his central concern to discover as much of the truth as we are privileged to discover. For it is his contention that madmen usually see the world more clearly than the so-called sane, and that their judgments are consequently more trustworthy. If this is so, Wiesel should consider himself in good company, since, as one of his characters in *The Town Beyond the Wall* comments, "God loves madmen. They're the only ones he allows near him."[1] Another character later picks up the refrain: "Since the beginning, madmen have represented the divine presence."[2]

Madness

In *Twilight*, his most recent novel,[3] Wiesel extends the logic of his concern for discerning the divine by giving us not only an occasional madman but a whole asylum full, inmates of Mountain Clinic in upstate New York. They have an interesting trait in common: with the exception of Zelig, they all think they are biblical characters: Adam, Cain, Abraham, Nadav (the son of Aaron), Joseph, the Messiah, and even, in the closing climactic pages a character who has assumed the role of God. In another part of the story, Yoel Lipkin takes upon himself the mantle of Jeremiah. Just to round out the cycle, Raphael Lipkin, the protagonist in the novel, from the very first words (which Wiesel says always stamp the nature of the story he is about to tell), thinks he is probably going mad, too, and spends a considerable amount of time testing his hypothesis.

This might sound like a dismal theme, even for serious readers who probably have enough reminders of madness in their own daily lives not to need further reinforcement from the world of fiction. But to those who think so, some countervailing factors should be noted.

One of them is that the madmen we encounter through the eyes of Raphael Lipkin are (like madmen in earlier Wiesel novels) extraordinarily perspicacious and offer perspectives on the world and God that are not only novel but profound. We stand to learn a great deal from them. This is particularly true of Abraham (to whom I shall return), if less so of the Messiah, who suffers from the existential handicap of being the son of a Protestant minister—which I consider an extremely clever theological riposte on Wiesel's part. We learn to sympathize with Cain and his overbearing father's preference for another sibling who may or may not exist, and, in the closing pages to agonize with God, who, it must be acknowledged, carries an extremely heavy burden of responsibility, particularly when pinned to the dialectical mat by the relentless questioning of Raphael, whose entire family and closest friend were devoured by the behemoth called the Holocaust. We will return to this episode also.

The most telling of these biblical characterizations, to my way of thinking, is the one of Adam, who devotes himself unremittingly to intercessory prayers. He has a very clear and unwavering agenda; he pleads day and night with God to call off the whole creation process immediately, since, as Adam can see with a prescience apparently denied to God, God peaked too early and from the moment of creation onward things are destined to go downhill. "Countless souls who will escape the curse of being born only to die," will applaud such divine self-restraint, Adam tells God. So will the trees that men will never cut down and burn, the animals who will never be slaughtered and eaten. All of creation, in fact, will laud the putative Creator who "does not shrink from admitting His error,"[4] and has the courage to close the book on creation before the first page has been turned. In a burst of generosity, Adam even offers to let God take credit for Adam's proposal, content that it be perceived as having emanated from a divine rather than a human source, so long as its content is honored.

If the portrayal of Adam is the most telling, the portrayal of Abraham is the most poignant. Jews (and all readers of the Bible) continually have to wrestle with the figure of Abraham, who is called upon by God to sacrifice his only son—a theme Wiesel has already dealt with powerfully in *Messengers of God*.[5] How would this heaviest of all burdens have a counterpart in the lives of Jews hiding from the Nazis in World War II? Wiesel shows us another Abraham who is able to command the trust and loyalty of his son, and yet who, like his biblical counterpart, fills the son with illusions that turn out to be destructive.

While the modern Abraham and his son are in hiding, the father keeps transmitting the Jewish heritage to the son through study and yet more study. The peasant who is protecting them cannot understand: why all the attention to books? The son will only be able to survive by learning to outrun his pursuers and live on herbs and pass as a Christian if captured. Abraham will have none of it. The power of the Word is everything, and the Word will protect them all.

But of course, as Abraham is later forced to acknowledge, "the Word did not save us."[6] Many Jews were rounded up. Many escaped because they could outrun their pursuers, live on herbs, and pass as Christians. But not Isaac. He had not been trained in those survival skills. And Abraham feels, knows, that it was the father's fault that the son did not survive.

Here a digression on madness is in order or we will miss the point. For Wiesel, there are varying degrees, or levels, of madness. We all know about clinical madness, infecting those who have simply lost touch with reality, see elephants under toadstools, receive messages from Martians through dental fillings, or feel mandated to kill all redheads because God has told them to. Such people we isolate from society for their own protection and ours, particularly if we are redheads. This is not the kind of madness with which Wiesel is concerned, however, even though the madness about which he writes can have the similar consequence of the sending of people to asylums.

Wiesel, on the contrary, writes about what he sometimes calls "mystical madness," or the madness of the prophets, the madness of those who see life in such a different perspective from the rest of us that the rest of us become uneasy in their presence and seek to incarcerate them or, if necessary, put them to death. The Hebrew prophets got this sort of treatment from the defenders of the status quo, Jesus of Nazareth got it from the Romans, Archbishop Romero got it from the military, and six million Jews got it from the Nazis.

The threat of the "mystically mad" is that they have such a different view of reality from ours, that if we don't dispose of them we will have to listen to them and take them seriously. And if we did that, a gnawing feeling of unease might rise in us to the point that we could no longer stifle it: since we cannot both be right, *what if they are right and we are wrong?*

This thought is not to be entertained. So, if annihilation is not a socially approved policy, we have to settle for incarceration, or at least ridicule, and calling them mad is often sufficiently degrading to remove them from our purview.

So the threat of Wiesel's madmen is that they may have a surer, saner corner on the truth than we do. A proposal: listen to the tales of the various biblical madmen that Raphael Lipkin interviews, and ask whether they may not be closer to the way things really are than their hearers.

Madness and Caprice

A second reason the book does not pall in anticipation is that it contains other plot threads in addition to the stories of life in an asylum for the mentally disturbed. The central design in the overall tapestry is the story of the Lipkin family. It is not a happy story; indeed, it is an utterly tragic one, and it is possible to see how anyone who survived it might, like Raphael, always be fearful of going mad, clinically and not just mystically. But in contrast to the dreams of many madmen, the Lipkin story is drenched in all of the tangible horror of the "real world," a world of invasions, battles, informers, rare moments of beauty, frequent moments of epidemics, cowardice, courage, refugees, heroic actions, and tragic miscalculations. Once into it, no reader is going to be able to set it aside. It is the story, finally, of the annihilation of a Jewish family at the hand of the Nazis, a story Wiesel has told in many forms before, but never, perhaps, so sparsely or starkly.

The consistent theme in the story, it seems to me upon reflection, is caprice, and that is certainly a truth about the Holocaust we need to keep relearning. Yes, there was human design, and diabolical design, in the planning and carrying out of the Holocaust, but there was absolutely no logic, no rationale, no chain of events, that dictated why this person should survive and not that one; there was no relationship between virtue and survival, or even between wisdom and survival. There was only caprice: a safe hiding place would be discovered on the only day it was used; a brash act might (or, equally, might not) contribute to survival; an evasive action useful on one day would guarantee capture on the next or preceeding day; a plan that worked for one family would, under identical outward circumstances, mutate into a trap sprung on another family. The Greeks had an expression for all this: Whirl is king, having overthrown Zeus. Holocaust version: Caprice reigns, having displaced Yahweh.

The story of the Lipkin family's gradual but inexorable dismemberment may be a compelling reason for madness, a justification for seeing the utter folly of the universe, and asserting, as several characters in the book assert, that the only sensible way to view the destruction is to posit that God, too, is mad, mad enough to let such things happen. In such a mood one could embrace the sanity of the mad Adam in suggesting that the whole venture of creation was at best (or at worst) a divine miscalculation, and that, once inaugurated, it could not be (or at least was not) retrieved in time.

So the first and second stories—of the mad inmates and the vortex of the Holocaust—intersect more fully than might appear on an

initial reading, and it is a matter of artistic skill as well as philosophical achievement to have interwoven them as skillfully as Wiesel
does, by the device of having the sole survivor of the Lipkin family
spend a summer interrogating the self-avowed biblical characters at
the Mountain Clinic. Raphael arrives there as a result of an impetus
provided by his involvement in a third story, the story of Pedro, a
story that turns out to be a powerful thread holding together the
apparently disparate stories of the inmates of the asylum and the
visitor Raphael.

Caprice and Friendship

Our knowledge of Pedro's story unfolds with tantalizing slowness,
which we must grudgingly acknowledge to be another mark of Wiesel's artistry. From the first page on, there are frequent italicized
portions representing Raphael's interior dialogues with Pedro (more
of them, interestingly enough, in the English translation than in the
original French, *Le crépuscule au loin*). it would not be fair to the
author to unmask too much of the Pedro story to those who have not
read the book, and even if the attempt were made it might be
inaccurate, for Pedro is an enigmatic character, and Wiesel keeps
his tracks pretty well covered until it is in his own interest to divulge
more. I mistakenly thought for about two-thirds of the book that
Pedro represented the reappearance of a central character from Wiesel's earlier novel *The Town Beyond the Wall*. Both are named Pedro,
both are redemptive presences, both comment very astutely on the
human scene, both give good advice and example to younger compa-
triots, both take inordinate risks to save others. But the earlier Pedro
was explicitly not Jewish, while the Pedro of *Twilight* was originally
named Pinhas, a fact that, just to make matters more ambiguous, is
omitted in the English translation. (The creation of such dilemmas
for the reader is vintage Wiesel.)

But whoever he may be, Pedro not only tracks Raphael down after
the war as a Jewish child with no family left and therefore in need of
help, but he subsequently promises to rescue Raphael's brother,
Yoel, when it is discovered that Yoel is in a psychiatric ward in

Krasnograd, a likely place for him to have ended up, considering the horrors to which he was subjected during the war.

Pedro estimates the odds of succeeding on this wild mission as fifty-fifty, and elaborate plans are made for the rescue. The odds are insufficient. The attempt fails. Yoel does not escape. Pedro does not return.

Much of Raphael Lipkin's subsequent quest in life is to find out what happened to Pedro, and to secure his freedom if he is still alive. Several years later, after writing a laudatory article about Pedro, Raphael begins to receive ugly, anonymous phone calls that impugn Pedro's integrity, asserting that he became an informer in captivity. The calls leave Raphael outraged and frustrated, until the caller cryptically suggests that he go to the Mountain Clinic where he may perhaps receive enlightenment about the "true" Pedro.

Departure of Raphael to the Mountain Clinic. He starts interviewing patients, ostensibly to continue a study of mysticism and madness, and we wait with mounting suspense for a denouement in which the mystery of Pedro will be unveiled and the calumnies against him exposed for what they are. Is Pedro one of the biblically inspired madmen? Has one of the members of the staff had contact with him elsewhere? Is someone at the clinic the originator of the mysterious phone calls, perhaps Dr. Benedictus himself?

How neatly the threads of these three stories could have been woven together by a second-rate novelist. But how true to his theme and the lives of his characters that Wiesel refuses to succumb to such an artifice. And how powerfully communicative of the uncertainty that persists for all Holocaust "survivors," that the threads of the many stories do *not* come together, and that ambiguity has the last word. Raphael even wonders at one point whether the phone calls were simply the product of his demented imagination.

The title is, after all, *Twilight*, a time when things are ambiguous, hard to see, and our vision plays tricks on us. Readers of Wiesel are aware that his first three books are entitled *Night*, *Dawn*, and *Day* (the latter rendered as *The Accident* in English).[7] *Night* was the story of his time in Auschwitz and the title was grimly and straightforwardly descriptive. Both *Dawn* and *Day*, however, were ironic titles, describing what turned out to be the moral cul-de-sacs of being an executioner or attempting to deal with the permanently searing experience of "the kingdom of night." *Twilight*, like *Night*, seems to be a descriptive rather than ironic title, though its symbolism is powerful. "Twilight," as Raphael informs Pedro, "is the domain of madness.[8] It is the time when things often appear other than they are, and vision is not as keen as one would wish. It is the time of madmen who may see clearly in the twilight hour what is hidden from the rest of us, for whom ambiguity remains the order of the day.

Friendship and God

It is in the twilight that the climactic interview with God takes place. Raphael's bags are packed, a farewell dinner has been held, and yet before going to the station he takes a final walk around the grounds of the asylum, sensing intuitively that there is still something more he has to learn before his departure.

And there he finds, as though waiting for him, the patient who thinks he is God. [God is brooding over the way creation has gone astray.] Raphael feels the need to pursue the subject. Where, after all, is the divine pity, and why has it always been used so sparingly? How can God justify all the human suffering, of which Raphael has seen more than his share?

God is taken aback by Raphael's insistent probing, but attempts a response. God "could have prevented the killer from being born, his accomplice from growing up, mankind from going astray." Yes. But there is still a problem: "Can you tell me," God asks Raphael, "at what precise moment I should have intervened to keep the children from being thrown into the flames? At the very last moment? Why not before? But when is 'before' "?[9] God turns the enigma back to the interlocutor.

And Raphael responds, first calmly and then in agitation: "Merciful God, God of Love, where were you and where was your love when under the seal of blood and fire the killers obliterated thousands of Jewish communities?" These are words, Raphael tells himself, "demanding to be spoken."[10]

God, described now by Wiesel as "the patient," is deeply hurt.

And Raphael, discerning what he thinks are tears on the cheeks of the other, regrets his harsh words.

But after an interlude in which Raphael remembers three individual heart-rending episodes that illustrate God's complicity with human evil, the conversation continues. And the important thing that emerges in the concluding exchanges is that God urges Raphael not to cry for himself. Rather, "Cry for the others. And for me too."[11]

The last four words seem to have been wrenched out of God's mouth. Are we to cry not only *to* God but also *for* God? Could God need human beings to share God's burden of sorrow as much as human beings need God to share their burden of sorrow? The theme echoes an exegesis of Ecclesiastes that a Midrashic scholar had once shared with Raphael, in which the constant theme goes We Must Pity God.

The mystery of evil is not resolved in this interview with the patient who thinks he is God. It never will be in any interview, no matter who the participants are. But the exchange provides the possibility of a new link between ourselves and God. Yes, we must challenge God, we must be angry with God, we must even on occasion rebuke God. But we can also feel sorry for God. We can, in the words of the Midrashic jester, "pity" God. God, too, is saddened by the state of creation. God, too, feels the pain of others. We can believe that it is a pain that wounds the heart of God as well as the hearts of God's children. Perhaps such recognition is a way of coming closer to God.

Further credence is given to this suggestion when we reflect on the name of the protagonist in the novel, chosen, as in all Wiesel's novels, with special care. In *Twilight*, the name is Rapha-el, which means "the healer of God," or as it can also be rendered, "God the Healer." Perhaps in heaven as on earth it is also true that the only authentic healer is the wounded healer.

God and Friendship

But the novel does not end in heaven. It ends on earth. What remains, at the end, when the author refuses to let the plot fall into a tidy pattern on either the human or the divine level? What remains a positive part of human experience in the midst of much that is negative, is a story of human friendship. In a world that seemed continually to scoff at the notion that anything like friendship or commitment or concern could survive, it was an act of courage to be committed to anything. We are privileged to share in the creation of deep bonds between two brave people—Pedro and Raphael—people who will risk everything for the sake of others, people who enlist our admiration because at a time when it would have been easy for either of them to turn inward and say, "I've suffered enough," both are ever willing to turn outward and say, "There are people in need, we must help them."

Is this enough to justify the creation that scars all survivors and destroys all victims? Raphael and God, as we have just seen, are still debating that question at the end of the novel, and the question is unanswerable from any perspective to which we have access. But, as [Wiesel says time and again, it is the questions, not the answers, that are the important thing] We will never know the answers, but we can keep refining the questions and refusing to surrender them to easy speculation, and it is this relentless pursuit of what can never be found but must always be sought, that marks Elie Wiesel as not only a thinker of importance but an artist as well.

One cannot chart the future path of a creative artist. Perhaps not even the artist knows what will come next, and if he does he must always be open to events that may intervene to change his course. Even so, I am intrigued by the possibilities of a continuation in a sequence that goes, at present, *Night, Dawn, Day, Twilight.* What comes next? A demon, perhaps, suggests to me that there should be a volume entitled *Midnight,* exploring the profound Kierkegaardian question, "Do you not know that there comes a midnight hour when all must unmask?"

What Wiesel could do with such a theme . . .

Notes

1. Elie Wiesel, *The Town Beyond the Wall*, trans. Stephen Becker (New York: Holt, Rinehart and Winston, 1964), 19.
2. Ibid., 101.
3. Elie Wiesel, *Twilight*, trans. Marion Wiesel (New York: Summit Books, 1988).
4. Ibid., 39.
5. Elie Wiesel, *Messengers of God: Biblical Portraits and Legends*, trans. Marion Wiesel (New York: Random House, 1976).
6. Wiesel, *Twilight*, 98.
7. Elie Wiesel, *Night* (New York: Avon Books, 1960); Elie Wiesel, *Dawn* (New York: Avon Books, 1970); Elie Wiesel, *The Accident* (New York: Avon Books, 1970).
8. Wiesel, *Twilight*, 202.
9. Ibid., 208.
10. Ibid., 208–9.
11. Ibid., 213.

16

Night: The Absence of God?
The Presence of God?
A Meditation in Three Parts

Jean-Marie Lustiger

How can one discuss the work of Elie Wiesel without speaking about the man? To separate one from the other would amount to betraying both, for Elie Wiesel is completely in his work. He is *one of the great theologians* of our century.

Such an assertion may come as a surprise. Elie Wiesel himself will not admit to being a "theologian." He shies away from what those who consider themselves theologians call theological thinking. He even goes so far as to continually remind us that strictly speaking Jewish theology does not exist.

Elie Wiesel dismisses the idea that he is a theologian doing theology. Yet, he is certainly cognizant of the theology that talks about God, but tends to culminate in a kind of rational and coherent whole that leads some people to deny its very object. Those who wrote the theologies of the death of God or even the atheistic theologies claimed to be theologians. Elie Wiesel is clearly not a theologian in that sense. "How strange," he wrote, "that the philosophy denying God came not from the survivors. Those who came out with the so-called God is dead theology, not one of them had been in Auschwitz." [1]

But one may also conceive of a theologian in another way: it is a person to whom God speaks and who, in turn, speaks to God and then tells the story; it is a person whom God seeks and who himself searches for God and then communicates the experience; it is a person whom God nourishes with the scroll of his Word, commanding him to utter it. God's Word is as sweet as honey on the tongue, even when it voices "lamentations, wails and reproaches" (Jer. 2 and 3).

In this sense, Elie Wiesel has been a theologian since he was a child, and he has never ceased to be one. He could not help it — even during the dark night of Auschwitz. Quite the opposite is true. He tells us that as a child, "at night I ran to the synagogue to weep over the destruction of the Temple . . . I wept [when I prayed] because — because of something inside me that felt the need for tears."[2]

When he returns to the devastated sanctuary of his childhood soul, Elie may find there the "gift of tears" that God grants to those He loves. Tears and joy without cause are inexpressible yet certain signs of God's presence. This sanctuary of his childhood was burnt to the ground when Elie witnessed the Germans hurl into the "huge flames" of the furnace a truckload of small children still alive. "Babies! Yes, I saw it — saw it with my own eyes . . . those children in the flames."[3]

The blaze dried his tears. The Word became both silence and absence, and in his exile, which no words can describe, Wiesel wrote: "My eyes were open and I was alone — terribly alone in a world without God and without man."[4] This unimaginable ordeal of faith is part and parcel of the struggle of faith. This is what Elie Wiesel ceaselessly keeps telling us, ever since he recovered the ability to speak the Word. To be a theologian is to chart this path and to struggle continually with God's incomprehensible love for His forsaken and distressed people.

Nor can one ever cease questioning the unfathomable patience of the Almighty. Before Noah, God established an everlasting Covenant with all flesh. In His Mercy, He promised that He would never destroy His creation again, even though, strictly speaking, justice might require Him to do so. And yet, why does God allow men to commit the absurd injustice of destroying each other and the earth along with them? And how and when will He fulfill the promise made to Abraham and the oath sworn to David? Yes, whoever questions and even challenges God, all the while desiring to obey His Word and listening to His silence, that person *is* a theologian.

To be a theologian is to acknowledge how incomprehensible God's ways are, and yet never cease to follow them. Is Elie Wiesel a theologian? Yes, in the same way as is any Jew who realizes that he rests in the hand of God, even as he contemplates the history of his people. True theology is a life that is faithful to God. We recognize it in the works of writers like Charles Peguy, in the diaries of St. Thérèse of Lisieux, who spent her life in prayer, the great achievements of Catholic theology in this century.

Do not conclude that this definition of the theologian—already given by the Fathers of the Church—is intended to reject as worthless the speculative power of human reason. On the contrary, in the expectation of the Final Judgment, it gives rationality its rightful place. Whoever, in order to justify his avoidance of God, would be tempted to make use of the dreadful confession of the child whose soul was devoured by the black flames[5] ought to ponder the following words: "Anyone who is an obstacle to bring down one of these little ones who have faith would be better thrown into the sea with a great millstone round his neck!" (Mark 9:42).

Elie Wiesel received the Nobel Prize for *Peace*, not the Nobel Prize for Literature. Therefore, it is not his literary oeuvre that has been celebrated, but that to which he himself and his writings bear witness: the fate of the Jewish people recognized as a sign of peace for all men and women.

The granting of this award is not an expression of atonement for the six million Jews who were slaughtered by the Nazis. Elie Wiesel told us that the honor bestowed upon him "belongs to all the survivors and their children and, through us, to the Jewish people with whose destiny I have always identified."[6] For the "final solution" was not meant to annihilate some individual Jews but the entire Jewish people. The alleged scientific nature of the racist definitions of the Jewish identity cast the light of the glaring inferno upon God's promise.

In his commentary on the Book of Job, Elie Wiesel writes: "Job was not Jewish; but his ordeal concerns all humanity, just as the suffering of the Jewish people ought to concern all humanity. Will

the day ever come when the crimes against the Jews will be considered as crimes against humanity, and the crimes against humanity
as crimes against the Jewish people?"[7]

How and why can one claim the privilege of such a mission?
Should one support his prerogative by keeping a tally of sufferings,
or by measuring abominations, or by computing countless numbers
of victims? On what sort of scales could we weigh history and its
forgotten crimes? Who would dare explore, for example, the bottom-
less depths of contempt into which over three centuries the slave
trade flung forty million black Africans? Or was it sixty million?
Historians are unable to agree when it comes to these numbers. And
yet the Jewish people received this mission against which it struggles
but which it will never give up, as Elie Wiesel constantly reminds
us. "I had believed that the mission of the Jews was to represent the
trembling of history rather than the wind which made it tremble,"
says Elisha, the hero of Wiesel's second book, *Dawn.*[8]

It is precisely upon this unbearable question that the ovens of
Auschwitz cast a somber light. But the answer remains an enigma—
a "mystery," as we should say together with Elie Wiesel, who without
hesitation uses this word so familiar to Christians. Totalitarian paganism stages an attack on God Himself by striving to annihilate His
people. "Why are the nations in turmoil? Why do the people hatch
their futile plots? The kings of the earth stand ready and the rulers
conspire together against the Lord and His Anointed" (Ps. 2).

For Nazi paganism wanted to proclaim the Aryan race as the only
human one and the master of all others. But Israel, the elect of God,
is the disturbing witness to the truth that God alone is God and He
created all humans in His image and likeness. Thus, Nazi ideology
did not find a better way to wrest the divine election and messianic
mission from the Jewish people than by stripping Jews of their dignity
and depriving them of their humanity. "I was a body. Perhaps less
than that," Wiesel wrote.[9] Remember these final lines: "I wanted to
see myself in the mirror hanging on the opposite wall. I had not seen
myself since the ghetto. From the depths of the mirror a corpse gazed
back at me. The look in his eyes, as they stared into mine, has never
left me."[10]

But the test Jews were put to exceeded all measure, not only because of the excess of their suffering, but because of their election by God, who established them as the Jewish people, even if they sometimes dream of becoming at last "a people like any other." When you are a witness of man's humanity, how can you consent to being excluded from the human family? It is unbearable to the point of madness to think that God would allow the worst possible disaster to crush the people He created to bring salvation to all humankind.

Peace is one of the messianic blessings. To honor Elie Wiesel and, therefore, as he himself said, "the entire Jewish people," with the Nobel Prize for Peace, is to implicitly recognize that the destiny of Israel is linked with the messianic salvation of all humankind. On the part of the "nations" (see Ps. 2:1) it is a timid sign of hope, a veiled expression of bashfulness in regard to the Lord and His Anointed. Elie Wiesel hinted at such an insight in his acceptance speech at Oslo, while focusing on negative events ("crimes against humanity, crimes against Israel"). He had gone a few steps further in his novel, *A Beggar in Jerusalem*, speaking through the character of Kalman, the Kabbalist: "The Jews are God's memory and the heart of mankind. We do not always know this, but the others do, and that is why they treat us with suspicion and cruelty. Memory frightens them. Through us they are linked to the beginning and the end. By eliminating us they hope to gain immortality."[11]

In the September 1980 issue of *Esprit*, A. Derczanski noted quite perceptively: "There is much resignation in Elie Wiesel's endeavor. It is grounded in the election which grabs him by the throat, but he wants to decipher it and figure it out through the Holocaust. He is too self-conscious to raise his people to the level not of the martyred but of the Messiah. Perhaps this is why he leaves us thirsting for more."[12]

Indeed, the underlying question is: What is the relationship between the election, the divine vocation of the Jewish people, and the Messiah? And does this messianic vocation provide any significance or justification to the suffering of both the people and the Messiah Himself?

The unimaginable event of the *Shoah* prompts Wiesel to respond: "The further I go, the less I understand. Maybe there is nothing to understand. I still fail to understand what happened — either the how or the why." The disaster has created "a mystery which overwhelms and subjugates us."[13] Let us recall Isaiah: "Time was when many were aghast at you, my people; so now many nations recoil at the sight of him, and kings curl their lips in disgust. . . . His form, disfigured, lost all the likeness of a man, his beauty changed beyond human resemblance" (Isa. 52:14–15; 53:2).

Both the fifty-second and fifty-third chapters of Isaiah ought to be quoted entirely here, even though their application to Israel remains so painful—if not downright unbearable. As far as I am concerned, I receive these words unreservedly and yet with the same bewilderment when they refer to Jesus, the Messiah of whom I am a disciple. Why was it necessary for the Messiah to endure such suffering in order to enter into His glory? That remains an unfathomable mystery, a folly and an obstacle for faith. Only the Spirit of the Lord who changes human hearts can reveal the depth of God's wisdom. Yes, the Son walked freely to his death, saying to God, His Father: "Burnt offering and sin offering you have not required, then I said: 'Lo, I come!' " (Ps. 40:7–8).

After these words of revelation, all violent sacrifices, all the hatred transferred on any scapegoat are proscribed. What an unbelievable trial this must be when a vast force of destruction comes to crush God's beloved people. It is an unbelievable ordeal. What word can be uttered in front of the bloody furrow ploughed like scourges by evil through the destiny of all humanity? I can bear the night into which Israel was plunged only by sharing the night into which the Messiah willingly entered in order to open to all the way of life and to bring forth the light of the world, the light of Resurrection, a light more dazzling than all the suns. When I believe this, I do not consider myself separated before God from Elie Wiesel whom I love as a brother.

For the Nazis, the *thought* that negates both God and man gives way to a systematic *enterprise:* sending both God and man back to nothingness. This shift to action, this translation of abstraction into destruction is truly an infernal form of nihilism. The young Elie could *see* it even before he left his village. The Hungarian police made the last group of deportees walk faster: "They were our first oppressors," wrote Wiesel. "They were the first of the faces of hell and death." [14] Experimental logic did not allow Hitler's plan to remain an abstract generality. Any theory can abstractly deny both God and man. But in order to justify its supremacy, the so-called Aryan race had to eradicate the Jewish people as the one through whom God in history had revealed Himself to man and revealed man to himself. This is how and why men sank into the infernal logic of the camps.

Only those who were plunged down into this abyss know what it was like. They ought to bear witness to it, but such hell is unspeakable, since it is the very negation of the Word. "The language of night was not human, but animal or perhaps mineral: hoarse screams, howls, muffled groans, wild laments, blows with a club . . . A beast striking out and a body collapsing; an officer raises his arm and a community marches to a common grave; a guard shrugs his shoulders and a thousand families burst to pieces and are brought together again only in death. This was the language of the concentration camp. It substituted itself for all other kinds of expressions and suppressed them all. Rather than a link, it became a wall. Was it possible to get over it? Should the reader be made to overcome it? I knew that the answer was 'no' but I also knew that the 'no' had to be changed to 'yes.' " [15]

Elie Wiesel brings us to the realization of the infernal character of this moment in our history, in the history of the Jewish people and of all humanity. Had anyone before Wiesel led us so far into the depths of this diabolical enterprise? For Wiesel has remained a man of faith, even when all evidence of God's presence was destroyed. His testimony—all his work—brings us back not to the horror of the past, but to the threshold where our personal responsibility still operates. He warns us about the nature of the danger that can always surface again.

This is Elie Wiesel's mission and what makes his message unique. He did not take it on himself, but he received it from the fervent Jewish saints who preceeded us, *tsadikim, hassidim;* he received it from On High.

He never told us who suggested to him the title of the French edition of his first story. But it seems to me that he gives the key, for the word "night" keeps coming up in these few, short pages. "In the work of Wiesel there are certain marks of a liturgy."[16]

The image of an inverted Passover springs out of Weisel's sentences; it is an infernal experiment made by the Nazis; no one but a Jewish witness can unmask it. "It was night" is the refrain of a Seder poem which spells out the manifestations of God's power and fidelity. But who is the master of the night of Auschwitz? "Hitler," answers one of the faceless prisoners, to the astonishment of the young Elie. "Hitler has made it very clear that he will annihilate all the Jews before the clock strikes twelve, before they can hear the last stroke . . . I've got more faith in Hitler than in anyone else. He's the only one who's kept his promises, all his promises, to the Jewish people."[17]

It is an infernal Passover where Hitler wants to show his power by destroying the people created and saved by God. References to the Passover abound throughout the story, beginning with the departure from Sighet. It is an infernal, perverted, inverted Passover that replaces the people's election by God with the selection by the SS; the Assembly of the people in the desert, the *Qahal* of the Exodus, is replaced by the roll call for extermination. "I understood," said Elie Wiesel, "that evil is frightening, even though it is powerless. In its very essence, it releases a sort of physical terror."[18] This is why Auschwitz has become a symbolic name for hell. It is a place of silence. A place of silence that allows the dark terror of evil to be made manifest. A place of silence that cries out to heaven, like Abel's spilled blood. A place of silence that must master the beast crouching at the door, eager and waiting to turn man into a murderer like Cain (Gen. 4:7). Because of their vocation, Christians ought to understand what such a silence signifies. The liturgy of the Church makes all the disciples of the Crucified face this emptiness. When all is accomplished on Good Friday and until the end of the night of Holy Saturday, we have to survive in God's obscure silence. How could we fail to understand and accept the fact that the Jewish people fulfill their sacred mission, which is to allow humankind to listen to the silence to which it has condemned the people blessed by God?

This emptiness of time and place can only be gazed upon "from afar" (Luke 22:54) by those whose eyes meet the dereliction of Good Friday before they can turn to the Rising Sun of the First Day.

Notes

1. Franklin H. Littell and Hubert G. Locke, eds., *The German Church Struggle and the Holocaust* (Detroit: Wayne State University Press, 1974), 271.
2. Elie Wiesel, *Night*, trans. Stella Rodway (New York: Avon Books, 1960), 12–13.
3. Ibid., 42.
4. Ibid., 79.
5. Ibid., 44.
6. Elie Wiesel, *The Nobel Peace Prize 1986* (New York: Summit Books and Boston University, 1986), 15.
7. Elie Wiesel and Josy Eisenberg, *Job, ou Dieu dans la tempête* (Paris: Fayard-Verdier, 1986), 41.
8. Elie Wiesel, *Dawn*, trans. Frances Frenaye (New York: Avon Books, 1961), 29.
9. Wiesel, *Night*, 63.
10. Ibid., 127.
11. Elie Wiesel, *A Beggar in Jerusalem* (New York: Pocket Books, 1970), 137.
12. A. Derczanski, "Elie Wiesel," *Esprit*, September 1980, 93–94.
13. Elie Wiesel, *Le chant des morts* (Paris: Editions du Seuil, 1972), 200–201.
14. Wiesel, *Night*, 29.
15. Elie Wiesel, *Paroles d'étranger* (Paris: Editions du Seuil, 1982), 8.
16. Derczanski, "Elie Wiesel," 93–94.
17. Wiesel, *Night*, 92.
18. Brigitte-Fanny Cohen, *Elie Wiesel, qui êtes-vous?* (Paris: La Manufacture, 1987), 57.

17

Sending Forth the Dove:
Elie Wiesel and the Temptation to Hope

Douglas K. Huneke

One of my students at the University of Oregon was particularly tormented by what he had learned of the Holocaust from reading Elie Wiesel's memoir, *Night*. He searched other works by the author looking for a word of hope, a glimpse of light. Finally, the day came when he could speak with the writer. His question silenced the audience, "You have a son, I believe. You experienced so much in the camps and after, and the condition of the world today is hardly less threatening. Why did you have a child? What are you saying when you bring a life into the world?"

After a long pause and in reverent tones the survivor responded, "I had been waiting many years before I brought life into this world. For many, many years I thought the world did not deserve it. By this I mean, that the world does not deserve to have our children. I was convinced that my generation would be the last. However, at one point I explored the texture of my life and I came to different questions. If we stopped having children, the killers do not. One day the world will be inhabited only by killers . . . Then the Jew in me spoke. It said, to have lived through 3,500 years of extraordinary events and to have it all end with me. That many years of prophets, princes, scholars, students, beggars, merchants, wanderers, and dreamers. I could not do that, so I brought life into the world to continue the line. This is all philosophy before it happened. It became very real when I had a son. He was the best answer to my question. You know, the first word, the first smile, the first movement, justified more than my words, my faith in the world"[1]

The answer justified the student's struggle, transformed his mood, perhaps changed his life. Why do so many of Elie Wiesel's readers wait expectantly on his expressions of and struggles with hope? How could they not, given the description of his first night in Auschwitz?

Not far from us, flames were leaping up from a ditch, gigantic flames. They were burning something. A lorry drew up at the pit and delivered its load— little children. Babies! Yes, I saw it—saw it with my own eyes . . . those children in the flames.[2]

After reading his response to that horrific vision, is it any wonder that the world needs a word of hope?

Never shall I forget that night, the first night in camp, which has turned my life into one long night, seven times cursed and seven times sealed. Never shall I forget that smoke. Never shall I forget the little faces of the children, whose bodies I saw turned into wreaths of smoke beneath the silent blue sky.

Never shall I forget those flames which consumed my faith forever.

Never shall I forget that nocturnal silence which deprived me, for all eternity, of the desire to live.

Never shall I forget those moments which murdered my God and my soul and turned my dreams to dust. Never shall I forget these things, even if I am condemned to live as long as God Himself. Never.[3]

There is a fragile, almost imperceptible measure of hope that sustains the victims in Wiesel's account of the *Shoah*. The reader, however, is lost in a taut, unflinching account of human evil, the absolute contradiction of even the possibility of hope. A first significant glimmer of hope comes for both survivor and reader in Wiesel's fourth book, the novel *The Town Beyond the Wall*. In this story the character of Pedro provides an authentic friendship that renews and ultimately liberates Michael, the survivor, from the death grip of the *Shoah*. The story ends with Michael in a prison cell, about to move a step away from the precipice of the Shoah, and Wiesel concludes, "Michael had come to the end of his strength. Before him the night was receding, as on a mountain before the dawn."[4] The Holocaust survivor tentatively turns to embrace life, conditionally to reenter the world of human relationships, despite the inhumanity and the risk.

What is the origin of this ray of hope? Is it possible that "the weeping prophet," Jeremiah, was the inspiration for this halting metamorphosis? Sixteen years after the publication of *The Town Beyond the Wall*, Wiesel would write of Jeremiah,

[His] purpose is to teach his contemporaries and their descendants a lesson: there comes a time when one must look away from death and turn away from the dead; one must cling to life, which is made of minutes, not necessarily of years, and surely not centuries; one must fight so as not to be overwhelmed by history but to act upon it concretely, simply, humanly.[5]

Hope remained an unstated or understated motif in the ten books that followed *Night*. It was the domain of survivors who dared to look back in an attempt to understand what enabled the Jews in *l'univers concentrationnaire* to live and remain human, perhaps to remain faithful. Then, in 1973 Elie Wiesel's cantata, *Ani Maamin: A Song Lost and Found Again*, with music written by Darius Milhaud, was performed at Carnegie Hall in New York City. The title, *Ani Maamin* is translated "to firmly believe" and is taken from the twelfth of Moses Maimonides' "Thirteen Principles of Faith," which proclaims, "I firmly believe in the coming of the Messiah; and although he may tarry, I daily wait for his coming."

As a youth, Wiesel sang a version of the song while worshiping in the synagogue of Sighet. Later, it became the resistance song of the Jews locked in the Warsaw Ghetto and others who faced certain death at the hands of the Nazis. On the dust jacket of the book, Wiesel wrote,

I heard it sung inside the kingdom of madness by Jews who knew they were on the threshold of death. How could they believe in the Messiah over there? How could they go on waiting for him? They should have known better . . . When you think of the Holocaust, you are inevitably confronted by the questions: Where was God? What did he know? What did he do?

On the cover page of the book, Wiesel introduces the tension of a faith and hope that are simultaneously present and absent, the tension between faith and hope and the reality of the *Shoah*, "Rather than appeasing, rather than consoling the survivors, this faith discon-

certs them. Both affirmation and provocation, it cannot help but
evoke uneasiness. And yet . . ." If *Night* represents the despair of
one who watched babies burn and his God murdered, *Ani Maamin* is
the survivor's provisional statement of hope despite despair.

The hope represented in *Ani Maamin* is comparable to the hope of
Noah, who waited seven days each time he sent forth a dove to
determine if the destruction of the world had ended. The nature of
Noah's wait and hope involved uncertainty and restrained anticipation for the future. Could a survivor of the *Shoah* approach the matter
of hope with other than uncertainty, restraint, and trembling anger
for the betrayals and the unanswerable questions?

Ani Maamin begins in defiance and anger, with Abraham, Isaac,
and Jacob repudiating their task and reporting directly to the celestial
court on their mission, "to roam the by-roads near and far, gathering
the echoes of Jewish suffering in the world, and make them known to
heaven. They wanted to bring it to an end."[6] The three patriarchs
roamed central and eastern Europe during the darkest hours of the
Shoah, "When the world was being consumed by the black flames of
night," and they in turn were consumed with guilt, "guilty of having
seen, guilty of being helpless" (15). In turn, each, with but a few
vivid, unsparing words, describes, accuses, and questions. Throughout their testimony God is silent, unmoved, unmoving.

This is a cantata of interrogation as each patriarch addresses a
succession of questions to God. Isaac's questions are predictably
intense and personal: "Do you recall the *Akeda*" (the divine order to
sacrifice Isaac on Mount Moriah)? "Why me?" "Do you see?" "Why
do you give them to death?" "What is the world?" "What is man—
soul—voice—memory—God?" (19).

Jacob's questions are slightly abstract, more theological. "Where
are you [God]?" "What of your promise?" "Is this your blessing?" "Is
this your victory?" "Why do you rob me of hope?" "Do you hear?"
(23).

Abraham reminded the Creator of the universe,

I alone believed in you,
In you alone.
As a reward, you promised me:
My children and my children's children would live,

Would grow and bless us, you and me.
You promised us survival,
Not just eternity.[7]

Next, Abraham began asking the questions of one who believed and accepted God's promise, a promise seemingly going up in smoke with the children who were his seed: "Why do you rob me of my future?" "Could the judge of judges be unjust?" "Why should the survivors feel guilty for suffering—for living?" (31).

Isaac asks his personal, penultimate question, "Why the just?" Jacob asks, "Why the humble?" Abraham asks, "Why the innocent?" Together they ask the ultimate question, "Why?" (63).

In the tale, a chorus sings and its questions frame the more global, humanitarian issues of the *Shoah*. "How can you [God]?" "How is one to believe?" "How is one not to believe?" (25). "Who will hear? Who will listen?" "Who will understand—who will repeat?" (27). "Where are you [God] on this night?" "Why so many chastisements inflicted on so many children?" (65).

The questions of these witnesses restrain any precipitate rush to hope. Hope quickly or easily achieved would be falsely grounded, a denial of the anguish and ultimately destructive of the renewal of faith. The questions are like Noah's doves sent over the stormy sea in search of a secure place to land. The questions probe the limits of dark horizons and return without an olive branch. There are, there can be, no answers to the questions. If there is to be a renewal of hope, faith, or future, it must be born of uncertainty, in spite of the evidence and the silence.

Near the end of the cantata, a new character enters the drama. Identified simply as the "Voice," is it God or, as Wiesel's Narrator asks, is it "Surely the voice of an angel come to plead God's cause?" (65). The absence of God's personal responsibility, intervention, or presence recalls the distressing moment on Mount Moriah when God, having ordered the sacrifice of Isaac, sent an angel to stay Abraham's hand. Why, we ask, did not God personally stop the ritual? Implicit in virtually all of Wiesel's writings is the survivors' need, if not right, to know about God's role in evil and human suffering. The sudden appearance in the cantata of a defensive stand-in for God leaves the questions unanswered, the need unmet, and the heart unsatisfied.

The Voice is always firm, but like the voice that addresses Job from the whirlwind, its questions and assertions are often diversionary.

> The Master of the World
> Disposes of the world.
> His creatures
> Do their creator's bidding.
> Accept his laws
> without a question.   (65–66)

Unlike Job and to their credit, Abraham, Isaac, and Jacob do not submit to the protestations of the Voice. When the Voice challenges, saying, "God knows, that is enough . . . God wills, that is enough," Abraham responds, "No, it is not enough" (69, 71). Finally, Wiesel has the Voice ask on God's behalf the other essential question of responsibility.

> Does God owe you an accounting?
> God alone?
> All this —
> His sole responsibility . . . ?
> Does God have the right
> To question you, in turn,
> To ask of man:
> What have you done with my creation?[8]

God is still silent. God must know. The inquisitors are at a loss. Abraham, Isaac, and Jacob make their decision to go into exile, to join their descendants. The three alone will speak the truth, offer comfort, and be present. The chorus breaks forth in a farewell punctuated by repeated exclamations of "Amen" for what the three must do. The word comes from a Hebrew verb meaning to care for and support, to be firm, true, and reliable. That is their new mission. As an exclamation it bids the three to persevere, to affirm their readiness to accept the consequences of their task. As they depart Abraham says, "Let us go toward them"; Isaac says, "Let us go for them"; and Jacob says, "Let us go with them" (87).

They are not stopped and each recounts an incident in which a Jew remained faithful in spite of suffering inhumanity. Each tale of trust is followed by the affirmation of the chorus singing, "Ani Maamin." After the first rending tale and tormented affirmation the Narrator interrupts, "Having spoken, Abraham takes another step backward. He does not, cannot, see that God for the first time, permits a tear to cloud his eyes" (93). Isaac, ever faithful in spite of his experience, bears witness and affirms, "I believe in God. With the last of my strength I claim him as my own" (95). The Narrator indicates that Isaac "does not, cannot, see that for the second time a tear streams down God's somber countenance, a countenance more somber than before" (97). Finally, Jacob tells of horror and trust, and affirms, "I shall wait for you. And even if you disappoint me I shall go on waiting" (101). The chorus responds,

> Auschwitz has killed the Jews
> But not their expectation.   (103)

Again the Narrator speaks, "God, surprised by his people, weeps for the third time—and this time without restraint, and with—yes—love. He weeps over his creation—and perhaps over much more than his creation" (103).

The three leave the celestial court, each with a different blessing, not a curse. Again, the Narrator interrupts:

> Abraham, Isaac and Jacob go away, heartened by another hope: their children. They leave heaven and do not, cannot, see that they are no longer alone: God accompanies them, weeping, smiling, whispering: *Nitzhuni banai*, my children have defeated me, they deserve my gratitude.
> Thus he spake—he is speaking still. The word of God continues to be heard. So does the silence of his dead children.[9]

Could there be any other place for God? If God had broken the silence with answers for the patriarchs' questions, God would have been complicit with or powerless before the Nazis. An indifferent, absent God would have been unworthy of faith. If God had remained silent, unmoved, and unmoving could there ever again be trust or hope? Where is God? God, Wiesel posits, is present in the midst of the suffering that ends at a gas chamber, crematorium, or mass grave. In the absence of intervention anything other than presence would have been offensive and lacked integrity.

When Abraham, Isaac, and Jacob decided to join their people, they concluded that there was no hope. Does the unexpected presence of God at the side of Abraham, Isaac, and Jacob tempt survivor and reader to hope? As the tale ends the ray of hope pierces the darkness more deeply, "because of Belsen . . . because and in spite of Majdanek" (105). Prayers are offered to God, against God, and for God. The benediction is pronounced,

> Blessed are the fools . . .
> who help their brothers
> Singing, over and over and over:
> *Ani Maamin* . . . (107)

There is hope, because of God's tears, because and in spite of the silence of the dead children.

Forty-two years after the *Shoah* and nearly thirteen years after the performance and publication of *Ani Maamin*, Elie Wiesel sent forth another significant dove in his search for a word of hope that could be spoken with integrity in a post-*Shoah* world. Once again, the word was encased in melody. It was to be sung, this time in a cantata entitled *A Song for Hope*. Wiesel wrote the words, David Diamond composed the score, and it was performed on 10 June 1987 at the 92d Street Y in New York City. Familiar characters from Wiesel's fictional and biblical writings appear in the cantata: a madman (or presumably so—was it Moshe?), survivors from every age with ample memories, Jeremiah, and Ezekiel.

The cantata opens with a question, "Was he a madman?"[10] In *Night*, when Moshe miraculously returned from the mass grave in the forest of Galicia he explained the urgency of his mission to the twelve-year-old Wiesel,

I wanted to come back to Sighet to tell you the story of my death. So that you could prepare yourselves while there was still time. To live? I don't attach my importance to my life anymore. I am alone. No, I wanted to come back, and to warn you.[11]

In the cantata the alleged madman appears and speaks of suffering, dangers in the future, and about a "desperate but impossible hope" (1). As in Sighet, no one listens. Still, he calls "the living to life and

the survivors to faith. He was a dreamer who made others dream"
(1). He fights death, asks for joy, and yearns to unite humanity. Still,
no one listens.

In *Night*, when Moshe returned to Sighet his experience in the
forest had robbed his eyes of joy and his voice of song. The unnamed
Narrator says of the madman in *A Song for Hope*,

And so, this strange man, this ageless and friendless Jew, with a broken
heart and an infinite memory, had to choose between song and silence. He
chose to sing silently. Better yet: he made silence sing.[12]

Abraham Joshua Heschel was fond of quoting a certain Hasidic
teaching. "There are three ascending levels of how one mourns: With
tears—that is the lowest. With silence—that is higher. And with a
song—that is the highest."[13] Wiesel and many other survivors and
victims were robbed of their tears and denied the grace of mourning:
29 January 1945, upon waking and finding that his father had been
taken away, "I did not weep, and it pained me that I could not weep.
But I had no more tears" (*Night*, 116). Silence was a powerfully
compelling force, but after ten years Wiesel rejected it, choosing
words rather than silence to bear witness and to challenge. There is
hope when Wiesel's madman sings: "of stubborn faith . . . of the
wisdom of old men . . . of the beauty of young women . . . standing
under a flowering arch, ready to celebrate the future . . . even as the
enemy waited for a signal to cut their throats, he sang, he sang, he
sang" (*Song for Hope*, 14).

One madman could no longer sing, the other could not stop
singing. The temptation to hope grows, but not without conditions.
Prior to its performance, Wiesel wrote of the cantata, [emphasis
Wiesel's] "A SONG FOR HOPE AND NOT a song of hope—there is a
difference between them. The first is an appeal, the second an answer
to an appeal. To live in hope is one thing; to wait for hope, to long
for it, is another. In this song we are still waiting."[14]

In *A Song for Hope*, the madmen called upon Jeremiah.

and invited him to sing
in his place,
to say what no other
could say:

that the duty of man
the duty of a Jew
is to hold fast to faith
even in the midst of ruins
and to impose joy
even when the earth is covered
with cemeteries
both visible and invisible.[15]

Either a song of hope or a song for hope will deprive the killers of a victory over memory, over the survivors. Why then Jeremiah? Because there is a certain affinity between prophet and author. The former seems almost a paradigm for the latter. Of him Wiesel wrote,

Though alone, he defines himself in relation to his fellowmen, who reject him. Though shattered, he does not try to escape the present and seek refuge in the future; he works with the present, on the present. Living in a disorganized, dehumanized world, he forces himself to pick up the broken pieces and dreams of man's possibilities to create harmony.[16]

The prophet Jeremiah rejected facile expressions of hope. He sought a future beyond exile, a future that was not a repetition of the past or the present. To the Jews languishing in Babylon he sent a promising word, "The Lord says, 'I alone know the plans I have for you, plans for prosperity not destruction, to give you a future and a hope. Then you will call upon me and come and pray to me, and I will hear you. You will seek me and find me; when you seek me with all your heart, I will be found by you' " (29:11–13). Out of the tension between the suffering of his people and his trust in God, Wiesel's Jeremiah repeatedly proclaims the sanctity of life, the immortality of memory, and the future of the people of Israel. This Jeremiah shouts, "The Babylonian enemy has been swallowed by oblivion but the people of Israel lives on" (9). The oppressors and killers never have the final word.

The visionary prophet Ezekiel is the next one introduced into the cantata. In another context Wiesel wrote of him:

No prophet was endowed with such vision—no other vision was as extreme. No man has shed such light on the future, for no other light was as forceful in tearing darkness apart. But, then, no one had ever seen such darkness, the total darkness that preceeds the breaking of dawn.

It is enough to follow his gaze to be uplifted by the hope it conjures. Look when he orders you to do so, and you will be rewarded by the conviction that hope is forever founded and forever justified. Listen to his words, to his voice, and you will feel strong—stronger than death, more powerful than evil.[17]

It was to Ezekiel that the Lord showed the desert of dry bones, saying, "The people of Israel are like these bones. They say that they are dried up, without any hope and with no future" (37:11). It is Wiesel's Ezekiel who transcends the nightmare by announcing that "the people of Israel survives its killers" (11). What follows Ezekiel's bold words are a series of brief, evocative vignettes in which Jews tell of their faithfulness to God, even as they waited for the torturers and killers. Every persecution, whether in Rome or the Ukraine, evoked obedience and sanctification. A boy says, "I have seen the killers at work and I don't understand" (17). He remains faithful. No one understands, no one has discovered the meaning of human suffering. The absence of meaning or understanding does not always preclude the possibility of hope.

Like Jeremiah, Ezekiel is memory personified, a link between the past and the present, promising that life will come to the dry bones, to the tortured, massacred people. Wiesel, like his characters, remains faithful to his tradition by making the message and the messengers timeless. He concludes his earlier essay on Ezekiel in this way:

Finally, all the events, and all the prophetic visions in the book, are inserted in their proper calendar. Fourteen dates are indicated to help us place the speaker and his discourse—with one notable exception: the vision of the dry bones, meaning that the resurrection is undated.

And we understand why: that vision, that promise, that hope, is not linked to either space or time.

That vision, that consolation, is offered to every generation, for every generation needs it—and ours more than any before us.[18]

In the *New York Times* article that preceded the cantata, Wiesel wrote, "I must confess that, of all the mysteries that characterize the Jewish people, its capacity for hope is the one that strikes me most forcibly."[19] That hope is most apparent in Wiesel's writings with the prophets who carry God's promise, as summons and reminder, across the ages to succeeding generations, and to God.

The Narrator concludes the cantata with the same question that opened it, "Was he a madman?" (21). What follows is more a response than an answer, linking past with present, memory, silence, and song.

> He had a choice between silence and memory.
> He chose the memory of silence
> over the silence of memory.

The choir responds,

> A song of hope?
> A song for hope.
> In an inhuman world,
> humanity is hope.

The cantata ends with the choir singing,

> a song of hope
> a song for hope:
> for,
> the children of Israel
> are the answer of Israel.[20]

The song that was lost appears to have been found again. It is not that the *Shoah* found meaning or that the questions were answered. Let us return to Moshe and his insistence in *Night* that "every question possessed a power that did not lie in the answer."[21] A measure of Elie Wiesel's significance and artistry is his ability to continually refine and ask the questions. The victims and the survivors of the Nazi genocide, and those who both listen to the witnesses and confront the implications of the *Shoah*, understand from Elie Wiesel something of the power that does not need answers, that holds horror and hope in tension. In the *Times* article, Wiesel writes of *A Song for Hope.*

[The cantata] represents for me the desperate effort of my own generation to invoke its right to hope. In the end, this right will become a duty. Instead of discouraging us, the spokesmen of the tragic past incite us to tenacity and faith. It is because Jeremiah has suffered that he can, in good faith, demand that we rise above our suffering. It is because our martyrs chose the supreme sacrifice, in order to remain true to themselves, that they have the right to urge on us another way than that of death.[22]

Tradition teaches believers to anticipate the resurrection of the dead. Ezekiel with his divinely inspired vision and Wiesel with memory-inspired words point to a resurrection of hope in the living who survived death. This hope is not built on a foundation of blind optimism; it is a fragile hard-won hope that sees an ember of itself in those who suffer, and struggles to rekindle in the living, its word of hope-in-spite-of-despair. During the time of the *Shoah*, God was no longer an abiding constant, and the human world was disintegrating. God and humanity remain a question for survivors who have faith and seek to build a just and compassionate world. After such tragedy hope can only be understood as the art of perseverance. The power of Elie Wiesel's words, memory, and hope derive in great measure from his tenacious transcendence of the *Shoah*'s meaninglessness and his untiring commitment to a world where childhood is not plundered by murderers.

While it is neither the problem of the word or the author, hope has yet to find its fulfillment and freedom in the words of Elie Wiesel: "I remember the killers and I despair; I remember the victims and on their behalf and for their sake and for their children's sake, I must invent a thousand and one reasons to hope."[23] It is enough to know that he can find reasons to hope and that hope is a dominant melody: "And so *Ani Maamin*—I believe—that we must have hope for one another also because of one another. And *Ani Maamin*—I believe— that because of our children and theirs we should be worthy of that hope, of that redemption, and of some measure of peace."[24]

Thirty years after the English language publication of *Night*, and with the release of *Ani Maamin* and *A Song for Hope*, we are re-minded of Elie Wiesel's commentary on the life of Isaac and these unforgettable words, which bridge the lives of subject and author:

Isaac will become the defender of his people. Why he? Because he suffered, but that is not a reason good enough. We believe that suffering confers no privileges; it is what you do with your suffering that counts. And Isaac transformed his suffering into praise for man and praise of man, rather than into hate and bitterness.[25]

Through tears of anguish and hopefulness and gladness we find in the words and songs of Elie Wiesel the vision and courage to sanctify life in the face of death; the echoing call to choose life and blessing rather than death and curse; and the irresistible summons to hope, because and in spite of . . .

Notes

1. Douglas K. Huneke, "Elie Wiesel: Speaking the Unspeakable," *Willamette Valley Observer*, 18 May 1979, 5.
2. Elie Wiesel, *Night* (New York: Hill and Wang, 1972), 41.
3. Ibid., 43.
4. Elie Wiesel, *The Town Beyond the Wall* (New York: Holt, Rinehart and Winston, 1967), 178.
5. Elie Wiesel, *Five Biblical Portraits* (Notre Dame: University of Notre Dame Press, 1981), 120–21.
6. Elie Wiesel, *Ani Maamin: A Song Lost and Found Again* (New York: Random House, 1974), 15.
7. Ibid., 19.
8. Ibid., 75.
9. Ibid., 105.
10. Elie Wiesel, *A Song for Hope.* (New York City: The 92d Street Y, 1987).
11. Wiesel, *Night*, 17.
12. Wiesel, *Song for Hope*, 3.
13. Abraham Joshua Heschel, *I Asked for Wonder: A Spiritual Anthology*, ed. Samuel H. Dresner (New York: Crossroad, 1983), viii.
14. Elie Wiesel, "Of Hope and the Abyss," *New York Times*, 7 June 1987, sect. 2, 42.
15. Wiesel, *Song for Hope*, 6.
16. Wiesel, *Five Biblical Portraits*, 121.
17. Elie Wiesel, "Ezekiel," in *Congregation: Contemporary Writers Read the Jewish Bible*, ed. David Rosenberg (New York: Harcourt, Brace Jovanovich, 1987), 167.
18. Ibid., 186.

19. Wiesel, "Of Hope and the Abyss," 42.
20. Wiesel, *Song for Hope*, 23.
21. Wiesel, *Night*, 15.
22. Wiesel, "Of Hope and the Abyss," 43.
23. Elie Wiesel, "The Nobel Lecture: Hope, Despair and Memory" in *The Nobel Peace Prize 1986* (New York: Summit Books and Boston University, 1986), 30.
24. Ibid., 31.
25. Elie Wiesel, "The Binding of Isaac" (Public lecture at Stanford University, Palo Alto, California, 4 May 1974).

Select Bibliography

Unless otherwise noted, all translations are from the French.

I. Works of Elie Wiesel

A. Books

1. Semiautobiographical

Night. Translated by Stella Rodway. Foreword by François Mauriac. New York: Hill and Wang, 1960.

2. Fiction

Dawn. Translated by Anne Borchardt. New York: Hill and Wang, 1962.

The Accident. Translated by Anne Borchardt. New York: Hill and Wang, 1962.

The Gates of the Forest. Translated by Frances Frenaye. New York: Holt, Rinehart and Winston, 1966.

The Town Beyond the Wall. Translated by Stephen Becker. New York: Holt, Rinehard and Winston, 1967.

A Beggar in Jerusalem. Translated by Lily Edelman and Elie Wiesel. New York: Random House, 1970.

The Oath. Translated by Marion Wiesel. New York: Random House, 1973.

The Testament. Translated by Marion Wiesel. New York: Summit Books, 1981.

The Fifth Son. Translated by Marion Wiesel. New York: Summit Books, 1985.

Twilight. Translated by Marion Wiesel. New York: Summit Books, 1988.

3. Biblical and Hasidic Legends

Souls on Fire: Portraits and Legends of Hasidic Masters. Translated by
   Marion Wiesel. New York: Random House, 1972.
Messengers of God: Biblical Portraits and Legends. Translated by Marion
   Wiesel. New York: Random House, 1976.
Four Hasidic Masters and Their Struggle Against Melancholy. Foreword by
   Theodore M. Hesburgh, C.S.C. Notre Dame: University of Notre Dame
   Press, 1978.
*Images from the Bible: The Paintings of Shalom of Safed, the Words of Elie
   Wiesel.* Introduction by Daniel Doron. Woodstock, N.Y.: Overlook Press,
   1980.
Five Biblical Portraits. Notre Dame: University of Notre Dame Press, 1981.
Somewhere a Master: Further Tales of the Hasidic Masters. Translated by
   Marion Wiesel. New York: Summit Books, 1982.
The Golem. Illustrated by Mark Podwal. Translated by Anne Borchardt.
   New York: Summit Books, 1983.

4. Drama

Zalmen, or the Madness of God. Based on a translation by Nathan Edelman,
   adapted for the stage by Marion Wiesel. New York: Random House,
   1974.
The Trial of God (As It Was Held on February 25, 1649, in Shamgorod).
   Translated by Marion Wiesel. New York: Random House, 1979.

5. Cantatas (Text by Elie Wiesel)

Ani Maamin: A Song Lost and Found Again. Translated by Marion Wiesel.
   New York: Random House, 1973.
The Hagaddah. New York: S. French, 1982.
A Song for Hope. Translated by Marion Wiesel. New York: 92d Street Y,
   1987.

6. Essays

Legends of Our Time. Translated by Steven Donadio. New York: Holt,
   Rinehart and Winston, 1966.
The Jews of Silence: A Personal Report on Soviet Jewry. Translated from the
   Hebrew by Neal Kozodoy. New York: Holt, Rinehart and Winston, 1968.

One Generation After. Translated by Lily Edelman and Elie Wiesel. New York: Random House, 1970.

A Jew Today. Translated by Marion Wiesel. New York: Random House, 1978.

Against Silence: The Voice and Vision of Elie Wiesel. Edited by Irving Abrahamson. New York: Holocaust Library, 1985.

The Nobel Peace Prize. New York: Summit Books and Boston University, 1986.

With Albert Friedlander: *The Six Days of Destruction: Meditations Towards Hope.* New York: Paulist Press, 1988.

B. Other

"Sighet, Sighet." Images Film Archives, 300 Phillips Park Road, Mamaroneck, N.Y. 10543. Broadcast April 1972.

"The Itinerary of Elie Wiesel: From Sighet to Jerusalem." *The Eternal Light.* National Broadcasting Co. TV script written and narrated by Elie Wiesel, broadcast 21 May 1972.

"Elie Wiesel's Jerusalem." Canadian Broadcasting Corporation [CBC] Television Transcript, Easter 1979.

"Breaking the Silence." Documentaries for Learning, Massachusetts Mental Health Center. New York: Cinema Guild, 1984.

II. Works About Elie Wiesel

A. Books

Berenbaum, Michael. *The Vision of the Void: Theological Reflections on the Works of Elie Wiesel.* Middletown, Conn.: Wesleyan University Press, 1979.

Brown, Robert McAfee. *Elie Wiesel: Messenger to All Humanity.* Notre Dame: University of Notre Dame Press, 1983 (Rev. ed., 1989).

Cargas, Harry James. *Conversations with Elie Wiesel.* New York: Paulist Press, 1976.

―――. *Responses to Elie Wiesel: Critical Essays by Major Jewish and Christian Scholars.* New York: Persea Books, 1978.

Estes, Ted L. *Elie Wiesel.* New York: Frederick Ungar, 1980.

Fine, Ellen S. *Legacy of Night: The Literary Universe of Elie Wiesel.* Albany: State University of New York Press, 1982.

Freidman, Maurice. *Abraham Joshua Heschel and Elie Wiesel.* New York: Farrar, Straus and Giroux, 1987.

Frost, Christopher. *Religious Melancholy or Psychological Depression: Some Issues Involved in Relating Psychology and Religion as Illustrated in a Study of Elie Wiesel.* Lanham, Md.: University Press of America, 1985.

Rosenfeld, Alvin, and Irving Greenberg, eds. *Confronting the Holocaust: The Impact of Elie Wiesel.* Bloomington: Indiana University Press, 1979.

Roth, John K. *A Consuming Fire: Encounters with Elie Wiesel and the Holocaust.* Atlanta: John Knox Press, 1979.

Stern, Ellen Norman. *Elie Wiesel: Witness for Life.* New York: KTAV Publishing, 1982.

Walker, Graham B., Jr. *Elie Wiesel: A Challenge to Theology.* Jefferson, N.C.: McFaland, 1987.

B. Journals

"Building a Moral Society: Aspects of Elie Wiesel's Work." *Face to Face: An Interreligious Bulletin,* Spring 1979.

"Elie Wiesel." *America.* 19 November 1988.

C. Dissertations

Baker, Marilyn J. "Against Humanism: Alienation in the Works of Elie Wiesel, Gunter Grass, and Kurt Vonnegut." University of Southern California, 1977.

Bernstein, Derora. "How Shall We Sing the Lord's Song in a Strange Land: The Journey Back to Life in the *Midrash* of Elie Wiesel." Ohio University, 1973.

Cedars, Marie M. "Speaking Through Silence: The Art of Elie Wiesel." University of Texas at Arlington, 1984.

Christ, Carol P. "Elie Wiesel's Stories: Still the Dialogue." Yale University, 1974.

Frankel, Sylvia H. W. "Jewish Sources in Elie Wiesel's Work." University of Oregon, 1981.

French, Ellen M. B. "Archetype and Metaphor: An Approach to the Early Novels of Elie Wiesel." Middle Tennessee State University, 1981.

Frost, Christopher J. "Some Issues of Approach and Method Involved in Relating Psychological and Religious Studies, as Examplified in a Study of Elie Wiesel and His Hasidic Masters." Boston University, 1984.

Horowitz, Sara R. "Linguistic Displacement in Fictional Responses to the

Holocaust: Kosinski, Wiesel, Lind, and Tournier." Brandeis University, 1985.

Jauchen, John S. "The Messianic Ideal in Ludwig Lewisohn and Elie Wiesel." Baylor University, 1986.

Leizman, Reva B. "The Road Towards Regeneration and Salvation in the Novels of Elie Wiesel." Case Western Reserve University, 1977.

Modini, Robert J. "Longing in Exile: The Dialogue with Despair in the Fiction of Walker Percy and Elie Wiesel." Syracuse University, 1984.

Schaneman, Judith C. "The Force of Memory in Elie Wiesel's Novels: A Survivor's Tale." University of Colorado at Boulder, 1986.

Walker, Graham B., Jr. "Elie Wiesel: A Challenge to Contemporary Theology." Southern Baptist Theological Seminary, 1986.

D. Bibliographies

Abrahamson, Irving. "Elie Wiesel: A Selected Bibliography." In *Confronting the Holocaust: The Impact of Elie Wiesel*, edited by Alvin Rosenfeld and Irving Greenberg, 207–12. Bloomington: Indiana University Press, 1979.

———, ed. Bibliographies to *Against Silence: The Voice and Vision of Elie Wiesel*. New York: Holocaust Library, 1985. Vol. 1, pp. 75–83 and vol. 3, pp. 339–72.

Abramowitz, Molly. *Elie Wiesel: A Bibliography*. Metuchen, N.J.: Scarecrow Press, 1974.

Bigelbach, Betty. "Selected Bibliography of the Works of Elie Wiesel." *Proceedings of the Center for Jewish-Christian Learning* 3 (Spring 1988): 30–32.

Fine, Ellen. *Legacy of Night: The Literary Universe of Elie Wiesel*. Albany: State University of New York Press, 1982, 166–94.

Roth, John K., "Elie Wiesel." In *Dictionary of Literary Biography Yearbook: 1987*, edited by J. M. Brook, 388–401. Detroit: Gale Research, 1988.

Contributors

Irving Abrahamson, Ph.D., Professor of English at the City College of Chicago, is an author, editor, and television script consultant. He is the editor of *Against Silence: The Voice and Vision of Elie Wiesel.*

Robert McAfee Brown, Ph.D., Professor Emeritus at Pacific School of Religion in Palo Alto, California, is a well-known Protestant Christian theologian who is the author of many books and essays, including *Elie Wiesel: Messenger to All Humanity.*

Harry James Cargas, Ph.D., Professor of Literature at Webster University, Webster Groves, Missouri, is the author of twenty-three books, including *Harry James Cargas in Conversation with Elie Wiesel.*

Marcel Dubois, O.P., Ph.D., is a member of the Department of Philosophy, Hebrew University, Jerusalem, Israel. Father Dubois is the author of nine books, including most recently, *Jerusalem: In Time and Eternity.* He is the editor of the ecumenical journal, *Emmanuel.*

Eugene J. Fisher, Ph.D., is Executive Secretary of the Secretariat for Catholic-Jewish Relations of the National Conference of Catholic Bishops, Washington, D.C. He is the author and editor of numerous books and essays, including *Faith Without Prejudice* and *Twenty Years of Jewish-Catholic Relations.*

219

Eva Fleischner, Ph.D., Professor of Religion and Philosophy at Montclair State University, Upper Montclair, New Jersey, is the author of *Judaism in German Christian Theology Since 1945*, and the editor of *Auschwitz: Beginning of a New Era?*

Lea Hamaoui, Ph.D. candidate, The Graduate Center of CUNY, teaches at Baruch College, Brooklyn, and is completing a longer study of Holocaust literature.

Douglas K. Huneke, M.Div., Senior Minister of Westminster Presbyterian Church, Tiburon, California, and Visiting Lecturer at San Francisco Theological Seminary, San Anselmo, California, is the author of *The Moses of Rovno.* Pastor Huneke is also a Trustee of the Marin Community Foundation and the author of innumerable essays and articles.

Rosette C. Lamont, Ph.D., is Professor of French and Comparative Literature at Queens College and the Graduate Center of CUNY, New York. She is the author of a number of books and articles published in France and the United States.

Mary Jo Leddy, N.D.S., Ph.D., a Sister of Sion, is founding editor of *Catholic New Times*, an independent national Catholic newspaper in Canada, and coeditor (with Mary Ann Hinsdale, IHM) of *Faith That Transforms*. She is a widely published Canadian Catholic essayist and journalist.

Jean-Marie Cardinal Lustiger, Ph.D., studied literature, philosophy, and theology at the Sorbonne, before entering the seminary. The author of several books, including most recently in English *Dare to Live*, Cardinal Lustiger is the Archbishop of Paris.

Dow Marmur, Ph.D., is Senior Rabbi of Holy Blossom Temple, Toronto, Ontario, Canada. He teaches contemporary Jewish thought at the Toronto School of Theology. His books include *Beyond Survival* and *Walking Toward Elijah*.

Carol Rittner, R.S.M., Ed.D., a Sister of Mercy, directs The Elie Wiesel Foundation for Humanity, New York. She was the coeditor (with Sondra Myers) of *The Courage to Care.*

John K. Roth, Ph.D., is Russell K. Pitzer Professor of Philosophy, Claremont McKenna College, Claremont, California. Included among his publications are *A Consuming Fire: Encounters with Elie Wiesel and the Holocaust* and *Approaches to Auschwitz: The Holocaust and Its Legacy* (with Richard L. Rubenstein).

George Schwab, Ph.D., is Professor of History at the City University of New York (Graduate Center and City College), New York. He is an author, editor, and translator of numerous works on power politics, legal and political theory, and German history.

Daniel Stern, Director of Humanities at the 92d Street Y, New York, is the author of ten books, including *Who Shall Live, Who Shall Die,* for which he received the 1978 International Remembrance Award from the Bergen-Belsen Association.

Elie Wiesel, author, teacher, witness, and human rights activist, received the 1986 Nobel Peace Prize. He is Andrew Mellon Professor in the Humanities at Boston University and the author of more than thirty books and hundreds of essays.

Index

223